The Essential Persona Lifecycle

The Essential Persona Lifecycle
Your Guide to Building and Using Personas

Tamara Adlin and John Pruitt

AMSTERDAM · BOSTON · HEIDELBERG · LONDON
NEW YORK · OXFORD · PARIS · SAN DIEGO
SAN FRANCISCO · SINGAPORE · SYDNEY · TOKYO
Morgan Kaufmann Publishers is an imprint of Elsevier

Morgan Kaufmann Publishers is an imprint of Elsevier
30 Corporate Drive, Suite 400, Burlington, MA 01803, USA

This book is printed on acid-free paper.

Notices

Knowledge and best practice in this field are constantly changing. As new research and experience
broaden our understanding, changes in research methods, professional practices, or medical
treatment may become necessary.

Practitioners and researchers must always rely on their own experience and knowledge in evaluating
and using any information, methods, compounds, or experiments described herein. In using such
information or methods they should be mindful of their own safety and the safety of others, including
parties for whom they have a professional responsibility.

To the fullest extent of the law, neither the Publisher nor the authors, contributors, or editors, assume
any liability for any injury and/or damage to persons or property as a matter of products liability,
negligence or otherwise, or from any use or operation of any methods, products, instructions, or
ideas contained in the material herein.

Library of Congress Cataloging-in-Publication Data
Application submitted

British Library Cataloguing-in-Publication Data
A catalogue record for this book is available from the British Library.

ISBN: 978-0-12-381418-0

For information on all Morgan Kaufmann publications,
visit our web site at www.mkp.com or www.elsevierdirect.com

Typeset by MPS Limited, a Macmillan Company, Chennai, India
www.macmillansolutions.com

Printed in China

10 11 12 13 14   5 4 3 2 1

This book is dedicated to the hundreds of brave souls who have participated in our workshops and worked with us as clients or colleagues over the past 10 years. Your creativity and experiences helped us build this process, and we couldn't have done it without you.

Oh, and we both adore our families and friends. Your support (and patience) mean the world to us.

CONTENTS

Tamara Adlin is the president of adlin, inc., a user experience strategy company in Seattle, Washington. Tamara's focus is on…focus! She's an expert at wrangling executive teams until they agree on a shared, crystal-clear, and prioritized set of key users and their goals; she believes that teams who can develop and stick with a solid focus on their users are in the best position to create really great products. She has tons of fun running workshops with executives, and then diving in to help teams who are working 'in the trenches' to design and develop great products. Tamara co-authored *The Persona Lifecycle: Keeping People in Mind Throughout Product Design* with John Pruitt, has been featured in several other books, and has been invited to speak on user experience strategy all over the world. In her recent work life, Tamara co-founded Fell Swoop, a user experience design company, and she ran a customer experience and usability team at Amazon.com. She cut her professional teeth at a series of Seattle tech startups after getting her Master's Degree in Technical Communication from the University of Washington. Today, she's happily focusing on practical methods that help business people increase their bottom lines by focusing on their customers, and she's got her work cut out for her.

John Pruitt is a Senior Program Manager at Microsoft, currently working on the next version of SharePoint as part of the Microsoft Office 2010 suite of products. Since joining Microsoft in 1998, he has conducted user research and designed UI for several versions of Windows (including Windows 98SE, 2000, ME, XP, and Vista) as well as Microsoft's integrated Internet client, MSN Explorer (versions 6, 7, and 8), and innovative mobile PCs like the Tablet PC and the super small form factor UMPC (Ultra-Mobile PC). Prior to Microsoft, he was an invited researcher in the Human Information Processing Division of the Advanced Telecommunications Research Laboratory in Kyoto, Japan, and also worked as a civilian scientist doing simulation and training research for the U.S. Navy. John holds a Ph.D. in experimental psychology from the University of South Florida and has published a variety of journal articles and book chapters on usability methods, skill training, naturalistic decision-making, speech perception, and second-language learning. He has been creating and using personas for more than 10 years, continually developing his approach and mentoring numerous product teams around Microsoft and companies worldwide. John co-authored the book, *The Persona Lifecycle: Keeping People in Mind Throughout Product Design*, with Tamara Adlin, and has presented broadly on the topic of personas at both academic and industry events.

What are personas?

INTRODUCTION

Personas are fictitious, specific, concrete representations of target users. The notion of *personas* was created by Alan Cooper and popularized in his book *The Inmates Are Running the Asylum: Why High Tech Products Drive Us Crazy and How to Restore the Sanity* (Sams Publishing, 1999). Personas put a face on the user—a memorable, engaging, and actionable image that serves as a design target. They convey information about users to your product team in ways that other artifacts cannot.

Personas have many benefits:

- Personas make assumptions and knowledge about users explicit, creating a common language with which to talk about users meaningfully.
- Personas allow you to focus on and design for a small set of specific users (who are not necessarily like you), helping you make better decisions.
- Personas engender interest and empathy toward users, engaging your team in a way that other representations of user data cannot.

In other words, personas will help you, your team, and your organization become more user focused.

WHY A PERSONA LIFECYCLE?

We originally wrote *The Persona Lifecycle: Keeping People in Mind Throughout Product Design* because lots of people were excited about personas, but:

- No one had described, in practical terms, how to create personas.
- No one had described specific tools for using personas during a product development process.
- Practitioners who had tried personas had failed in their efforts more often than they had succeeded.

1

We looked into why so many persona efforts were failing, and we found four common reasons:

1. The effort was not accepted or supported by the leadership team.
2. The personas were not credible and not associated with methodological rigor and data.
3. The personas were poorly communicated.
4. The product design and development team employing personas did not understand how to use them.

The Persona Lifecycle was a solution: an end-to-end set of methods and tools designed to support persona practitioners from the moment they decided to try personas until well after the completion of a project. The persona lifecycle is built on several core assertions, all of which arose from our research and experience:

- Building personas from assumptions is good; building personas from data is much, much better.
- Personas are *not* documents. They are shared ideas around who your users are that must come to life in the minds of the people in your organization.
- Personas are a highly memorable, inherently usable communication tool *if* they are communicated well.
- Personas can be initiated by executives or first used as part of a bottom-up grass-roots experiment, but eventually they require support at all levels of an organization.
- As long as personas are well built, data driven (or otherwise validated and agreed upon), and thoughtfully communicated, the product team can use the personas that come to exist to generate new insights and seek out the right details when they need them.
- Personas are not a stand-alone, user-centered design (UCD) process but should be integrated into existing processes and used to augment existing tools.
- Effective persona efforts require organizational introspection and strategic thinking.
- Personas *can* be created and show their value quickly, but if you want to obtain the full value from personas you will have to commit to a significant investment of time and resources.

We understand that the devil is in the details when it comes to launching a persona effort within an organization, and we are excited to share specific techniques that will help you succeed in your own persona efforts and in turn help your organization realize the benefits of truly UCD.

The five phases of the persona lifecycle

The persona lifecycle is a metaphoric framework that breaks the persona process into phases similar to those of human procreation and development. As shown in Figure 1.1, the five phases in this framework bring structure to the potentially complicated process of persona creation and highlight critical (yet often overlooked or ignored) aspects of persona use:

- *Family planning*—Before you begin any persona effort, you should figure out what problems you're trying to solve and what materials (specifically, data sources) are already available for you to use.
- *Conception and gestation*—Organize assumptions; turn data into information and information into personas.
- *Birth and maturation*—Create a persona campaign and introduce the personas to your organization.
- *Adulthood*—Use the personas in specific ways to help during the design, development, evaluation, and release of your product.
- *Lifetime achievement and retirement*—Measure the success of the persona effort and create a plan to reuse or retire the personas.

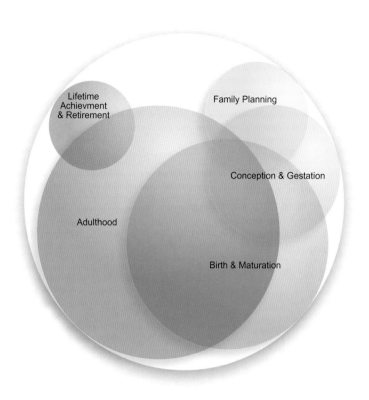

FIGURE 1.1
The five phases of the persona lifecycle. This diagram is designed to show both the order of the phases (from family planning through conception and gestation, birth and maturation, adulthood, and finally lifetime achievement and retirement) and the relative amount of effort and importance related to each phase. Each lifecycle phase is covered in detail in subsequent chapters of this book.

As the name indicates, the persona lifecycle is a cyclical, largely serial, process model. As Figure 1.1 shows, each stage builds on the next, culminating but not ending at the *adulthood* phase. Note also that the final stage, *lifetime achievement and retirement*, is not immediately followed by a cyclical return to the first stage. This is because different persona efforts culminate and restart in different ways. Personas can be reused, reincarnated, or retired depending on the project.

More importantly, although each phase does build on the previous, some are more important than others, and some you can complete in just an hour or two if need be. *Conception and gestation* and *adulthood* are the vital steps. As you read this book, remember that you can (and should) customize your own persona process in accordance with the amount of time, resources, and data you have.

The persona lifecycle doesn't have to take a long time. You can, and should, be selective in the techniques you choose to integrate into your persona effort. Although we do not think it is a good idea to skip any of the lifecycle phases completely, we do believe it is completely acceptable to take some shortcuts within any of the phases. Giving some attention to every phase will increase the odds that your persona effort will ultimately be successful. Your overall goal should be to create helpful and well-used personas, not to follow the process described in this book to the letter. Throughout the book, we suggest both complete end-to-end processes and helpful shortcuts. We point out the processes we believe to be the most important and effective, and you can treat each chapter as a menu of techniques and tools that can be used together or independently.

WHY ANOTHER PERSONA LIFECYCLE BOOK?

The original version of *The Persona Lifecycle: Keeping People in Mind Throughout Product Design* is rich in details, examples, philosophy, and stories from the field. It was written to give you the full context around every aspect of persona creation, communication, and use, in addition to as many tools and tricks as we could find. The original is a reference tome that will help practitioners navigate the specific needs of their own organizations … and get past the inevitable hurdles everyone faces during a persona effort.

This book is for people who just need to know what to do and what order to do it in. It is completely focused on practical tools and methods, without much explanation on why the particular tool or method is the right one. For that reason, we have significantly shortened the entire book, and we have further abridged the chapters that did not include critical steps in the persona creation and use process.

We have focused the content as follows:

- *Family planning*—Basic ideas and a few tools that will help you get organized
- *Conception and gestation*—Step-by-step instructions to move from assumptions to completed personas
- *Birth and maturation*—Strategic techniques to get the right information about your personas out to your teammates at the right time
- *Adulthood*—Specific tools that will ensure your personas are used by the right people at the right times (and in the right ways!) during the product development cycle
- *Lifetime achievement and retirement*—Basic ideas and a few tools that will help you measure the success of your persona effort … and prepare for the next one

Again, we don't recommend that you skip any step in the persona lifecycle (even those that we cover very briefly here). In this book, we include some guidelines that will help you with every phase, no matter how much time you have. Our goal is to help you give some thought to important issues and jot down some basic information. A little upfront work will be incredibly helpful when you need to justify your project, capture lessons learned, and plan for your next persona effort.

WHAT ADDITIONAL MATERIALS WILL I FIND IN THE ORIGINAL PERSONA LIFECYCLE BOOK?

Our original book, *The Persona Lifecycle: Keeping People in Mind Throughout Product Design*, is a lot longer than this edition, which provides a very practical—in some cases, a step-by-step—description of the basics of the persona lifecycle; the original includes much more in-depth content. Several chapters in this edition, including those on family planning and retirement and lifetime achievement, have been radically shortened; they tell you *what* you need to do but do not include details on *how* to do some of these steps. The chapter on birth and maturation is shortened, but not as drastically; it still contains some specific how-to methods and suggestions. The chapters on conception and gestation and adulthood are also still quite detailed, and they include a few important updates based on lessons we've learned since our original book was published.

Having said that, one of our most important insights into persona projects is that the devil is *always* in the details. If you find yourself stuck during the process, don't despair. Instead, consult the original persona lifecycle book for many more details and suggestions, including:

- A complete history of the origin of personas
- Detailed analysis of why personas work and what causes them to fail
- Many "bright ideas" to help streamline your persona efforts

- Dozens of stories from the field written by other persona practitioners that will give you first hand insights based on their experiences and ideas for new methods and tools that have worked for them
- An extensive case study based on our fictitious company, G4K, which provides examples of all the materials related to a successful persona effort

In addition, the original book includes five invited chapters written by persona experts:

- "Users, Roles, and Personas," by Larry Constantine
- "Storytelling and Narrative," by Whitney Quesenberry
- "Reality and Design Maps," by Tamara Adlin and Holly Jamesen
- "Marketing Versus Design Personas," by Bob Barlow-Busch
- "Why Personas Work: The Psychological Evidence," by Jonathan Grudin

But don't worry: we've made sure to provide you with all the basics you'll need as you embark on your persona effort right here in this book.

The five phases of the persona lifecycle

INTRODUCTION

The persona lifecycle is a metaphoric framework that breaks the persona process into phases similar to those of human procreation and development. As shown in Figure 2.1, the five phases in this framework bring structure to the potentially complicated process of persona creation and highlight critical (yet often overlooked or ignored) aspects of persona use:

- *Family planning*—Before you begin any persona effort, you should figure out what problems you're trying to solve and what materials (specifically, data sources) are already available for you to use.
- *Conception and gestation*—Organize assumptions; turn data into information and information into personas.
- *Birth and maturation*—Create a persona campaign and introduce the personas to your organization.
- *Adulthood*—Use the personas in specific ways to help during the design, development, evaluation, and release of your product.
- *Lifetime achievement and retirement*—Measure the success of the persona effort and create a plan to reuse or retire the personas.

As the name indicates, the persona lifecycle is a cyclical, largely serial, process model. As Figure 2.1 shows, each stage builds on the next, culminating but not ending at the *adulthood* phase. Note also that the final stage, *lifetime achievement and retirement*, is not immediately followed by a cyclical return to the first stage. This is because different persona efforts culminate and restart in different ways. Personas can be reused, reincarnated, or retired depending on the project.

More importantly, although each phase does build on the previous, some are more important than others, and some you can complete in just an hour or two if need be.

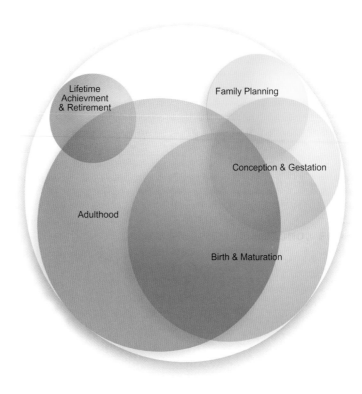

FIGURE 2.1
The five phases of the persona lifecycle. This diagram is designed to show both the order of the phases (from family planning through conception and gestation, birth and maturation, adulthood, and finally lifetime achievement and retirement) and the relative amount of effort and importance related to each phase. Each lifecycle phase is covered in detail in subsequent chapters of this book.

Conception and gestation and *adulthood* are the vital steps. As you read this book, remember that you can (and should) customize your own persona process in accordance with the amount of time, resources, and data you have.

THE PERSONA LIFECYCLE ENCOURAGES AND SUPPORTS USER-CENTERED DESIGN

The persona lifecycle will work for you whether or not you have already incorporated user-centered design (UCD) methods into your product development cycle. The persona lifecycle does not *replace* existing processes; rather, the phases of the lifecycle help to structure user-centered thinking throughout whatever design and development process you have in place. In this section, we illustrate the ways the phases of the persona lifecycle will introduce UCD into your organization (if UCD methods have not yet been adopted) or enhance UCD methods already in practice.

Phase 1. Persona family planning

Persona development begins with family planning. This is the research and analysis phase that precedes the actual creation of personas. During family planning, you will focus on:

- Creating a core team of colleagues to help you with the entire persona effort
- Researching your own organization (which we call *organizational introspection*) to evaluate the problems and needs of your company, organization, or product—once you understand the needs you hope the persona effort will address, you can evangelize the persona method and prepare the product development team for the persona effort

- User research and identification of data sources that will provide the raw materials for your personas
- Thinking strategically about how you will introduce and support the personas in your organization

Family planning ends when:

- You have established that personas are right for your organization and current project.
- You have buy-in from key individuals and have completed initial research and data gathering.
- The persona core team is in place.
- You have created a solid plan for the rest of the persona effort that suits your product team's needs.

Phase 2. Persona conception and gestation

In the chapter on persona conception and gestation, we explain how to extract useful information from disparate data sources and use this information to build personas. We have included some new suggestions, process descriptions, and insights in this edition of our book; these reflect the evolution of our process since the publication of *The Persona Lifecycle: Keeping People in Mind Throughout Product Design*.

During the persona conception and gestation phase, the lifecycle process helps you decide:

- How many personas you will need to create to communicate the key information in your data
- Which qualities and descriptive elements you should include in your persona documents and how to tie these elements back to your original data sources
- How to prioritize and validate your personas
- How to decide when your personas are complete and ready to be introduced to your product team

A lot of the work during the conception and gestation phase centers on collaboratively filtering data and organizing information—information that arises out of the data you collect in *family planning* and information that arises from other sources, such as inherent knowledge of how people behave, your business or product strategy, the competitive marketplace, and technological affordances related to your product domain. The information you identify will help you understand the particular user roles, user goals, and user segments that uniquely describe your target users. When you have isolated information about your users' roles, goals, and segments, you will be able to determine what personas you should create to capture and communicate the most relevant qualities of (and differences among) target users related to your product domain and business strategy.

When you have completed the process described in the chapter on conception and gestation, you will have translated raw data and insights into a set of complete, robust personas that are ready to participate in the product design process.

Phase 3. Persona birth and maturation

Like parents sending young children off to school, you and your core team will send your personas into your organization to interact with other people. The personas are fully formed but may continue to evolve slightly over time. Moreover, throughout the remainder of the development cycle, your personas will continue to develop in the minds of your product team. Problems at this phase might involve a lack of acceptance or visibility and other problems that lead to personas that die on the vine and disappear from the project. More subtly, your personas may come to be misconstrued and misinterpreted. Successful persona birth and maturation require a strong, clear focus on communication to ensure that your personas are not just known and understood but also adopted, remembered, and used by the product team. The chapter on birth and maturation includes:

- Creating a persona campaign plan to organize your work in birth and maturation and adulthood
- Introducing the personas (and the persona method) to the product team
- Ensuring that the personas are understood, revered, and likely to be used (for example, creating artifacts to progressively disclose persona details)
- Managing the minor changes to the persona descriptions that become necessary after the personas are introduced

We help you decide which of many artifacts to create and when and how to use them to keep the personas (and the data they contain) fresh in the minds of the product team. We also give you pointers on maintaining the delicate balance of sharing ownership of the personas (and the details they contain) while ensuring that new or altered details don't threaten the integrity of the underlying data.

Phase 4. Persona adulthood

Personas are all grown up in the adulthood phase, and have a job to do. You have introduced the personas to the product team and have worked to clarify the role and importance of the personas. You have encouraged the product team to embrace the personas and the information they contain, and now it is time to help everyone use the personas to inform the design and development of the product.

The effective persona practitioner must understand the many ways personas can be involved in *existing* processes and ensure that the personas work hard in an organization during the core development phases.

Personas can be used to help you plan, design, evaluate, and release your products. Personas can also inform marketing, advertising, and sales strategy. The chapter on adulthood is full of practical tools and suggestions to ensure that your personas have real impact—that they get used in a meaningful way by your product team.

Phase 5. Persona lifetime achievement, reuse, and retirement

Once the project or product is completed, it is time to think about what has been accomplished and to prepare for the next project. You will want to assess how effective the persona method was for your team and product development process. If you are beginning to think about the next product (or next version of the product just released), you will need to decide whether and how you will reuse your existing personas and the information they contain.

The end of a product design and development cycle is a good time to assess the effectiveness of personas for the team and to take stock of lessons learned for the next time. How did the development team accept the method? Were your personas useful? To what extent were they accurate and precise? We provide suggestions and tools you can use to validate the use of personas in the development process and to determine if the persona effort was worth the exertion and resources it required. Did personas change the product? Did they change your design and development process? User-centered designers are constantly under pressure to validate the worth and return on investment (ROI) of their activities, and personas can be useful tools for measuring the success of both the product and of the UCD (user-centered design) activities as a whole.

Persona family planning

WHAT IS FAMILY PLANNING FOR PERSONAS?

Family planning is the first phase in your persona process. It is the time when you will do some investigation and strategic thinking about your organization and its approach to user-centered design (UCD) and development. Your personas will not be introduced to the rest of your organization until the *birth and maturation* phase, but the ultimate success you have with them depends a lot on the work you do during the family planning phase. It is critical that you use this time to think up front about what happens after the personas are created.

There are four major activities during the family planning phase:

- Building a core team
- Researching your own organization (organizational introspection)
- Creating an action plan
- Collecting data

In this version of our book, we introduce the basic steps you should complete during the family planning phase. As you'll see, much of family planning is about thinking, planning, assessing, and gathering materials. For more detailed suggestions related to family planning, see the related chapter in *The Persona Lifecycle: Keeping People in Mind During Product Design.*

ORGANIZATIONAL INTROSPECTION: ARE PERSONAS RIGHT FOR YOUR PROJECT?

Your first job is to take a realistic look at the problems your team and organization are trying to solve and decide if personas will help. Don't skip this step to save time, even if your team needed personas a month ago. We define *organizational introspection* as the process of evaluating the problems and needs of your company, organization, and product team. Organizational introspection is, in simple terms, working to answer the following questions:

- How user focused is your company?
- How do people think and communicate about users?
- How is user information incorporated into the product design and development process?

Do a thorough job in examining the personalities and politics that surround you. Only then can you decide if personas are the right way to address the problems facing your organization and product team and, if so, how you should introduce and maintain the personas to ensure maximum acceptance. If you conclude that personas are appropriate for your team, process, and product needs, you will then be ready to assemble a team, create a plan to ensure that your personas will be used and found helpful, and begin collecting data.

STEP 1. BUILD A CORE TEAM

Even if your team is just you and one other person, the discussions you will have will provide you with a critical perspective on your work and on the decisions you are making that you simply cannot arrive at by yourself. You need a persona core team because:

- Personas can be a lot of work for just one person.
- Discussion and debate are critical activities in the persona creation process.
- Getting your personas accepted and used requires cross-organizational buy-in.

In most cases, we have found that effective persona core teams include a minimum of two and a maximum of ten members. In our experience, teams with over ten members require too much coordination and quickly become unmanageable. The ideal persona core team has three to five active members and several other members in an advisory or on-call role.

Plan to include the people who are already involved in user research, market research, business analysis, task analysis, or any other user- or customer-focused research or profiling activity. If you have colleagues in any of the following specialties, you should put them on the short list for inclusion on the core team:

- Information architects, interaction designers, and human–computer interaction (HCI) specialists
- Usability specialists, user researchers, and ethnographers
- Technical writers, documentation specialists, and training specialists
- Market researchers, business analysts, and product managers

STEP 2. IDENTIFY GOALS

One of your jobs, as a user-centered designer, is to help build focus in your organization. Personas will help you to do this, but they aren't the only tool at your disposal. Before you dive head-first into creating personas, you should do everything you can to articulate (and get sign-off on!) a very specific set of goals. These goals will help you keep your executive team on track during the adulthood phase of the lifecycle, and they will help you measure the success of the project.

We recommend this (deceptively simple) set of questions:

1. What are the top three to five business goals for your product or service? Business goals are expressed in numbers. They describe the needles that this project should help to move. A statement such as "increase revenue and decrease costs" isn't specific enough

to be a useful goal. Instead, ask for extremely specific numbers—for example, "increase number of purchases on our website by 20%" or "decrease number of customer service calls related to returns by 50%."

2. What are the top three to five brand goals for your product or service? Brand goals are expressed in terms of the way you want the new product or service to articulate, advance, or modify the perception of your brand.

3. What are the top three to five user experience goals for your product or service? Customer experience goals express the problems you want your site to solve for your customers. Try writing these as quotes you would like to hear coming out of your users' mouths after they see your new product or service—for example, "Wow, I didn't know that I could find information about all of my accounts in one place!"

4. What are the most important differentiators for your product or service? What are you offering your customers that no one else can? Remember, these really need to be different. It's not enough to say, "We have the best customer service in the industry." That's too vague, and it's not really defensible.

5. What are the most important value propositions for your product or service? Why should your customers care about your differentiators?

You'd think that any business would have a list of all of these available to anyone who asks. Maybe your company is different, but we have never encountered any company that could just hand over the answers to these questions on request. Remember to approach this carefully. Your role is not to challenge the executive team or accuse them of being disorganized. Instead, let them know that it's your job to *understand* what these goals are and to ensure that everyone working on the project is crystal clear on the most important goals for the company.

We suggest you try to find these types of goals in documents available to you or that you draft what you *think* the goals are. Ask your boss, and your boss's boss, to correct any misunderstandings you have.

Creating clear goals now will help you measure ROI later

Measuring the ROI of the overall project is very important; it's also important to measure the ROI of the persona effort itself. Personas aren't free. They cost time and effort and, in many cases, at least a little bit of money. Doing a little thinking now can set you up very well to measure the value of the personas to the overall project once everything is said and done.

There are several ways your personas can help, and each of these can be measured:

*   Personas can help improve your process; for example, personas can help your teams communicate more effectively, agree on and document design decisions, or achieve resolution on key issues faster.
*   Personas can help improve your products; for example, your products can (and should!) suffer from fewer bugs and require less support and user-facing documentation.
*   Personas can help improve your organization; for example, personas can ease political disputes, improve internal communication between departments and from the executive teams, and even noticeably increase the overall customer focus of the entire company.

You'll see that the ways to measure change aren't necessarily numeric (in fact, they are seldom numeric). But, you'll find that it certainly is possible to think about the way things are today, how we want things to be, and what things will have to change in order to make that dream come true. Not all measures of ROI have to be expressed in numbers. See Table 3.1 for a sample Persona Effort Goals Worksheet.

TABLE 3.1 Persona Effort Goals Worksheet

Goal or issue	How things are today	How we want things to be tomorrow	Ways to measure change
Use personas to create a clear, shared focus across the entire organization. (Or state another process, product, or organizational improvement goal or issue.)	We're just getting started, so we're still driving to clarity on exactly who our target users are and the relative business value of each.	We want a set of personas that everyone knows and business goals for each release or project articulated in terms of personas' needs.	After the first release, ask everyone to describe the three most important users. Collect current business and vision documents—note the ways users are referenced. After the persona effort, all documents should reference the personas. (Before beginning this process, we should have asked everyone to describe the three most important users of the product or service.)

Family Planning: Create a plan	Lifetime Achievement: Measure ROI
What resources do we have for personas and other UCD activities?	How much did the persona effort actually cost?
What product problems do we want to solve with personas?	Has the product improved? How much, and in what ways?
What process problems do we want to solve with personas?	Has the process improved? In what ways?

FIGURE 3.1
Measuring the return on your persona-effort investment is much easier if your plan includes specific references to the improvements you hope to realize. If you create your action plan to explicitly cover the questions on the left-hand side of the table shown here, you will thank yourself during the lifetime achievement and retirement phase.

STEP 3. CREATE AN ACTION PLAN

The action plan is a translation of all of the analysis you have done into a roadmap or specification for your persona effort. Although they can be of different formats, all persona action plans incorporate the following:

- A definition of the scope of the project and the associated goals for the persona core team
- A description of a communication strategy
- A listing of milestones and deliverables

If you know you will need to explain the value of your persona-related work at the end of your project, create your action plan to explicitly answer the questions on the left-hand side of the table shown in Figure 3.1. Figure 3.2 shows a generic action plan and how to detail milestones and deliverables.

Note that you will be able to use your action plan to assess the value of your persona effort during the lifetime achievement and retirement phase by measuring the changes that result from your work.

STEP 4. GET YOUR HANDS ON SOME DATA

During the family planning phase, your goal is to figure out what your data sources should be and to collect the raw data. We believe that the best personas come from a variety of

Persona Effort Action Plan	
Elevator Pitch	
	We're going to use personas to help our entire organization stay focused on what our customers need and how they think. The personas will be prioritized by the exec team according to our business goals, so they'll help us with user-focus and with business-focus!
Process-Related Goals for the Persona Effort (if our work is successful …)	
	• It will take less time to agree on the set of features we'll include in the product. • We will have a common language around users and business goals, which will make meetings and discussions more effective. • It will be easier to create QA test plans.
Product-Related Goals for the Persona Effort	
	• 20% reduction in customer service calls. • 50% fewer bugs at launch. • 2% increase in conversion rates for new customers.
Resources Available for Our Persona Effort	
	List: • core team members • person hours available from the core team members • time available from the advisory members of the core team • financial resources, etc.

Milestones & Deliverables			
Phase	**Activities and Deliverables**	**Timeline**	**Related Development Cycle Milestones**
Family Planning	Include persona-specific work and deliverables during each period (e.g., field research, data assimilation, skeleton personas, communication activities, etc.)	Include the date of completion or expected duration of the activity	Include the broader product or project milestones here to provide context for the plan (e.g., spec complete date, code complete date, release date)
Conception & Gestation	–	–	–
Birth & Maturation	–	–	–
Adulthood	–	–	–
Lifetime Achievement and Retirement	–	–	–

15

FIGURE 3.2
Your action plan should include a mission or vision statement (which we recommend be in the form of an "elevator pitch"), overall goals, and resources for completing the work. You will also need to detail the milestones and deliverables for your persona project, which we recommend you complete in terms of the lifecycle phases.

sources, especially those including both quantitative and qualitative data. Further, although we have seen great personas created after an extensive data collection and analysis effort, we have also seen useful personas based completely on assumptions. During this step, we suggest you look for:

- *Existing primary data sources (internal)*—What sources of user and customer data are readily available to you? What are the central and peripheral topics or domains that would be pertinent to your project? What are the other possible sources of data in your company? Who currently owns each data source?

- *Existing primary data sources (external)*—What are the possible external sources of data relevant to your domain, company, or product? Are there institutions or other companies that might have conducted research related to your domain? If you need to purchase such data, do you have the money to do so? We have had great luck finding lots of data on the Internet. Some of it is free, and some you have to pay for, but it's out there.
- *Original primary data sources (doing your own research)*—After seeking out existing data sources, what information is missing? What do you really need to learn? Who do you need to study, and how do you need to study them? In many cases, the remaining need for data is qualitative, as existing external data tend to be quantitative in nature. You'll want to go deep with a few carefully selected participants, observing and interviewing them in their own context to really understand their situations, needs, and goals. This information will also be immensely helpful later in the process as you craft the details of your personas.
- *Secondary data sources*—Who are the subject-matter experts in your company? Who has the most contact with existing customers? Your support organization, sales force, and account representatives can be great sources of information about your users.

Stay organized

As you collect data from primary (both internal and external) and secondary sources, it is a good idea to keep a data source index, which includes a master list of all data sources and a short description of the content of each source. At the very least, each source index should include:

- Name of the source
- Date the data were collected or analyzed
- Where you found the source
- Types of data the source contains—qualitative data, quantitative data, or both? Demographic, psychographic, behavioral, or some other type of data?

16

An example of an index is provided in Figure 3.3.

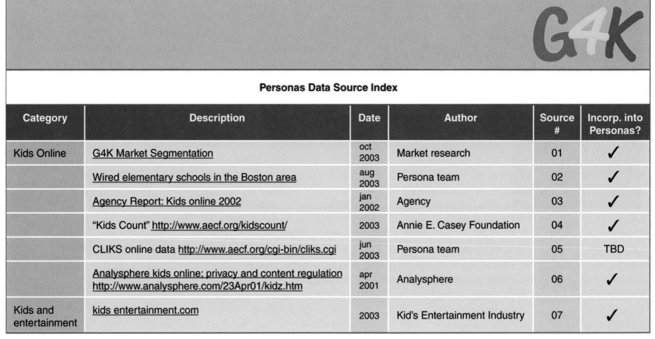

Personas Data Source Index

Category	Description	Date	Author	Source #	Incorp. into Personas?
Kids Online	G4K Market Segmentation	oct 2003	Market research	01	✓
	Wired elementary schools in the Boston area	aug 2003	Persona team	02	✓
	Agency Report: Kids online 2002	jan 2002	Agency	03	✓
	"Kids Count" http://www.aecf.org/kidscount/	2003	Annie E. Casey Foundation	04	✓
	CLIKS online data http://www.aecf.org/cgi-bin/cliks.cgi	jun 2003	Persona team	05	TBD
	Analysphere kids online: privacy and content regulation http://www.analysphere.com/23Apr01/kidz.htm	apr 2001	Analysphere	06	✓
Kids and entertainment	kids entertainment.com	2003	Kid's Entertainment Industry	07	✓

FIGURE 3.3
Create a data source index. Note that this example includes the category for the data, a link to the primary source, the date of creation, author, source number, and a final column for whether and when the source was used in the creation of the personas. You will use the final column during the conception and gestation phase to keep track of which data sources have been mined for their persona-related information.

GET READY FOR CONCEPTION AND GESTATION!

Now that you have a team to help you, you have thought about what problems you want to solve, you have identified goals, and you have gathered up data, you're ready to begin creating personas. Remember, don't skip the steps in family planning; even spending just a few hours thinking about the issues in this chapter and recording some measurable goals will help you immensely as you embark on your persona effort. The notes you jot down during this phase will be invaluable when you are (inevitably) asked to justify the time, effort, and money you spent on creating and using personas.

17

Persona conception and gestation

19

WHAT IS THE CONCEPTION AND GESTATION PROCESS FOR PERSONAS?

Conception and gestation is the phase of the persona lifecycle in which you actually create your personas. It is the phase in which you use data to create engaging representations of individual users that your team can use for planning, design, and development. During this phase, you will face the tricky question of how many personas to create and how to prioritize them. You will process the data and assumptions you have collected (by prioritizing, filtering, and organizing) to discover information about your users. Using this information, you and your core team will create bulleted persona "skeletons" that key stakeholders can prioritize according to business goals. You will develop your prioritized skeletons into complete personas that are then ready to be introduced to your organization in the *birth and maturation* phase.

Unlike some of the other chapters in this new edition of the book, this chapter retains almost all of the detail we included in the first book, with a few exceptions; for example, we have removed the ongoing case study and a few of the additional sidebars. We've also made a more significant update to this chapter in that we put far more emphasis on *ad hoc personas* and their role in the persona lifecycle. Since our first book was published, we have both participated in many more persona efforts and both experienced first-hand the importance of the ad hoc persona creation process in:

- Developing and articulating a shared focus on project goals and priorities
- Illuminating and aligning assumptions that exist about users in the minds of key project stakeholders

In the original book, the first step in the conception and gestation process was to "describe categories of users." Like the ad hoc persona creation process, this step focused on identifying the way the organization *currently* thinks and talks about the key differences between users (i.e., *before* the persona process). The ad hoc persona workshop starts with this step, but it doesn't stop there.

Based on our experiences since we wrote the original book, we believe there are two persona creation processes you can use. They align to the ways each of us has evolved our own work.

As a consultant, Tamara works with a variety of different companies. John is still at Microsoft, where he has moved on to become a Program Manager with the SharePoint team. He continues to be consulted by teams throughout Microsoft on their persona efforts. In short, Tamara comes in from the outside and works with organizations who have varying amounts of time, resources, and data to apply to personas, and John works internally with teams who rely on data to create personas to be accepted and used. Tamara has built her process on ad hoc personas that are created collaboratively with high-level executives and stakeholders and then validated with existing and new data. John uses ad hoc personas as one step of his overall data-driven persona creation process.

If you are working as a consultant, we recommend you insist on working with people as high in the food chain as possible and rely heavily on the ad hoc persona process. This way, whether or not you move on to a full data analysis, you will end up with personas that reflect and communicate the key goals and priorities of the executive staff and are therefore supported from the top down.

If you are working internally and don't have extensive access to the executives—and are facing the task of convincing the higher-ups that personas are useful and worth supporting—we recommend you plan to use as much data as humanly possible. There is no substitute for being able to show that you have analyzed and incorporated data findings from as many sources as possible when you present the personas throughout any organization. In other words, if you are working from the bottom up, you'll need those data as you try to move the personas up the food chain.

No matter which process you intend to use, we recommend you read this chapter end-to-end before you get started. You'll see that some of the steps and methods in this chapter are appropriate for both approaches (e.g., prioritization and validation of the personas).

THE SIX-STEP CONCEPTION AND GESTATION PROCESS

Persona creation is largely a serial and straightforward process in which you summarize, cluster, and analyze the data to discover themes (see Figure 4.2). You use these themes to generate rough persona skeletons. You then cull and prioritize the skeletons to focus on only the most important, most appropriate targets. Finally, you enrich the skeletons into full personas by making the details concrete and adding personality and a story line.

As shown in Figures 4.1 and 4.2, we recommend a six-step persona conception and gestation process that includes the following activities:

- **Conception**
  Step 1. Identify ad hoc personas—Work collaboratively with your stakeholder team to create quick, ad hoc personas that capture and communicate the organization's current thinking about who your users are and what they want and need. Creating ad hoc personas

- Create ad hoc personas
- Process data
- Identify & create skeletons
- Evaluate & prioritize skeletons
- Develop skeletons into personas
- Validate the personas

FIGURE 4.1
The six-step persona creation process.

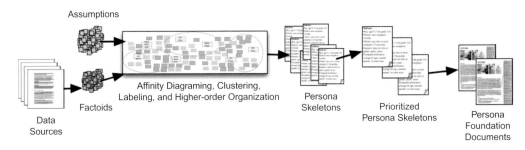

Assumptions

Factoids

Data Sources

Affinity Diagraming, Clustering, Labeling, and Higher-order Organization

Persona Skeletons

Prioritized Persona Skeletons

Persona Foundation Documents

FIGURE 4.2
The flow of persona creation: Start with ad hoc personas to organize all of the current thinking about your users. If you are going to move on to create full, data-driven personas, you'll filter and organize your data sources to pull out factoids, assimilate the factoids into clusters, and use these to create brief skeletons. Finally, you'll augment the skeletons into completed foundation documents, which capture and communicate your personas.

now (even if they are based solely on assumptions) will help you structure your data processing and build a bridge between the ways people think of users today and the data-driven personas you will create.

Step 2. Process the data—Process your raw data to extract information relevant to your user and product domains and then identify themes and relationships. We suggest that you do this by conducting a collaborative data assimilation activity.

Step 3. Create skeletons—Evaluate your processed data to verify the categories of users and to identify subcategories of users. Create skeletons, which are very brief (typically bulleted) lists of distinguishing data points for each subcategory identified.

- **Gestation**

Step 4. Prioritize the skeletons—Once you have a set of skeletons, it is time to get feedback from all stakeholders. You will evaluate the importance of each skeleton to your business and product strategy and prioritize the skeletons accordingly. Your goal is to identify a subset of skeletons to develop into personas.

Step 5. Develop selected skeletons into personas—Enrich the selected skeletons to create personas by adding data, concrete and individualized details, and some storytelling elements to give them personality and context.

Step 6. Validate your personas—Once you have added details, it is important to double-check to make sure your final personas still reflect your data.

Because we recommend either an ad hoc persona effort or a data-driven persona effort, we believe there are two basic variations on the six-step process listed above:

1. Ad hoc personas with either light validation (when you have very little time) or more rigorous validation (which may include some data analysis and additional data collection):
   o Identify ad hoc personas (step 1).

○ Create skeletons (step 3).
○ Prioritize the skeletons (step 4).
○ Develop selected skeletons into personas (step 5).
○ Validate your personas (step 6).
2. Data-driven personas (which incorporate ad hoc workshops, but only as a preliminary step in the overall persona creation process):
○ Complete all six steps listed above.

We know that many of you have short windows of opportunity in which to create personas that will be available and useful throughout product design. Many of you are also probably wondering how many personas you will need to create for your product. We address these important questions before describing the six-step conception and gestation process in detail.

HOW LONG DOES THE CONCEPTION AND GESTATION PROCESS TAKE?

The amount of time you spend on conception and gestation activities will depend on your project schedule, the amount of data you have, and your goals for the persona effort. You can create useful ad hoc personas in less than a day, or you could take months to fully analyze mountains of data and create personas that link every detail back to a data source. In most cases, you and your team will compromise between these extremes and create useful data-driven personas in about one to two weeks.

In our original book, we included several sample schedules. Today, we believe that you should (and must, really) work backward from your existing project schedule.

STORY FROM THE FIELD
A Quick but Effective Persona-Building Process

Colin Hynes, Director of Usability, Staples.com

When I was ready to create personas, I began by blocking off my calendar for two days. Then I wrote out one defining sentence on each persona. For example, "Comes to the website to research so she can buy in our store." While writing the descriptions, I recalled vividly the experiences I had while visiting offices during our extensive contextual inquiry studies and when listening to customer phone calls through customer service representatives. I used this information to build the persona descriptions, which were then reviewed with members of the Usability team.

As a team, we filled in color about the personas' motivations, goals, up-sell potential, defining quote, onsite conversion potential, and other key factors that created the whole of each persona. We started with nine personas and then cut it back to six when there seemed to be too much overlap. Even though the process wasn't as rigorous as some, it was incredibly useful to get the personas down on paper so I would have something for stakeholders to react to.

HOW MANY PERSONAS SHOULD YOU CREATE?

This is one of the first questions we hear when we talk about personas. While the answer is, of course, "it depends," we have found that roughly three to five personas are a good number to target. However, we believe that, although you may choose to communicate just a few personas to the development team, your data and the goals of your business should drive the number of personas you create. During the conception and gestation phase, your goal is to create a set of personas that are:

- Relevant to your product and your business goals
- Based on data or clearly identified assumptions
- Engaging, enlightening, and even inspiring to your organization

Note that your goal is *not* to describe every possible user or user type nor to detail every aspect of your target users' lives. Your personas will aid decision making by both narrowing the field of possible targets and highlighting user data that are important and highly related to the product you are creating. This chapter will help you analyze your data sources, decide how many personas to create, and determine what (and how much) information to include in each persona and which personas to prioritize.

The argument for a single primary persona

In their book *About Face 2.0* (Wiley, 2003), Alan Cooper and Robert Reimann include an axiom that states, "Design each interface for a single, primary persona." Cooper argues that you must prioritize your personas to determine which single persona should be the primary design target for any given interface. We have noticed that many people assume that this means there should only be one primary persona for the entire product. We believe this is a misinterpretation of Cooper's axiom. Yes, there should be one primary persona per interface, but many products have several interfaces (e.g., the interface you use when you read e-mail is quite different from the interface used by the administrator who maintains the e-mail server, but both interfaces are part of the same product). There are also secondary personas—perhaps those that use the product less often or use a particular interface as a peripheral aspect of their job.

Cooper recommends that we start by creating a cast of characters. We should then identify primary (preferably one) and secondary (probably several) personas within that cast. By definition, each primary persona will require a unique interface, because to be primary the persona must be satisfied, and it cannot be satisfied by any other persona's interface. If you must create more than three primary personas (and therefore three interfaces), Cooper argues that the scope of the project is probably too broad.

Cooper's insistence on clearly identified primary personas is the cornerstone of his approach, for good reason. One of the benefits of personas is that they focus and clarify communication around the qualities and needs of target users. Of course, personas are only clarifying if they are actually used by the product team. If people don't remember who the personas are and don't use them in their everyday communication, then the focus and clarity will be lost. Thus, your personas need to be visibly representative of the customer base and unfalteringly credible to your product team.

Strictly limiting the number of personas also forces stakeholders to make difficult and important decisions very early in the design process. Your work will be a forcing factor for clarifying business goals as early as possible, and the earlier you understand clear business goals the easier it is to build a product to suit those goals.

CREATING ONE PERSON TO DESIGN FOR: GREAT IN THEORY, COMPLICATED IN PRACTICE

In many cases, you, your core team, the product team, and business stakeholders will not accept a single primary persona. This might be because focusing so specifically may simply not *feel* right. It is difficult to convince an executive team that all design efforts should target a single persona because the thought of building a product that will only appeal to one person is sometimes too difficult to combat. Top-down buy-in for your persona effort is important. If people (especially stakeholders) are uncomfortable with your cast of personas, they will not support or use them.

Even if you do have a go-ahead from the executive team to create one primary persona per product interface, you may not know how many unique interfaces (and therefore how many primary personas) you should create. Many find themselves facing a chicken-and-egg dilemma: Should you decide how many unique interfaces your product needs and then create personas, or should you create the personas first and then create user interfaces accordingly?

In addition, if it is so important to create a single primary persona for each unique interface (or for the entire product), why create secondary personas at all? And, if you do create secondary personas, how should you use them to enhance but not interfere with the design process?

Because each project, product, and team is different, there is no "right" number of personas to create; however, saying "it depends on your project" is certainly not very helpful. The type of product you are building, the nature of your target audience, the information you discover in your data, and the particulars of your business goals should help you answer the following questions:

- How many personas do I need?
- Which personas do I need?
- Which personas should be primary or secondary?
- How do I use secondary personas without designing for everyone?

PERSONA CONCEPTION: STEPS 1, 2, AND 3

When we published our original book, we asserted that, if at all possible, personas can and should be created using data. This is certainly still true today. Over the past few years, however, we've seen and participated in many ad hoc persona projects that offered tremendous value to the products they supported, despite the lack of hard data used in the creation of the personas (see above).

Why not always create personas from data? Why create personas at all if you don't have data? The answer is simple. Sometimes you just don't have the money or the time, and sometimes a company is so far away from user-centrism that a full data-driven persona effort is a practical impossibility. If you decide to use ad hoc personas, you will complete step 1, below, and then move on to the gestation process.

Step 1. Identify ad hoc personas

Ad hoc personas are persona sketches that you and your core team can create to articulate your organization's existing assumptions about the user population. We recommend that you create assumption personas whether or not you plan to collect first-hand data about your target users. If you cannot perform your own user research, you and your team will still realize many of the persona-related benefits for your process and product. If you are planning on collecting data directly from users, creating assumption personas first can:

- Help stakeholders understand the need for the persona effort.
- Streamline your product-related communication.
- Help you target your field research to validate (or contradict) current impressions of who users are.
- Provide some practice with persona conception and gestation methods before you need to create your "real" personas.

ASSUMPTIONS EXIST; AD HOC PERSONAS ARTICULATE THEM

The truth is that everyone on your team (from marketing to design to development) has assumptions about users, and these assumptions do exert influence over the design of the product. These assumptions could be based on anything from hard data to personal biases. If you articulate the assumptions—draw them out into the light, where they can be examined and evaluated—you gain more control over them and the ways they impact the product. At the very least, your persona effort will make all of your organization's assumptions about target users very explicit—a perhaps painful but nonetheless valuable outcome.

Assumptions are usually formed after data have been internalized, combined, and interpreted. Assumptions almost always reflect some misinterpreted, poorly recalled, and

25

improperly combined aspects of original data, but they do contain some data and they do reflect the ways your company has digested and understands information about your users and your business. It is likely that some elements of your company's strategy with respect to your competition, the changing market, and your evolving technology exist only in the minds of stakeholders. Eliciting assumptions helps you understand some valid and important information affecting the design and development of your product.

AD HOC PERSONAS ARE EASY TO CREATE AND HELP PEOPLE UNDERSTAND WHY PERSONAS ARE VALUABLE

Ad hoc personas are much easier to create than data-driven personas. In a short time, you and your core team can collect, analyze, and categorize many of your organization's assumptions and create ad hoc persona sketches. Because these sketches relate directly to your product and will contain information that is familiar, they will help everyone in your organization see the value of personas to the design and development effort. The exercise can also help your persona core team practice the techniques you will use during "real" persona creation. Ad hoc personas are excellent tools for clarifying and focusing communication in meetings. (See also "Story from the Field: Ad Hoc Personas and Empathetic Focus" later in this chapter.)

Ad hoc personas can help make it clear to your managers that different assumptions exist and that therefore a common definition of the target audience needs to be created and communicated. At the very least, making assumptions explicit will help ensure that everyone's assumptions *match*, which is no small feat! Unclear communication and mismatched assumptions can be very damaging to a product. It is actually *riskier* to allow these factors to impact your product than it is to create "bad" personas by guessing and making assumptions. Once everyone in the organization sees their assumptions collected, organized, and expressed as personas, they usually find it easier to discuss the assumptions coherently and to agree on changes as a group—or to agree that allowing extra time for data collection is a good idea.

AD HOC PERSONAS CAN PROMPT DATA COLLECTION

Ad hoc personas can be the eye-opening catalyst that gets your team interested in some real user research. When your assumptions are exposed, so are gaps in your knowledge of your users. Ad hoc personas can lead your organization toward more rigorous user-centered design (UCD) techniques. For a nice example of how ad hoc personas can trigger interesting methods for user data collection, see "Story from the Field: Personas at Zylom.com" later in this chapter.

AD HOC PERSONAS, COMMUNICATED AND USED PROPERLY, ARE SIMPLY NOT THAT RISKY

If you create ad hoc personas in collaboration with high-level stakeholders and executives, the ad hoc personas will reflect the business goals of the company and will therefore be extremely helpful during the design and development process. If you create the ad hoc personas without the involvement of high-level stakeholders, you must either:

- Get their buy-in during the prioritization process so you have top-down support, or
- Make it painfully clear that your ad hoc personas are based on assumptions and not on data.

The risk of assumption-based personas comes when the team *forgets* or *ignores* the fact that the information contained in the personas is based merely on assumptions and begins to treat it like data.

Ad hoc personas align the organization's thinking around a set of common referents, which makes them valuable. If you end up using ad hoc personas and never move on to data-driven personas, you can still reap many of the benefits of personas; however, the entire organization must understand and agree that ad hoc personas are there primarily to improve communication.

WHEN ARE AD HOC PERSONAS A BAD IDEA?

If you believe that your organization harbors long-held "sacred cow" assumptions that people will be unable or unwilling to bring forth in a meeting, or you know that you will never get buy-in from high-level stakeholders, proceed with extreme caution. When you explore assumptions, you run the risk of exposing bad decisions that were made in the past and other "dirty corporate secrets" some of your colleagues may not want illuminated. If you suspect or discover this is the case, create personas only from primary data sources. Ad hoc personas are good for exposing, communicating, and aligning assumptions, but they are not effective tools for challenging highly political assumptions. If you want to challenge assumptions, do it with data.

HOW LONG DOES IT TAKE TO CREATE AD HOC PERSONAS?

If your organization is small, you will probably be able to identify and organize existing assumptions quite quickly, perhaps in one or two short brainstorming meetings. If you have a large organization, it could take quite a long time to schedule interviews with all of the key stakeholders, to review strategy documents, and so on. In this case, the time it takes is worthwhile because you will probably find wildly disparate assumptions that are affecting both the development cycle and your finished products in negative ways.

THE AD HOC PERSONA CREATION PROCESS

We recommend conducting an ad hoc persona workshop to create your ad hoc personas. The process is as follows:

1. Identify participants and schedule the workshop.
2. Clarify business, brand, and user experience goals.
3. Identify current language used to describe categories of users and customers.
4. Complete the assumption-gathering sticky note exercise.
5. Assimilate assumptions.
6. Identify skeletons.
7. Prioritize skeletons.

You'll need some basic supplies during your ad hoc persona workshops:

- Pads of yellow sticky notes—one pad per participant (the 3-inch-square variety works well)
- Two or three pads of sticky notes in at least two colors *other* than yellow
- Fine-point black permanent markers (one per participant)
- Easel paper (you can use the non-sticky variety, which is much less expensive than the super-big sticky note kind)
- Masking tape and Scotch tape
- Whiteboard and whiteboard markers
- Snacks

1. Identify participants and schedule the workshop

If you plan to use the ad hoc personas in your persona effort (as opposed to using the process as a first step in your data-driven persona effort), try to involve senior members of the project and executive team (if possible) in your ad hoc persona workshops. The more senior the ad hoc persona creation team, the better the results.

We recommend you schedule two consecutive four-hour meetings, preferably in the mornings, for the initial workshops. It takes time to have the conversations required to get everyone aligned in their thinking. Schedule a follow-up meeting at least a week later to review the results with the core team and to plan the next steps.

2. Introduce the workshop and clarify business, brand, and user experience goals

It is especially important to be clear about your goals when creating ad hoc personas—for example, "Our goal is to create a temporary set of target personas that will be used for initial planning discussions but validated later with research" or "The outcome of this meeting will be that each of the stakeholders has a clear and agreed-upon vision of our most strategic customer targets." Make sure that everyone involved knows why you are doing this exercise and why you believe it is worthwhile.

In Chapter 3, Persona Family Planning, we recommended that you articulate goals for your company, your product, and your persona effort. These include:

- Business goals
- Brand goals
- User experience goals
- Value propositions
- Differentiators
- Persona effort goals

If possible, ask the stakeholder team to provide as many details as possible on these goals before the workshops. If this isn't possible, spend some time gathering this information during the workshop. Be careful, though; these conversations can take on a life of their own, and your entire workshop can be taken over. Set a time limit for the conversation, and make it clear that the objective of the current conversation is to create a rough first draft of a document that will require quite a bit of additional thinking, discussion, and iteration.

Although it is possible that everyone in your organization is crystal clear on all of these goals before they walk in the door for the workshop, we've never found that to be the case. A primary reason for having this discussion as part of the ad hoc persona workshop is to allow the stakeholders to prove to themselves that they have some work to do to get to clarity within their own ranks. Because one of the major benefits of personas is to create and maintain clarity and focus throughout the organization, the personas themselves depend on clearly articulated goals and the shared focus of the key stakeholders in the organization.

3. Identify current language used to describe categories of users

This part of the process is usually quite quick, because your goal here is to simply list the current language used to describe the users and customers of your products. Why do this step at all? Because, inevitably, it becomes quite clear that the current language in your organization is not very helpful when it comes to making design decisions that impact your product.

When we conduct these workshops, we often hear categories of users or customers described in very basic ways. Here are some examples from our actual workshops:

- For an online commerce company:
  - Customers (people who have made a purchase)
    - One-time purchasers
    - Multiple purchasers
  - Inactives
    - Attrited one-time purchasers
    - Attrited multiple purchasers
  - Customers by category (e.g., people interested in this type of product versus another type of product)

- ○ Prospects
  - Highly qualified
  - Not highly qualified
- For a B-to-B product company:
  - ○ Small to medium businesses (SMBs)
  - ○ Enterprise
  - ○ Education
  - ○ Legal
  - ○ Financial
  - ○ IT managers
  - ○ CIOs
  - ○ Power users
  - ○ Casual/ad hoc users
  - ○ Facilities managers
  - ○ Project managers
  - ○ Approvers
  - ○ Expert users
  - ○ Novices/first-time users
  - ○ People who want to save time
  - ○ People who care about saving money

In the first example, the terms relate to segments of users or customers. This is one typical scenario, and you'll see it in organizations with a strong marketing focus. Marketers focus on segments to help them figure out the best ways to get the product in front of the people who are part of the purchasing funnel.

In the second example, the descriptions are more diverse. They include sizes of companies, types of companies, roles of users, job descriptions, and goals. This type of list is typical when you involve senior team members from multiple departments. For more discussion regarding roles, goals, and segments, see below.

Listing the current language used to describe users is incredibly important. After you have made this list on a whiteboard or easel pad (and it usually only takes a few minutes to do so), you can point at the list and demonstrate that there are two problems:

1. The terms are a mish-mash of descriptions that are useful to specific teams but not easily understood by the entire organization.
2. There are too many terms.
3. None (or perhaps few) of the terms is helpful to anyone trying to make a specific design decision.
4. None of the terms helps the entire organization understand the overarching goals of the company or product.

We often find that this is a very important "a ha" moment, especially when many people in a company believe they are already very user focused.

If you believe that the workshop participants simply won't believe that most people in the organization are confused about goals or don't have a good way to describe users, you should consider sending out a pre-workshop questionnaire and reviewing existing documents before the workshop. You can present your findings as part of the process.

ALTERNATIVES TO THE WORKSHOPS: SEND OUT AN E-MAIL QUESTIONNAIRE

As an alternative to a direct, in-person meeting, you can create a short questionnaire asking members of your organization to send you their assumptions about your target users. Ask them to describe, in as much detail as possible, how they envision the various people who use or will use your product. Be prepared to follow up on the questionnaire to collect more

29

details as necessary. Also keep in mind that e-mail is fairly easy to ignore and that you might not get many responses. Your questionnaire might include questions such as the following:

- Can you describe one or two typical users of our product?
- Can you name and describe a person you know who is most similar to the types of people using our product?
- At what times of day do our users use our product?
- Where do people use our product?
- Do our users use our product because they like to or because they have to?
- Are we trying to attract different types of users with our new product? Who are they?
- What (besides using our products) do our users like to do?
- Are the people who pay for our products the same people who use the products on a daily basis?

REVIEW EXISTING PRODUCT VISION, STRATEGY, AND DESIGN DOCUMENTS

If for some reason you can't gather assumptions directly from your team, you might be able to find a wealth of assumptions about target users in some of your team's planning documents. Find a copy of the company's business plan, product strategy documents, design and vision documents from existing versions of the product, and marketing strategy documents. Look for any document that records strategic decisions made by your company. These decisions often hinge on expressed or implied assumptions about the target users of the product. Write down all references to users or customers and capture the exact wording as well as the implied characteristics you find. If you plan to share this analysis with anyone, be careful to be tactful and work to avoid offending any of the original authors of the documents you are dissecting.

HANDY DETAIL

Categories of Users Usually Reflect Roles, Goals, and Segments

There are two reasons to identify categories of users early in the process. The primary reason is to ensure that your data assimilation exercise produces results that are relatively easy to create personas from. The second is to establish a clear connection to the existing language used to describe users.

The data assimilation process is typically a bottom-up deductive process in which you find important relationships between and among the data sources. Using high-level categories to provide structure to assimilation adds a layer of top-down inductive analysis. The use of categories ensures that you will be able to express the information you find in the clusters of data as personas. Without categories, your clustered data will yield interesting information but you might have a difficult time using this information to form personas.

When you are ready to communicate and use your personas, you will find it much easier to do so if you can describe them in language that is already familiar—even in the case where your data suggest that the initial categories should be replaced by different ones. In the next three sections, we describe three differences between target users that can be used to discover and define the categories important to your business and product: differences in user roles, user goals, and user segments. Each of these is accompanied by an example scenario. All of the scenarios describe the same company (a bank) and project (an online banking system). In the example scenarios, we show you how differences in roles, goals, or segments can be used to create high-level categories of users depending on business objectives and the existing corporate environment.

In our banking examples, no matter which personas the team ends up creating, all of them should be traceable back to the categories of users. When people ask, "Why did you create these particular personas?" (and this question will come up), the answer will be something similar to the following:

"We created at least one persona for each major category of user. We created these categories for one of the following reasons:

- Stakeholders identified *user roles* our product had to support to be successful.
- Stakeholders identified *user goals* we had to satisfy to have a successful product.
- Stakeholders identified *user segments* we had to satisfy to have a successful product."

Thinking About User Roles, User Goals, and User Segments

The sections that follow explore processes for thinking about user roles, goals, and segments.

User Roles

When you describe a person according to sets of tasks, job descriptions, responsibilities, or other external factors related to his or her interaction with your product, you are describing the user in terms of his or her *role*. For the purpose of software development, a user role is often defined with regard to the relationship between the user and a system. Specific roles don't necessarily map to specific users. Individual users might find themselves in any of these roles at different times. Roles are generally related to business, work, and productivity. In fact, sometimes they are directly related to job type, position, or responsibilities; however, they may also be related to an activity that defines a person as a type of consumer (e.g., the "shopper," the "browser," the "agent," or the "assistant").

Scenario 1: Create categories based on user roles. Your bank is large and offers many services for many different tiers of customers. Everyone at the company knows that the bank's website is going to continue to evolve over the next few years and will eventually support the specific needs of many types of customers. However, for now you have to figure out what features you need to build *first*. That is, which ones will give the bank the most bang for the buck as it tries to attract more customers and reduce its current customer support costs? You decide to create your categories of users based on various user *roles*. In this scenario, it would be appropriate to describe the following role-based categories of users:

- The new account shoppers
- The existing account holders
- The borrowers
- The investors

31

User Goals

When you describe a user in terms of what he or she is trying to achieve—in his or her own terms— you are describing the user's *goals*. Individuals have general goals that apply to many things they do in their lives, including the way they approach products. People also have specific goals that relate to tasks. Goals have a timelessness that roles do not. Whether or not you use goals as your primary differentiator, communicating your personas' goals will be critical during the *birth and maturation* and *adulthood* phases.

Scenario 2: Create categories based on user goals. Your group has been assigned to create an online banking experience to help the bank catch up with its main competitor. You also need to satisfy some of the customer requests that have been coming in for online access to account information and management tools. Your bank has been working hard to build a reputation as a trustworthy, solid financial institution, and you know that the online banking application needs to reflect this reputation. Your research shows that many people are dissatisfied with current online banking options because they are not sure the Internet is completely safe and reliable. You decide to create your categories of users based on different user *goals*. In this scenario, it would be appropriate to describe the following goal-based categories of users:

- Users who "want my financial life to be simpler"
- Users who "want my money to work for me"
- Users who "want to feel like my money gets as much attention as a millionaire's money"
- Users who "want to feel safe when I'm banking online"

User Segments

When you describe a user in terms of characteristics he or she shares with many other users, you are describing the user in terms of a segment. Segments are defined according to shared demographics, psychographics, attitudes, and behaviors. In marketing, segments are often used to create targeted messaging and advertising to increase product sales. Marketing teams, product planners, and business development groups often define their objectives in terms of segments they have built to reflect the existing market and opportunities for innovation and new sales.

Segments can be rigorously defined through quantitative analysis of data, but they can also evolve through casual references to groups of users or customers (which, by the way, are sometimes referred to as "user classes"). Because segments are often used as shorthand when business stakeholders are talking about users and customers, they exist (are embedded) in the culture and lingo of many companies regardless of how rigorously they are defined. If segments already exist in your company's vocabulary, they will influence your persona project.

Scenario 3: Create categories based on user segments. The bank executives have been walking around for weeks talking about critically underserved markets for your bank's service and their desire to fulfill some of these unmet needs through the new online banking services. The executive team asked the marketing team to identify segments of consumers who would be likely to sign up for a new online banking service. The marketing team did some research and identified three main segments, which they described as enthusiasts, ostriches, and neophytes. You know that if your personas don't fit within these segments your executive staff will reject them. You decide to use the segments (as they are currently defined by market research) to describe the following categories of users: have debt and credit concerns and think of money in terms of "what I can afford today."

- *Financial enthusiasts*—35 to 65 years old, urban or suburban, professional, college educated, yearly household income of $50K to $250K, make decisions related to finances and review all account balances and activity at least once a month, aware and wary of Internet security issues, careful researchers and informed consumers of financial services
- *Financial ostriches*—25 to 40 years old, urban or suburban, professional, college educated, have children, yearly household income of $35K to $90K, busy with life and work, seldom balance checkbook, seldom review financial decisions, have several accounts at various financial institutions (including IRAs from old jobs), not entirely sure what they have at any given time, feel overwhelmed whenever they think of organizing finances
- *Financial neophytes*—18 to 25 years old, some college, yearly household income of $10K to $60K (with potential for considerable income growth), newly financially independent, tend to be interested and motivated but nervous, very aware of current financial status

No matter how your organization initially categorizes users, all of your completed personas will include information related to that persona's role, goals, and segment.

HANDY DETAIL

Roles Are Not Always the Best Choice—Beware of Automating the Misery

If you are working on a redesign of an existing product or process, be very cautious about creating personas based on existing roles. Remember that your redesign might automate some tedious chores, enable some advanced activities, and so on. If you create personas based solely on existing roles, tasks, and activities, you will miss the opportunity for revolutionary change in your product.

4. Complete assumption sticky note exercise

Distribute one pad of yellow sticky notes and one permanent marker to each participant (see supply list above). Ask each participant to use the next 20 minutes or so to list one possible target end users of your product, one per sticky note.

You'll get some funny looks when you make this request. Here are some guidelines to help smooth the process:

- Each sticky note should include a person and a situation or problem (see Figure 4.3). Alternatively, each sticky note could be written from a user's point of view—for example, "I'm looking for information on starting an account."

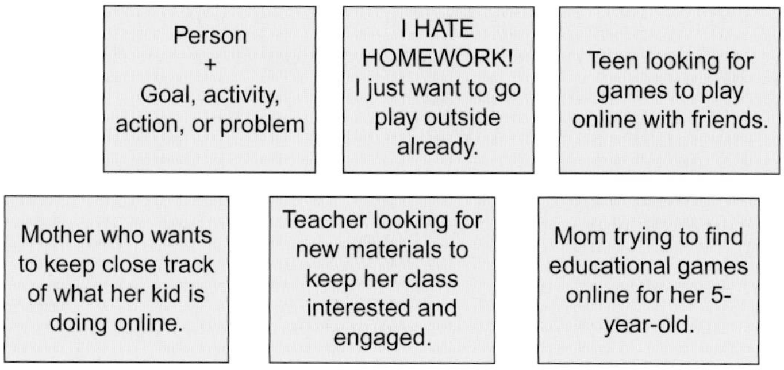

Person + Goal, activity, action, or problem	I HATE HOMEWORK! I just want to go play outside already.	Teen looking for games to play online with friends.
Mother who wants to keep close track of what her kid is doing online.	Teacher looking for new materials to keep her class interested and engaged.	Mom trying to find educational games online for her 5-year-old.

FIGURE 4.3
Create a slide showing examples like these to project during the sticky-note exercise.

- Remind everyone that there is a list of categories of users on the whiteboard to refer to. If they feel stuck, tell them to look at the categories and think of specific individuals who fit into each category and record one per sticky note.
- Participants will either run out of things to write quickly (see previous suggestion) or insist they could create "hundreds of these things." As a rule, we find that people will run out of steam in around 15 to 20 minutes, and that's fine.
- Remind everyone to write legibly!

As the stakeholders create the sticky notes, you should be doing two things:

- Use one of the other sticky-note colors (e.g., green) and transcribe the categories of users you identified in the previous step. If there are more than ten, consider finding ways to identify the most important or obvious categories and use those.
- Do your own yellow sticky notes! You've been thinking about users as you've prepared for the workshop. It's important to get your own thoughts into the mix.

ASSIMILATE ASSUMPTIONS

This is when you're going to ask everyone to actually stand up and do some hands-on participation! While you might get some groans when you tell everyone to put away their laptops and cell phones, the process tends to engage people quickly and most find it both challenging and fun.

You can assimilate assumptions on a wall, table, or even the floor. If you have a large conference-room table, ask everyone to clear *everything* off of the table. Cover the table with sheets of easel paper.

If you're going to use a wall, you'll need a pretty big wall, and it would be helpful in this case to use the easel-sized sticky pads instead of plain easel paper.

Assimilating on the floor is sometimes the most practical option, given the space constraints of many offices (and has the extra added benefit of forcing very important stakeholders to get down on the floor!).

In the previous step, you used some of the time to transcribe the categories of users onto green sticky notes. When everyone is standing up and the paper is ready:

- Tell everyone that each of the green sticky notes lists one of the categories of users you identified together.
- Spread the categories of users out across the paper, leaving plenty of room for participants to place their sticky notes.

33

- You might want to organize the categories from left to right if that makes sense; for example, an ecommerce team might have identified users according to where they are in the purchase decision process, so you can put the "prospects" on the left and the "existing customers with questions" all the way to the right. This isn't critical, but if some kind of order makes sense then go with it.

Now it's time to assimilate. Here are the instructions we recommend you give to the workshop participants:

1. Encourage everyone to get all their sticky notes down on the paper quickly. This will make it easier to do the next step. So, put sticky notes related to each category near that category. If you have sticky notes that don't relate to any of these categories, use a green sticky note to create a new category. After all the sticky notes are down on the paper, you have an opportunity to make an important point. Ask everyone to stop and look at the paper and notice how many sticky notes there are. The sticky notes are probably placed on the paper rather haphazardly, and the whole scene will look fairly chaotic and disorganized. It's the perfect time to make the point that this illustrates a problem you are trying to address with the personas: All of these assumptions exist about users, and the ones you're looking at now only reflect the assumptions of people in the room. It's easy to imagine the confusion that exists throughout the organization regarding who the key users are and what they want and need.

2. Assimilate the sticky notes. If you are familiar with affinity diagramming, this is the same process. Ask participants to group around sections of the sticky notes and look for patterns. The sticky notes are already somewhat organized according to the categories of users, each of which is represented by a green sticky note. The workshop participants should be looking for subcategories within each category and any new categories of users. Put some green sticky notes on the table and instruct the participants to create new category or subcategory labels as they identify them. Remind them that these are just sticky notes, so they can and should be moved around. The green sticky notes don't have to be considered set in stone during the process. In other words, encourage the participants to be very actively involved with the sticky notes and to try not to get into analysis paralysis as they do the exercise. Physically rearrange the sticky notes during this exercise. We find it very helpful to array the green sticky notes across the top of the large sheets of paper, with the yellow sticky notes arranged in columns under each label. Ask your participants *not* to overlap the yellow sticky notes, as this makes the notes more difficult to read and more likely to fall off the large sheets when the whole thing is moved.

3. People will lose steam after a while. Encourage them to switch to different areas of the diagram to work on something new if you see energy flagging. Also make sure that people are talking and working together during the workshop. If you are planning to move on to create data-driven personas, plan to spend some time on this step. If you plan on using ad hoc personas, allocate around 30 minutes to this process, and stop even though there will probably still be work to do to finish the clustering.

4. Ask participants to divide up puddles of sticky notes. If you see a cluster of more than around ten yellow sticky notes, ask a few participants to find subcategories within the cluster (if possible).

5. Discuss the process with the participants.

6. Take a photo of the assimilated clusters for your records.

If you are going to move on to data-driven personas …

If you are using this exercise as a first step in a data-driven persona exercise, stop here and move on to identify skeletons and analyze what you've found.

If you are going to use ad hoc personas …

Reassimilate based on goals. You've just spent a lot of time clustering your assumptions according to the categories of users you identified at the beginning of the process. This is an important step; however, it will not necessarily help you create the kinds of ad hoc personas that will help your organization refocus on the differences between the goals and needs of your customers.

It's time to recluster all of the yellow sticky notes. Instead of relying on existing categories of users, you'll use yet another color of sticky notes (e.g., pink) to create new categories of users and rearrange the sticky notes accordingly. One method we suggest is to remove all of the green sticky notes from the worksheets, so you can get a fresh start. You'll get some big groans at this point. Press on!

Instruct the participants to recluster the yellow sticky notes under new category labels, all of which *must* start with the words "I want …" or "I need ….", or another similar phrase as long as it starts with "I."

HANDY DETAIL

What's the Difference Between "I Want" and "I Need"?

For the purposes of this exercise, the difference is not critically important. Encourage your participants to use whichever of the two sentence starters feels right to them. Generally, people tend to use "I need" statements for anything that is related to business, money, family, or other critical activities. "I want" statements tend to feel right for activities or needs that are related to leisure or other noncritical activities.

Demonstrate the new categories you want the team to create. Find several sticky notes that are related in terms of "I want …" or "I need …." They will probably be scattered across several of the existing clusters; for example, after the earlier exercise, you might have clusters that look like this:

- New account shoppers
  - Freshman arriving at college
  - Businessman switching banks to escape fees
  - Man who has too much in one of his other accounts and is worried about FDIC limits
- Checking account customers
  - Person setting up online bill pay
  - Woman who wants to know if the bank is open in the evenings
  - Someone looking for the customer service phone number
  - "What was this charge on my statement?"
- Savings account customers
  - Person who wants to transfer money from savings to checking
  - "I need to talk to a real human about this transfer fee!"
  - "How much are wire transfers?"
  - "Did my wire transfer go through?"
  - "Do you insure savings accounts?"
- Loan customers
  - First-time home purchasers looking for info on mortgages
  - Person who has a mortgage with this bank that has been sold to another bank
  - "Do you do student loans?"
  - "I want to pay off my loan right now."
  - "What are your fees?"

Here are examples of recategorization according to "I want ..." or "I need ..." statements:

- "I need help."
  - Someone looking for the customer service phone number
  - "I need to talk to a real human about this transfer fee!"
- "I have a general question."
  - Woman who wants to know if the bank is open in the evenings
  - "How much are wire transfers?"
  - "Do you insure savings accounts?"
  - First-time home purchasers looking for info on mortgages
  - "Do you do student loans?"
  - "What are your fees?"
- "I have a question about my statement/account."
  - "What was this charge on my statement?"
  - "Did my wire transfer go through?"
  - Person who has a mortgage with this bank that has been sold to another bank
- "I want to make a payment/move money."
  - Person who wants to transfer money from savings to checking
  - "I want to pay off my loan right now."
- "I want to set up new services on my account."
  - Person setting up online bill pay
  - Person who wants to transfer money from savings to checking
- "I want to find out how you are better than other banks."
  - Businessman switching banks to escape fees
- "I need a new bank account."
  - Freshman arriving at college
  - Man who has too much in one of his other accounts and is worried about FDIC limits

Note that a single yellow sticky can show up in more than one category. If this is the case, simply copy the yellow sticky and place it in both categories on your worksheet.

The magic, and pain, of this exercise

This recategorization is both painful and fairly miraculous. It's painful because it is a transition from an old way of thinking about users and customers to a new way of thinking about users and customers.

In many cases, it is a transition from a company-centric way of thinking about the needs of users (e.g., we have a mortgage department, so all mortgage customers are in a category, and all checking account users are in another category) to a user-centric way of thinking (e.g., from the *user's* point of view, what do your company, products, and services do for *me*?).

There will be a few categories and sticky notes that will cause the team trouble and require a lot of conversation, but be persistent. Once you get through this process, the magic happens.

What's the magic? Almost inevitably, this process results in a *major* epiphany for the workshop participants. They suddenly realize that they have been thinking about their users in the wrong way. They see that the existing categories of users and ways of talking about users don't help them or the rest of the organization really understand and address what users actually want and need.

But how do you know these needs and wants are real? You haven't used any data!

Yes, it's true that this process doesn't use any hard data. What it does use is the embedded knowledge of the company and product's users that exists in the minds of the workshop participants. The people you are working with have been thinking about the business for months or years; there is a lot of very relevant and very accurate information in their heads about their users and customers. The participants know why the business exists and what problems it should be solving for people. Additionally, most businesses are *not* rocket science; for example, we wrote the categories and recategorization in the example above ourselves, and we are not bankers. It's impossible to argue, however, that these categories of users are not important just because we didn't use data to create them.

The truth is that most companies and teams are far from being user centered at all; simply recategorizing assumptions based on the users' point of view yields seemingly obvious insights that simply didn't exist before the workshop.

If you plan to use ad hoc personas as your final personas (that is, not continue on to data-driven personas), skip steps 2 and 3 and move on to step 4 (create persona sketches).

IDENTIFY CATEGORIES AND SUBCATEGORIES

After your reclustering exercise, you'll probably have 20 to 30 pink "I want/I need" sticky notes arrayed across your worksheet. Ask someone to read each pink sticky as you write it up on the whiteboard or on easel paper. Though this process does take a few minutes, it's important to do it while the whole team is assembled. The process allows everyone to step back and see the results of the work they've done.

After you've written all the pink sticky labels up, review them as a team. Usually, you will find that there are categories and subcategories that arise from the pink sticky notes. In our banking example, we might identify the following category/subcategory combinations:

- "I have an account, and want to do something new."
  - ○ "I have a question about my statement/account."
  - ○ "I want to make a payment/move money."
  - ○ "I want to set up new services on my account."
- "I am shopping for a new bank."
  - ○ "I want to find out how you are better than other banks."
  - ○ "I need a new bank account."

And so on.

In step 3 (below), you'll use these categories and subcategories to create your ad hoc persona skeletons.

STORY FROM THE FIELD

Ad Hoc Personas and Empathetic Focus

Donald A. Norman, Nielsen Norman Group

Personas as a Communication Tool

Design is in many ways an act of communication, but to communicate effectively the designer must have a clear, cohesive, and understandable image of the product being designed and the user of the product must be able to understand that communication. By emphasizing the several types of unique individuals who will be using the product, personas aid the designer in maintaining focus— concentrating on design aspects individual personas require and eliminating from the design things they will find superfluous. Personas are tools for focus and aids to communication, and for this they only need to be realistic, not real and not necessarily even accurate (as long as they are appropriate characterizations of the user base). Although it is often fun to read the detailed descriptions of personas and to pry into their private and social lives, I have never understood how these personal details actually aid in the design process itself. They seem completely superfluous.

Thus, a major virtue of personas is the establishment of empathy and understanding of the individuals who use the product. It is important that each persona seem real, allowing the designer to ask, "How would Mary respond to this? Or Peter? Or Bashinka?"

Personas also play an important communicative role within the design community and within the company producing the product. When one discusses the product in terms of its impact on the individual personas, the language of the discussion is automatically based on that of the people who use it and the benefits (or difficulties) that would accrue to them. This is in contrast to the technical language so often applied when talking about the features and attributes of the product. Personas make it easier to be human centered. As others have noted, personas provide a common language regarding experience so that designers, engineers, and marketing people can unambiguously communicate when they talk about the product. The same tool is valuable when the product is being designed by different groups within the company—and this is always the case with any large, complex product. The use of personas helps standardize the approach of each group, so there is continuity of level and function in the different parts of the product.

Empathetic Focus

Another purpose of the persona, I believe, is to add empathetic focus to the design. By focus I mean that the design must be clear and coherent. It is not a collection of features added willy-nilly throughout the life span of the product, even if each feature by itself makes sense. Rather, it is having a clear image of what the product is meant to be—and what it is not meant to be—and rejecting features that do not fit. By empathy, I mean an understanding of and identification with the user population, the better to ensure they will be able to take advantage of the product and to use it readily and easily—not with frustration but with pleasure.

Using Ad Hoc Personas

As a consultant to companies, I often find myself having to make my points quickly—quite often in only a few hours. This short duration makes impossible any serious attempt at gathering data or using real observations. Instead, I have found that people can often mine their own extensive experiences to create effective personas that bring home design points strongly and effectively.

In one case, for a major software company, one of their major customer bases was American college students. We quickly identified several classes (called *cases*) of students:

- *Case 1*—A student attending a two-year community college while holding a full-time job
- *Case 2*—A student in a four-year institution who wants to have a successful business career
- *Case 3*—A student who is only in school for lack of anything else to do and who has few desires other than to have a good time

We quickly invented one relevant persona per case: a hard-working, single mother (case 1); a serious full-time student with no outside experience or responsibilities (case 2); and a lackadaisical, laid-back goof-off (case 3). Unlike traditional persona studies, these were not based on data, but each was described in sufficient detail (including names) so that the group all agreed they felt like people they knew.

I have found that an excellent way of using a persona is to have someone role play the part. In this way, only one person has to develop an in-depth knowledge of the persona, and everyone else uses the role player as an expert informant in activities such as participatory design.

In this case, I divided the attendees at my workshop into three groups to do a design exercise, with someone role playing the relevant persona as expert informant. The result was wonderful to behold.

The teams all produced highly user-centered designs based on the products of their respective companies. The designs were all very different in type and spirit from the products of their company, even though some of the designers of those products were in the workshop. The differences were striking.

In regard to case 3, the student kept saying, "I don't care," when asked about choices, while simultaneously making it clear that he wanted a system that required no effort or thought on his part and that gave him his preferred outcome (receiving a degree, but with minimal impairment to his preferred lifestyle). In regard to cases 1 and 2, students were more involved, but because of their different requirements imposed different demands on the software. Everyone agreed that this simple exercise had altered their perspective on what a product ought to do and how they should approach design.

Another consulting job was for a major publisher of city-information products. This group of attendees consisted of the executive team for the company, and although none of them actually designed products, the product groups were all under their control. For this workshop, I had the group invent two couples. One couple was young, newly married, and about to have their first child. They had only a small apartment and did not have much money. Their task was to use the city guide to find a crib for the expected child. The other couple was older and retired, with significant discretionary income. All of their children were away from home, living independently. My original intention was to have this older couple book a travel adventure, but because we were running out of time I switched the exercise. I announced that the older couple were the parents of the expectant mother, and they wanted to purchase a crib for their new grandchild.

The new exercise was extremely rewarding because it demonstrated how the two couples approached the task very differently, with different emphases, different search characteristics, and very different values. Having the workshop attendees work on the same problem was serendipitous, for it revealed the deficiencies in the existing city guide. Interestingly enough, after the conclusion of the exercise several of the executives admitted that their own behavior mimicked that of the older couple, including the observation that they seldom turned to their own city guide as a first step. This sensitized them to the fact that their own behavior with their company's product was a relevant datum. "Realize that others might behave the same way you do," I admonished them. "Take your own behavior seriously."

The Final Assessment

These two different examples of personas are very different from the traditional usage of the concept. They were created quickly, did not use real data, and were employed without much background information and attention to detail. But, even so, they serve as wonderful tools for building understanding and empathy into the design process in a way that would be impossible with any other method.

Do personas have to be accurate? Do they require a large body of research? Not always, I conclude. Personas must indeed reflect the target group for the design team, but for some purposes that is sufficient.

A persona allows designers to bring their own life-long experience to bear on the problem, and because each persona is a realistic individual person the designers can focus on features, behaviors, and expectations appropriate for this individual. This allows the designer to screen off from consideration all those other wonderful ideas they may have. If the other ideas are as useful and valuable as they might seem, the designer's challenge is to either create a scenario for the existing persona in which these attributes make sense or to invent a new persona for whom the same applies. The designer then needs to justify inclusion of this new persona by making the business-case argument that the new persona does indeed represent an important target population for the product.

STORY FROM THE FIELD

The Benefits of Creating Assumption Personas

Laura Grange, Program Manager, and Rahul Singh, Software Developer, Amazon.com

At Amazon.com, we decided to create a quick set of assumption personas as the first step before creating data-driven personas—in this case, for a particular product being built for the software developer community. The product manager sent out an invitation to the entire team, inviting them to participate in the brainstorming session. She got a reply from her boss asking why we were creating personas in a brainstorming session. He thought, quite rightly, that "You don't brainstorm personas. You put them together through customer information, analysis, and feedback."

The product manager replied, "This is a valid point. We're using assumption personas as a method of jump-starting persona development. The team gets together to get all assumptions about the target user population out on the table. We create assumption personas out of these, which we can do quickly—in one or two two-hour meetings.

"We then use these assumption personas as the basis for evaluating the research and data we have, so the persona data effort becomes centered on validating the (usually) fairly accurate assumptions. Why do it this way? For several reasons:

- "The assumptions about the target user population typically reflect significant contributions from teams that have been working on products for a while. Creating assumption personas capitalizes on this rich but unarticulated information and quickly aligns all of the assumptions. This alignment is valuable even if the persona effort goes no further. There is value in creating the assumption personas simply for the benefits derived from aligning the team's assumptions.
- "Using data to validate assumption personas is a lot easier and quicker than creating personas from scratch (from data).
- "If you create personas from scratch without surfacing the assumptions first, you end up with personas that are more difficult for the team to use. Building assumption personas helps build buy-in."

This quick explanation was enough to give the manager confidence that the exercise was worth the limited amount of time it would take. It was great to hear that he already knew about personas and their relationship to data! After the first assumption persona session, we got the following e-mail message from one of the developers on the project, who was dubious at the start of the meeting but soon became an active and enthusiastic participant:

> I was one of the people in the persona brainstorm and I just wanted to say that it was really quite a good exercise IMHO [in my humble opinion]. I went into it thinking it was going to be a waste of time, but it wasn't. In fact, parts of it were quite scary and a bit too close to home.

This quote is especially interesting because I was working with developers to create assumption personas who were also developers! It was easy for the development staff to assume they knew the users because the users in this case share the same job description as the development staff. During our first two-hour session we identified several assumption personas that we were able to discuss and invite stakeholders to prioritize.

Step 2. Process the data

During the *family planning* phase, you collected and reviewed many data sources, including research reports containing summaries, highlights, and significant details extracted from raw data of some sort. Your next task is to process these research findings, pulling out the bits and pieces that are relevant to your team and product domain. Once you have isolated these relevant factoids, you and your core team will process them (through an assimilation exercise) using the user categories you agreed upon in step 1.

DATA PROCESSING METHODS

There are many ways you can go about processing your data to create personas, and we strongly recommend a specific approach: affinity diagramming (which we and others often refer to as *assimilation*). We use the assimilation method because it is quick, easily understood, and is overtly collaborative. It also works well across a variety of data types and formats.

As an alternative, you might consider doing quantitative analysis (such as factor analysis, cluster analysis, or some other multivariate statistical procedure) or qualitative analysis (with a tool such as Atlas.ti, HyperQual2, HyperRESEARCH, NUDIST, or Xsight, a trimmed-down version of NUDIST). These tools are quite useful for extracting the underlying themes from any type of data, as you possibly did with raw data during the family planning phase. For example, Rashmi Sinha [2003] describes a persona creation process using principal components analysis to identify the critical underlying dimensions. Her analysis uncovered independent clusters of needs (very similar to goals), which were then used in combination with other information as the basis for creating distinct personas. Such an approach is similar to cluster analysis and other statistical techniques typically used in the creation of quantitative market segments. Although we believe that analyses such as these can be a great starting point, we recommend that you also conduct a data assimilation exercise as the primary method of persona creation, particularly when combining data from a variety of sources.

COLLABORATIVE ASSIMILATION HAS SIDE BENEFITS

Because the entire core team is involved in the assimilation exercise, everyone has an opportunity to see the factoids from all data sources. By the time the assimilation exercise is complete, everyone on the core team will have been exposed to the data and to the inherent patterns, themes, and relationships in the data. This shared understanding is priceless. As a side benefit, through your assimilation exercise you create a core team that is fully cognizant of a huge amount of data from a wide variety of sources. Armed with your clustered and labeled data, you and your team are perfectly prepared for the next step: identifying and creating skeletons.

ASSIMILATION WORKS WELL, BUT IT DOES HAVE A FEW DRAWBACKS

Assimilation does have a couple of drawbacks you should be aware of before you begin:

- During an assimilation exercise, you and your team will group factoids that have been extracted from their original contexts. Factoids that are unrelated when you read them in context may seem related (and end up grouped) after they have been extracted from their sources and copied onto sticky notes. This opens the possibility for misrepresenting the original data in your final personas.
- Identifying relationships between factoids is a subjective exercise. Two different teams might group factoids in different ways and end up with different conclusions.

Because affinity diagramming does open the door to misrepresentations of your data, we encourage you to schedule enough time to validate your personas after you have created them. However, it is also important to remember that personas can never fully express or represent the data in the same way it is expressed in the original sources, and that this is not the point of the personas. Rather, personas will help you communicate the essential and helpful information the data contain. The danger that some aspects of the personas *may* misrepresent some aspects of the data is outweighed by the guarantee that the personas *will* convey important and data-driven information to your product team.

PLAN YOUR ASSIMILATION MEETING

An assimilation meeting typically lasts two to four hours. It should include all members of your persona core team. These meetings work best in medium to large rooms that have plenty of wall space (or floor space). Before the meeting, make sure you have plenty of sticky notes, markers, tape, and large sheets of paper on hand.

If you have a relatively small to medium amount of data, you should be able to assimilate all of it in a single meeting. If you have a large amount of data, consider distributing the data sources and request that your colleagues identify relevant factoids before the meeting. Alternatively, simply schedule multiple meetings that focus independently on each identified user category. If you do the latter, make sure to have a final meeting in which the assimilation results for all user categories are reviewed together. Generally, the agenda for an assimilation meeting should be as follows:

1. Describe the rules, goal, and outcome of the meeting.
2. Identify key data points (factoids) in the data sources.
3. Transfer key data points (factoids) to sticky notes.
4. Post user category labels in various locations in the room.
5. Assimilate the key factoids.
6. Label groups (and do some higher order organization).

DESCRIBE THE GOAL AND OUTCOME OF THE MEETING

Your goals for this meeting are fairly simple:

- Filter and prioritize the data down to the most important and relevant bits of information, or factoids, for your specific product and team.
- Organize these factoids into meaningful, related groups, paying attention to the user categories you identified in step 1.

These groups of factoids will serve as the core content and structure for creating personas, but note that when this meeting is over you will not have personas in hand.

IDENTIFY KEY DATA POINTS (FACTOIDS) IN THE DATA SOURCES

The first step in processing the data is to review and filter the information in each of the research reports. You do this because not every data point in a given study or report is relevant to the definition of your target audience or to the design of your product. Whether it is done before or during the meeting, ask your core team members to highlight findings they think are key in understanding your target audience or that are highly insightful toward defining aspects of your product. In other words, you want them to look for findings that are relevant to your market, industry, or domain. Highlight any facts that seem important to your product's audience or to the product itself. Figure 4.4 shows example highlighting in a market research report.

Determining what pieces of information are important may seem daunting at first. Don't fret too much over this until you have tried it. When in doubt, be inclusive. It is better to start with too many factoids than too few. You might be tempted to develop criteria ahead of time (e.g., criteria for factoids that are irrelevant, too detailed, too broad, or otherwise not very helpful). We recommend that you do not. In our experience, such criteria are not easy to come by and are difficult to apply. Attempting to generate them consumes valuable time that could be used more directly with the data. In fact, because your core team consists of key individuals across your organization and from different disciplines, each person will have different insights and perspectives on what is important. This is good. You will find that agreement on the importance of any individual piece of data actually happens through the assimilation process.

In the end, even your full personas will *not* include or reference all of the data you find and cluster. If you find yourself drowning in data or your team stuck in "analysis paralysis," just force yourself to move on to the next step and trust that the process will still work. Be willing to try things out, and plan to use your time on iteration (not initial perfection).

TRANSFER FACTOIDS TO STICKY NOTES

After everyone has had a chance to comb through the assigned research documents, it is time to go back through the items they highlighted, reevaluate their importance, and then transfer

What to Do if You Are Drowning in Data

If you have collected a lot of data during the *family planning* phase, you might find it difficult to get started with your data analysis. Staring at a huge stack of printouts can be incredibly intimidating. If you are having a difficult time getting started, try sorting your printouts into three stacks: very relevant (to your product domain and intended users), moderately relevant, and not very relevant. Conduct an assimilation exercise with only the very relevant documents and see what types of clusters you get. After you run your first assimilation exercise—even if it is just with a subset of the data resources collected—you will find that it is easier and much quicker to identify interesting factoids in future exercises. If you are then still dissatisfied with the depth of insights revealed initially, and have the time, you can continue assimilating with less relevant data.

Create quick data-driven personas

If you have had time to collect data but need to create and introduce personas on a tight schedule, you should spend as much time as possible understanding and assimilating your data to create meaningful and relevant skeletons (there is always time to add more detail after the personas are introduced). If you decide to create quick, data-driven personas, your process during the conception and gestation phase might run as follows:

- Step 1 (1/2 to 1 hour)—Meet with your core team and product stakeholders to identify categories of users that are important to your business and product domain.
- Step 2 (2 to 4 hours)—Process the data. The core team should thoroughly read the data sources, identify important factoids, and complete an affinity exercise to cluster the factoids around the categories of users.
- Step 3 (2 to 4 hours)—Identify and create skeletons (either in a meeting with your core team or independently). Evaluate your processed data to verify the categories of users and to identify subcategories of users. Create skeletons from the key data points for each subcategory you have identified.
- Step 4 (2 to 4 hours)—With your core team and product stakeholders, prioritize the skeleton personas. Add concrete details and personal facts to enrich and personalize the skeletons. If you need to speed up the conception and gestation process, spend your time making sure that the skeletons from which you create the sketches reflect the assimilated data and your conclusions about the resulting categories.

If you do need to create your personas quickly, be aware that the stakeholder review and prioritization can be an unpredictable and a time-consuming process. To get these done quickly, you will have to be well organized and very proactive; for example, you will need to provide clear goals, explicit instructions, and time lines to your stakeholders.

them to another medium to enable assimilation. Each important factoid should be copied or cut out of the original document. We prefer to do the factoid assimilation using sticky notes, though larger sheets of paper (e.g., 8-1/2 × 11 or easel sheets) can be useful for readability and easier collaboration. Figure 4.5 shows an example of some facts being pulled from a field study report (qualitative findings) and transferred to sticky notes. It may be more practical to simply physically cut the data points out of the research document with scissors and glue them onto 3 × 5 index cards. (You could also use printable sticky notes or 3 × 5 cards and have someone type them in and print them during the meeting.) Either way, remember to note the source and page number on each factoid. Remember to include the source and page number on every sticky note.

POST USER CATEGORY LABELS AROUND THE ROOM

Before starting your assimilation exercise, it is important to seed the room with the user category labels you identified in step 1. If your categories are based on quantitatively

While 38 percent of White non-Hispanic children and 35 percent of Asian and Pacific Islander children used the Internet at home, just 15 percent of Black children and 13 percent of Hispanic children did.[5]

More school-age children use computers at school than have access to them at home.

School is a major influence on children's access to computers. Among children of school age (6 to 17 years), 2 in 3 had access to a computer at home in 2000. However, 4 in 5 actually used a computer at school.

More than half of school-age children had access to computers both in school and at home (57 percent). However, many children had access in only one location or the other. Of them, far more had access in school than had access at home. Twenty-three percent of school-age children had access to a computer only at school, compared with just 10 percent who had access only at home. Adding all three groups together, 9 in 10 school-age children had access to a computer somewhere, leaving just 10 percent of children who had no access to a computer in any locale (Figure 2).

Schools level the playing field by giving computer access to children who have none at home.

For children 6 to 17 years old, computer use at school was more nearly equal across different income, race, or ethnic groups than computer access at home (Figure 3).

School-age children in family households with incomes of $75,000 or more had the highest rates of home

[5]The proportions of home Internet users among Asian and Pacific Islander and White non-Hispanic children were not significantly different. The proportions of home Internet users among Black and Hispanic children were also not significantly different.

computer access, at 94 percent, compared with those with incomes below $25,000, at 35 percent (a difference of about 60 percentage points). But at school, while 87 percent of those with the highest incomes used a computer, 72 percent of those with the lowest incomes did so, a difference of only 15 percentage points.

Figure 3 illustrates a similar equalizing effect observed among children of different racial or ethnic groups. At home, access varied from high to low by 41 percentage points. However, at school the range was much smaller, just 14 percentage points.

The net result of the effect schools have in giving computer access across income, racial, and ethnic groups is a leveling of the computer access that children of different groups have compared to what they would have had if home were the only place available for them to use computers. The absolute percentage-point gap in total computer access between children from family households with the highest and lowest incomes was only about one-third as large as the gap in

home access between these two groups. Similarly, the overall computer access gap between White non-Hispanic school-age children and Black or Hispanic school-age children was just over one-third the size of the gap between these groups in home computer access.[6]

ADULT ACCESS TO COMPUTERS AND THE INTERNET

More adults have computers and use the Internet at home than ever before.

More than half of all adults 18 years old and over, 55 percent, lived in a household with at least one computer in 2000, compared with only 46 percent in 1998. Thirty-seven percent of all adults used the Internet at home, compared with just 23 percent in 1998 (Table C).

The oldest adults had the lowest rates of home Internet use. Only 13 percent of those 65 years old or over used the Internet at home.

[6]The proportions of overall computer access among Black and Hispanic school-age children were not significantly different.

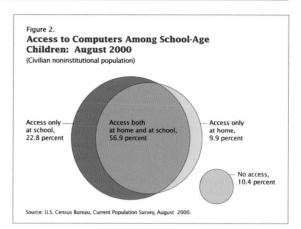

Figure 2.
Access to Computers Among School-Age Children: August 2000
(Civilian noninstitutional population)

Access only at school, 22.8 percent

Access both at home and at school, 56.9 percent

Access only at home, 9.9 percent

No access, 10.4 percent

Source: U.S. Census Bureau, Current Population Survey, August 2000.

U.S. Census Bureau   5

FIGURE 4.4
Data highlighting in a quantitative market research report. (Adapted from U.S. Census Bureau, 2001.)

derived segments, include the major defining characteristics of the segments as well. These labels will serve to direct your initial placement and high-level organization of the factoids. We recommend that you do this with larger sheets of paper instead of sticky notes to ensure that they are salient and visible (see Figure 4.6). Be sure to leave room between and underneath each label for the multitude of sticky note factoids that will be placed in relation to them. Your assimilation and prioritization activities, detailed in the following, will revolve around these predefined categories, so make sure everyone in the room is intimately familiar with them.

ASSIMILATE THE FACTOIDS

Now the interaction (and fun) begins. To do the assimilation, everyone will get up (at the same time) and place their factoids around the room, positioning related factoids near each

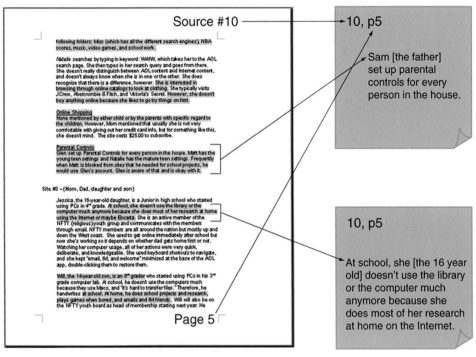

FIGURE 4.5
An example of two factoids identified in a qualitative research document (field study report) and transferred to sticky notes.

45

FIGURE 4.6
Seed the walls with your user category labels. (Photograph courtesy of Jonathan Hayes.)

other to form groups or clusters. Ask everyone to review their factoids and start putting them on the wall or floor in relation to other people's factoids (and in relation to the predefined categories).

For example, if one person has a factoid about children's Internet use behaviors after school and another has a factoid about children's daily entertainment activities in the home, these

FIGURE 4.7
An assimilation exercise in progress. In this case, the factoids are written on larger sheets of paper to facilitate collaboration. (Photograph courtesy of Jonathan Hayes.)

two factoids might be placed near each other. As everyone adds their factoids, similar or related factoids will cluster, and factoids that are not related will end up far apart. Figure 4.7 shows an assimilation exercise in progress.

During your assimilation exercise, you might find factoid "islands" of sticky notes that turn out to be difficult to cluster. If you find factoids that cause extended arguments or that you feel you have to force into a cluster, put them aside and return to them later. You won't use every factoid you have created and clustered in your finished personas.

You might also find that a single factoid fits well in more than one location. Make copies of the factoid and put it everywhere it belongs. As the assimilation progresses, you will find that your opinions on how to cluster factoids evolves. Your team will probably want to redistribute factoids and even move entire clusters as the exercise progresses, and you should encourage them to do so until they feel that the clusters make sense.

Look for "puddles" of factoids. If you see more than five to ten factoids clustered closely together (in a "puddle"), try to find additional distinctions between the factoids on those sticky notes. Instead of a single large cluster, try to create several smaller clusters that reflect these distinctions.

LABEL THE CLUSTERS OF FACTOIDS

As the clusters of factoids become stable, begin labeling the clusters with sticky notes. Be sure to use a different color for the labels (see Figure 4.8). Remember that assimilation is given structure by the categories you initially identified, but at its core the resulting clusters are determined by the data (i.e., it is a bottom-up process). Not all of your clustered factoids have to fit cleanly into your defined categories. When you label your clusters, you will identify supporting data related to your categories, distinctions in categories (subcategories), and new information about your targeted users (see Figure 4.9).

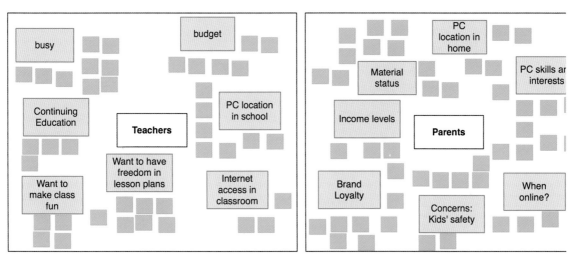

FIGURE 4.8

Categories of users (white), cluster labels (pink), and factoids (blue) after an assimilation exercise. In this illustration, we show the labels (pink) much larger than the sticky-note clusters. This is simply so you can read the cluster labels. We recommend that you use sticky notes to label the clusters of factoids (in this example, blue sticky notes) and assumptions (in this example, yellow sticky notes; see Handy Detail, below) you find during your assimilation exercise because this facilitates moving and changing the labels as needed.

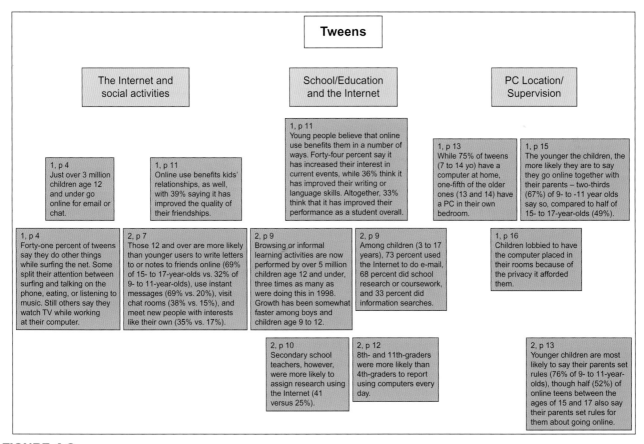

FIGURE 4.9

Some example clusters of factoids.

> ### HANDY DETAIL
> **You Can Include Collected Assumptions in Your Assimilation Exercise**
>
> If you collected assumptions during family planning (or to help you identify categories of users), you can assimilate these along with the factoids. Assign one sticky-note color to indicate assumptions so you don't confuse them with factoids. Assimilating assumptions along with your factoids allows you to easily see which assumptions are supported by data (those that end up clustered with factoids) and which ones are not (those that end up alone or in small clusters with other assumptions).
>
> Assimilating assumptions in with your factoids can produce some very interesting results; for example, you can create your categories, assimilate your assumptions (perhaps using yellow sticky notes), and then assimilate your factoids (using blue sticky notes). After your assimilation is complete and you have labeled all of your clusters of factoids (see material following), you will probably find that some clusters include only blue sticky notes (factoids) or only yellow sticky notes (assumptions). This is helpful information. If a cluster includes only factoids, it could mean:
>
> - Your organization doesn't have any assumptions about this topic.
> - Your organization does have assumptions about the topic but you have not surfaced these assumptions yet.
>
> To find out, you can ask your stakeholders to tell you their assumptions about the topic in question. If a cluster includes only assumptions, it could mean:
>
> - The data do not support the assumptions.
> - You did not find and use the data related to these assumptions in your exercise.
>
> If you find a cluster with only assumptions, look for more data to either support or specifically contradict the assumptions. You know that the assumptions exist and therefore could exert influence on the design of your product. It is worth looking for data now.

DATA TEND TO CLUSTER IN EXPECTED AND UNEXPECTED WAYS

The data you have assimilated had many different authors with many different purposes. It is not possible to determine before you assimilate it what truly insightful and compelling relationships in information you will find. Factoids will not all naturally cluster in ways that seem immediately relevant to your persona effort. This information may not map neatly to user types or goals, but it may contain domain-related insights that prove invaluable to your effort. If you find "odd" clusters developing, don't try to force them to fit. Examine them for insights into your user base. You may want to follow up any perplexing questions with additional user research.

KNOW WHEN TO STOP

Continue the assimilation and labeling exercise until:

- Everyone has placed their set of factoids on the floor or wall in relation to other factoids.
- The groups or clusters have started to settle.

Note that you may have to just force yourself to stop, as the organization of factoids, labeling, and reorganization can go on for a long time. One way to force the issue is simply to stop once every group has a label (even if you don't have agreement on the current organization and labeling).

IDENTIFY SUBCATEGORIES OF USERS

When you listed current language around categories of users in step 1, you thought about the differences in user roles, user goals, and user segments among the groups of your target users. To identify subcategories of users, you will now think about these differences *within* each of your categories based on key findings across the clusters. For example, if you created categories of users defined primarily by differences between user roles, you can now examine each of those categories for important differences in user goals and user segments. You may also find that there are specific subroles that form subcategories. You should create a subcategory to describe any product-significant differences you find within your categories that seem important and are clearly indicated in the assimilated data.

CLUSTERS IDENTIFY GROUPS OF FACTS; SUBCATEGORIES IDENTIFY GROUPS OF PEOPLE

Look at the data clustered under each of your user categories. As a team, evaluate and discuss the possibility that each category should be divided into two or more subcategories. Consider roles, goals, and segments in this assessment. As you identify subcategories, you can write them on a whiteboard. You might also find it helpful to transfer the subcategory names onto sticky notes and place them appropriately in your assimilated data. In doing this exercise, you are simply exploring the possible groups of users that have emerged from your data.

WHEN DOES A DIFFERENCE MERIT A SUBCATEGORY?

The most difficult part of this process is determining whether a difference is *meaningful and useful*. Step back and see if subcategories are bubbling up out of your assimilated data.

Your goal is to express what Bob Barlow-Busch (in his contributed chapter "Marketing Versus Design Personas" in *The Persona Lifecycle: Keeping People in Mind Throughout Product Design*) calls "the differences that make a difference" between the types of people described in your data sources. As your core team discusses the results of your assimilation, consider the following questions in determining which merit the creation of subcategories:

- *Does this subcategory represent a group of users important to the design of our product?* Does this subcategory likely require different features from other subcategories and different ways of interacting with our product?
- *Does this subcategory represent a group of users important to our business?* Does this subcategory produce revenue, bring mind share, or influence other people regarding your product?
- *Is this subcategory clearly unique compared to the other subcategories?* Is the subcategory different enough to warrant a separate and distinct persona?

WHAT IF WE END UP CREATING A LOT OF CATEGORIES AND SUBCATEGORIES?

As long as you feel you can distinguish the categories and subcategories you discover in the data, it is fine (and often a good idea) to create subcategories. Create as many categories and subcategories as it takes to capture your data. You will not necessarily create personas for all of them. The product design and development team will likely not be able to embrace more for consumer-facing products to have a minority of customers account for a majority of profits. It therefore makes sense to highlight their needs. (It might also be the case that noncustomers, who the company hopes to attract, want more out of the product than it currently delivers.) But the principle is the same as designing for the neediest users: See if, by satisfying a design problem for the most demanding users, you can satisfy a much larger group of users. Thus, this can be valuable complementary approach, but just use it with care.

Step 3. Create skeletons

By the time you get to step 3, you have identified important categories and subcategories of users. If you are planning on using ad hoc personas, you identified the categories based on logical groupings of your "I want" and "I need" statements. If you moved on to step 2, your categories and subcategories are based on the patterns you found in your data.

Once you have identified and agreed upon the categories and subcategories of users, you are ready to create *skeletons*. Skeletons are very brief, typically bulleted, lists of distinguishing

49

data ranges for each subcategory of user. Skeletons help your core team transition from thinking about categories of users to focusing on specific details. They also allow your team to present the key findings of the assimilation exercise to stakeholders.

AD HOC PERSONA SKELETONS

Use the groupings of pink sticky notes described at the end of step 1 (above) as your skeletons. Tape sheets of easel paper to the wall, and write the skeleton description at the top of each sheet. Under that, add the cluster labels that you used to create the skeleton. Continuing the example we started in step 1:

- Skeleton 1—"I have an account and want to do something new."
  - "I have a question about my statement/account."
  - "I want to make a payment/move money."
  - "I want to set up new services on my account."
- Skeleton 2—"I am shopping for a new bank."
  - "I want to find out how you are better than other banks."
  - "I need a new bank account."

You'll likely have 10 to 20 (or even more) of these skeletons from your assumption exercise. Don't worry about the numbers; we'll cull these down to a reasonable amount later. Also, you may feel the need to further elaborate some of these skeletons, but resist the temptation at this point. For now, simply number them so they are easy to identify during the prioritization exercise.

DATA-DRIVEN PERSONA SKELETONS

Create one skeleton for each of the subcategories you identified. On each skeleton, list the cluster labels that relate to that subcategory. These cluster labels will become headings in your skeleton. Because you will be comparing and prioritizing skeletons against each other, it is important that each contain at least somewhat comparable information. Consider including common characteristics or headings across all of your skeletons. If you do this, you may find that you are missing information for some skeletons. In these cases, either leave that information blank, perhaps marking it as "need data," or make an informed estimation

Skeleton	Sketch
Boy, age 10–13 **Computer use at school** • Has access to a shared computer in his classroom or a computer lab shared by the whole school • Has at least one computer-related assignment a week • Finds computer use at school boring **Internet use at home** • Shares a home computer with family • Uses Internet to play games and (sometimes) do school work **Interests/Activities** • Likes to talk about games with friends • Likes video games more than computer games • Participates in multiple organized sports	**Danny** Danny is 12 and he just started 6th grade, which is very cool. He has computer lab once a week and he likes it a lot. He usually spends recess in the computer lab looking for info about the Lakers and for new games to try. He thinks he's a computer pro; his mom's been coming to him for help with silly stuff for years now.

FIGURE 4.10
A skeleton versus a sketch persona. Note that the skeleton includes headings derived from cluster labels (from the assimilation exercise) and data points. For now, avoid any narrative details that might distract stakeholders as they try to prioritize the skeletons.

about what it might be. If you do the latter, be sure to indicate that it is an assumption to be followed up on.

Under each heading, create a bulleted summary of the information you found in the data. You are not exhaustively including every aspect of the associated factoids. Try to identify the key points that capture the essence of the subcategory. Do not give the skeletons names or other personal details that make them feel like people (which may relate to but are not specific to the data). As shown in Figure 4.10, skeletons are not sketch personas; they are selected facts that define and distinguish your subcategories of users.

How many skeletons should I create?

We recommend that you create skeletons only for subcategories of users you believe are interesting or important to your product. If you create a large number of skeletons, you can use the prioritization exercise following to narrow in on the few you will evolve into personas. However, it is much easier for stakeholders to prioritize fewer skeletons. Use the criteria listed previously in the "When Does a Difference Merit a Subcategory?" section to discuss each skeleton as you create it and to combine, augment, or discard skeletons.

HANDY DETAIL

Think About Your Users

Earlier in this book, we reminded you to think about the users of your own work products. Skeletons are a perfect example of the importance of this. Skeletons are documents you use to communicate with your business stakeholders. You will ask these stakeholders to prioritize the skeletons in accordance with business objectives. This is precisely why you do not want to include fictional details (such as a name, favorite color, or favorite activity). Any information in the skeleton document that is not obviously derived directly from data will distract the stakeholders and invite debate on details— and this is not the appropriate time for that debate.

HANDY DETAIL

What if You Find "Scary" Information in the Data?

What if you have some data that make you create a persona that inherently will not like your product? For example, maybe you are building a product for television and the data indicate that people in a key set of target users are too busy to watch television. What do you do? If you run into this type of problem, you can:

- Escalate the data you have found to the stakeholders, so they can reevaluate the strategy for the product. If they push back, show them the data that led to your conclusions.
- Reevaluate your data sources to consider whether they are really in line with the existing strategy with respect to target users.
- Build this information, and the related design challenges, into the personas you create. Given that your targets currently don't like to watch television, and that you cannot change the delivery medium, how do you get these people to change their behavior and turn on the television to access your product? How do you build a specific product that will appeal to them, given their needs and goals?

51

PERSONA GESTATION: STEPS 4, 5, AND 6

Once you have a set of skeletons, it is time to get feedback from your stakeholders. You will evaluate the importance of each skeleton to your business and product strategy and prioritize the skeletons accordingly. During gestation, you will identify a subset of skeletons to develop into personas.

Step 4. Prioritize the skeletons

It is time to prioritize your skeletons. To do this, schedule a meeting with members of your persona core team who understand the data you have collected and stakeholders empowered to make decisions about the strategic focus of the company. If stakeholders are not aware of the data and general process that led to these skeletons, present that information before introducing the skeletons to them. It is important to carefully plan and manage your prioritization meeting. Before you get started, remind everyone of the goals of the meeting and the impact their decisions will have on the project.

- *These skeletons were derived from data* and should map fairly clearly to the user types (categories and subcategories) you already reviewed together.
- *Prioritization should focus on immediate goals or low-hanging fruit.* Remind the team that the goal is to reduce the possible set of targets to just those that are critical *to your current product cycle.* Remember that you can prioritize the skeletons differently for subsequent versions of this product or for derivative or sibling products.
- *Prioritizing does not mean abandoning the interests of the lower priority skeletons.* It simply means deciding that, in the case of feature or functionality debates, the interests of the persona derived from the most important category or subcategory of users should be considered before anyone else's. If the stakeholders insist that all of the skeletons are critical, ask them to consider which would be *most useful* to the development staff. For example, have them do a Q-sort in which they can place a particular number of items in each of three priorities (high, medium, and low) and then have them sort within each category for one more gradation. You can always provide a slightly different set of personas to those teams who might benefit most from them (e.g., give your marketing team the set of personas closest to purchase decisions).
- *Prioritizing should be relatively easy if the business and strategic goals for the product are clear.* If prioritizing is difficult, it may mean that the stakeholders have some more work to do on their own. The skeletons and the detailed category and subcategory distinctions may be able to help them in this work (see information on articulating goals in Chapter 3).

It is important to reach consensus on the importance of the various skeletons, but it is not often easy to do so. When you ask your stakeholders to rank the skeletons you identified, they will probably respond in one of the following ways:

- "These three [or some subset] are the ones we really need to target."
- "They are all great."
- "They are all great, but we need to add X, Y, and Z customers to this list" or "You are omitting many of our major customer groups."
- "None of these is good."
- "I can't tell you which ones are the right ones."
- "Wow, we need to do some (more) customer research" or "We really need to know X about our users."

Although getting the first answer is the best, all of these answers are actually okay. They all provide useful, actionable information. Of course, you could get a completely different response from each stakeholder. If that happens, know that it is useful information and take note of it (in Chapter 7, we provide suggestions for expressing the value of the persona effort); also, demonstrating that key stakeholders had very different ideas about the target users before the personas were completed can be helpful.

Some of your stakeholders' answers may point to problems in your organization—problems in business strategy or lack of real knowledge about your customers. If this is your first time doing personas, we can pretty much guarantee that there will be difficulty and indecision. You are asking difficult questions that your stakeholders may not have been asked before or probably have not been asked this early in the product cycle.

STRUCTURE THE DISCUSSION

It is helpful to provide some structure to the prioritization exercise. The first step is simply to have them rank order the skeletons by perceived importance. There will likely be some disagreement as they sort the list. That is okay at this point. Once you have a rough order in place, we suggest assigning each skeleton one or more values that can more closely be tied to data:

- *Frequency of use*—How often would each skeleton use your product? Daily users would likely be more important regarding design decisions than those that only use your product once a month.
- *Size of market*—Roughly how many people does each skeleton represent? Larger markets are usually more important than smaller ones. Do you plan to aim your new product at a new market? In that case, you might consider the importance of a small market with growth potential.
- *Historic or potential revenue*—How much purchasing power does each skeleton encompass? If this is a new product, you may have to estimate this amount (e.g., through trade journals, market trends, market research, and understanding spending behaviors in related markets). In many cases, users might not directly make the purchase. Someone else buys such products for them. Still, they may influence those purchase decisions.
- *Strategic importance*—Decide who is your most strategically important audience. Is it those who make the most support calls, those who rely on your product for critical activities, those who use your competitor's product, or those who don't use yours or anyone's product yet? Are you trying to expand or grow your market? If that is your primary goal, do your skeletons include nonusers, technology pioneers, or trendsetters? Which target audiences will help your team innovate or stretch?
- *"The magic question"*—Sometimes it's just really hard for a team to say that one persona is more important than another. Try turning the question around: "If we don't make [persona name] ridiculously happy, we've failed." This is a great way to prioritize for many executive teams, because there are often a few personas who, when they are put into that sentence, are obviously critically important. For example, if you are creating a website for elementary-school children to introduce them to more of your company's games, then it's easy to say, "If we don't make Tanner (the 9-year-old who has one of our games but doesn't know about the others) ridiculously happy, we've failed." And this is likely to be *more* true than: "If we don't make Austin (the 12-year-old competitive gamer who has moved on to advanced gaming) ridiculously happy, we've failed."

You might derive other attributes that are more directly related to your line of business. Either way, you can use just one of these attributes or some combination of them to more accurately prioritize the skeletons. If time is critical for your stakeholders (which is usually the case), consider generating the values for these attributes yourself, and even doing the prioritization, prior to the meeting. To help your leadership team through the review process and toward a conclusion, remind the stakeholders that validation work can and will happen later in the process to ensure that the current decisions and resulting personas are on track.

ASK STAKEHOLDERS TO ASSIGN POINTS

Before you dive into a debate about which personas are most important, collect each individual executive's and stakeholder's opinions on prioritization. Ask everyone to take out a sheet of paper and write down all the names of the skeletons or sketch personas. Then ask them to indicate the relative priorities of each persona, using the following rules:

- You have a total of 100 points.
- Assign points to each persona to reflect the priority of that persona.
- You *cannot* give the same number of points to any two personas *unless* it's zero. (We guarantee that everyone will forget this rule and you'll have to ask for some revisions; for example, ask someone who gives both Tanner and Austin 20 points to change one to 19 and one to 21.)

53

- Create a grid on a whiteboard using persona names as the row headers and each executive's or stakeholder's name as the column headers.
- After everyone is done (*everyone* must be finished!), ask everyone to write their scores on the board.

This exercise inevitably brings to light discrepancies in thinking. It's very helpful to point out that these discrepancies are totally solvable and that one of the most helpful benefits of creating and using personas is that they highlight exactly these kinds of "not on the same page" issues for product teams. If these discrepancies had *not* surfaced, they still would have existed in the minds of key team members. Surfacing these issues is the first step toward solving them.

Record all the scores in a spreadsheet, and work with the meeting participants to come to agreement on the scores for each persona. You will need these when you move on to the adulthood phase. Note that the participants may have to continue the debate beyond a single meeting to reach agreement on the priorities.

Note that this method will not be as easy if you have more than eight to ten skeletons or sketches.

REMEMBER, IT'S *THEIR* DECISION

You are going to have definite opinions about which personas you think are most important and should be very high on the priority list. However, it's critical to remember that the prioritization process is an incredibly important step as you work to get buy-in, and therefore future support, from the executive team. It's the executives who should prioritize the personas, because the priorities should reflect business objectives. Remind the executives that you (and your team) can create excellent user experiences no matter which personas you are designing for (which you can!).

ASK IF ANYONE IS "MISSING"

Finally, you will want to ask your stakeholders if there are any missing skeletons (i.e., categories or subcategories of users) that are truly important to your company. If the answer is yes, have the stakeholders create those skeletons based on their collective knowledge and assumptions. You should include those additional assumption skeletons in the prioritization process.

BRIGHT IDEA

If You Are Stuck, Create Anti-Personas

Consider preparing skeletons of clear *non-targets* for your stakeholder review meeting. These are audiences that no one would refute as being outside your product's audience. Cooper refers to these as "negative personas" in *The Inmates Are Running the Asylum: Why High Tech Products Drive Us Crazy and How to Restore The Sanity* (Sams Publishing, 1999). These are usually quite obvious once described, but it is helpful to make it clear that your product is not for everyone in the known universe. For example, if you are developing an ecommerce website, your target audience probably shouldn't include people who are non-PC users, people without Internet connectivity, or (more ridiculously) infants and toddlers.

This is particularly useful if your team members see themselves as the target audience. It is also useful if there is a well-known audience or well-liked audience that is not a good business target. For example, anti-personas might include:

- Extreme novices ("My mom can't use this.")
- The seasoned expert or guru ("Macros and shortcut keys are critical!")
- The domain enthusiast (an obvious audience that might actually be very small in size and thus not a good target for the business).

Got a Lot of Possible Users? Plot Them by Critical Dimensions

Len Conte, BMC Software

Are you creating a product that will have many users? Not sure how to approach creating personas that will be useful? We suggest plotting large groups of users according to the critical dimensions of technical and domain expertise and looking for clusters of users (see Figure 4.11). For example, for an online media player you could collect a large group of assumption personas or sketch personas and cluster them according to their domain knowledge (how much expertise do they have with respect to media?) and technical expertise (how facile are they with computers and the Internet?).

Wherever you find a group of dots, that's where you need a persona. This can be a great tool for a reality check on assumptions. Perhaps one or more of the executives assumes that the target market is largely in the top right quadrant (perhaps highly technical music enthusiasts), but your data show that most potential users of your product cluster in other quadrants.

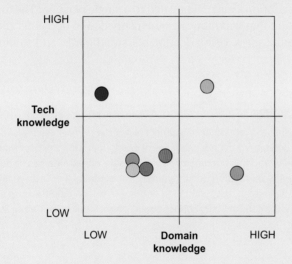

FIGURE 4.11
A plot of technical expertise and domain knowledge. Each colored dot represents a large group of current or target users. You'll need at least one persona wherever you see a cluster of dots.

Articulate the Role of the Non-Primary (or Secondary) Personas

Whether or not you decide to enrich the skeletons of your nonprimary categories and subcategories into full personas, you should make some solid decisions about how you might use them. These less important targets can serve, among other ways, as tie-breakers, brainstorming tools, or heuristics. Alternatively, there may be some critical scenarios with nonprimary personas; for example, one persona may be an IT manager who has to install the software.

You and your team can evaluate the design as it progresses from the points of view of the non-primary personas you build from these categories and subcategories. This will give you a perspective that is illuminating and still grounded in data. If you are clear on the role of the non-primary personas and communicate the fact that they will not be discarded despite not being selected, you will free your team and stakeholders to make the difficult decisions that will result in a streamlined set of primary personas.

Step 5. Develop selected skeletons into personas

You now have a reduced set of basic skeletons that your stakeholders helped select. Your task at this point is to enrich these skeletons to become personas by adding data as well as concrete and individualized details to give them personality and context. You will also include some storytelling elements and photos to make the personas come to life.

As you build on your skeletons, all of the details of your personas will be encapsulated in a *foundation document*. Depending on the available time and the needs of your product you might create full personas for just the small set of primary personas you defined, or you can create full personas for a larger set of primary and secondary personas. We have found that it is time and resource effective to first fully develop the high-priority primary skeletons and then to enrich, but not exhaustively complete, the nonprimary skeletons into sketch personas.

WHAT IS A PERSONA FOUNDATION DOCUMENT?

We use the term *foundation document* to describe whatever you use as a storehouse for all of your information, descriptions, and data related to a single persona. The foundation document contains the information that will motivate and justify design decisions and generate scenarios that will appear in feature specs, vision documents, storyboards, and so forth.

> **HANDY DETAIL**
>
> *The Foundation Document Is a Storehouse, Not a Communication Artifact*
>
> It is worth noting here that *the foundation document is not the primary means of communicating information about the persona to general team members.* In fact, don't expect many people outside the core team to actually read this document. You will create other materials to do that (see Chapter 5 for details). Likewise, the foundation document may not contain all or even most of the scenarios your personas will act in. Instead, the foundation document will contain the core scenarios that provide context and motivation for your product overall (see Chapter 6 for more information on using personas in scenarios).

Foundation documents contain the complete definition of a given persona, but they do not have to be long or difficult to create. Depending on your goals and the needs of your team, your foundation document could range from a single page to a long document. Creating a foundation document for each persona will provide you and your team with a single resource you can harvest as necessary as you create your persona communication materials. At the very least, complete personas must include *core information essential to defining the persona*: the goals, roles, behaviors, segment, environment, and typical activities that make the persona solid, rich, and unique (and, more important, relevant to the design of your product).

AD HOC PERSONAS VERSUS DATA-DRIVEN PERSONAS: TWO TYPES OF FOUNDATION DOCUMENTS

In this chapter, we have described two basic approaches to creating personas: ad hoc personas and data-driven personas. Each type of persona requires a different kind of foundation document.

Ad hoc persona foundation documents

Over time, we've created an ad hoc persona foundation document format that works very well, especially given the very practical needs of teams who don't have time or resources to create full, data-driven personas. Our ad hoc persona foundation documents include the following:

- Persona name, which is usually an alliterative, descriptive name such as "Ellen Everyday" or "Danny Drummer"

- Persona photo (see below for recommendations related to persona photos)
- Priority score (a summary index indicating the relative importance of this persona —
  likely generated in the previous step while evaluating your skeletons)
- Identifying quote, which is written to quickly communicate the key goals or needs of the
  persona with respect to the product
- Meet-the-persona write-up, which is a one- to three-paragraph narrative describing who
  the persona is
- Questions in [persona name's] own terms (which should capture the key questions and
  concerns that the persona has with respect to your product)
- Things the persona would be interested in but might not think to ask for ("Oh, by the
  way …" statements)—these allow you to recast the benefits or interesting new features of
  your product in terms that will resonate for the persona (see Appendix A)

Data-driven persona foundation documents

If you have gone through the data analysis and assimilation process described above, you
have lots of options when it comes to your foundation documents. If you have time, your
completed foundation documents should contain:

- Abundant links to factoids
- Copious footnotes or comments on specific data
- Links to the original research reports that support and explain the personas'
  characteristics
- Indications of which supporting characteristics are from data and which characteristics
  are fictitious or based on assumptions

As your foundation document grows, it is helpful to add headings and a table of contents.
Consider creating your foundation documents as an HTML page for each persona. This
will allow you to add links and keep your materials organized while providing access to
your various core team members and stakeholders during its development. We provide an
example of a more detailed and complete foundation document in Appendix B (see the
completed persona, Tanner Thompson).

The more details you include now the easier you will find the *birth and maturation* and
adulthood lifecycle phases. Complete multipage foundation documents can contain a
tremendous amount of information and require considerable effort to create. It is up to you
and your team to decide how rich your foundation documents need to be and how you will
collaborate on or divide the work required to create them.

If you are extremely time and resource constrained, you can start with brief one-page
description or resume-style foundation documents. Then, as you find the time you can always
come back and add to the information in these short foundation documents. Figure 4.12
shows one-page and resume-style outlines for these brief foundation documents.

CHOOSE PERSONA CHARACTERISTICS TO INCLUDE IN THE FOUNDATION DOCUMENT

Your assimilated data as well as your product and team needs will dictate what content
to include in your foundation documents. When you created your skeletons, you were
purposely selective in what information you included. Now you need to be more exhaustive.
This means that you need to include all headings and information appropriate and useful to
understanding your audience and developing your product. Different types of information
will be relevant for different people on your team and will have different uses toward
product development.

Your skeletons will serve as the starting point for the foundation documents. Each skeleton
has a bulleted list of characteristics. Your next step is to add important content headings

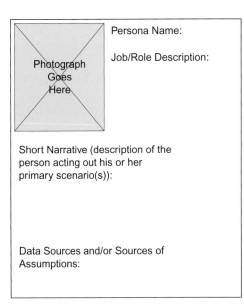
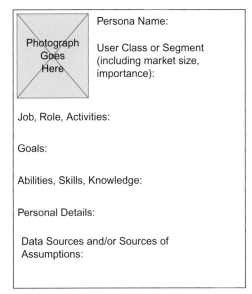

FIGURE 4.12

One-page (left) and resume-style (right) foundation document templates. These are the shortest possible data-driven persona foundation documents, and in most cases (unless you are extremely time and resource constrained) your foundation documents will include considerably more detail. Note that it is a good idea to develop your own template before you dive into creating your foundation documents. The templates help organize your work as you add and look for data to include in the document.

based on three things:

- The labels for the clusters that came out of the assimilation exercise
- Topics relevant to your product domain or business (e.g., if you are creating an Internet product you probably need a section on Internet activities, equipment, or Internet connection environments)
- Some common headings in persona documents that help create a persona that is well rounded, realistic, useful, and complete

Regarding the second and third of the previous items, consider the following list of persona characteristics that you can use as a content "menu" and template for your foundation documents. When you are deciding which characteristics to include in your foundation documents, think about the types of information that will be most helpful to your core team and to the development team. We recommend that you include at least rudimentary information in each of the following categories of persona characteristics:

- Identifying details
  - Name, title, or short description
  - Age, gender
  - Identifying tag line
  - Quote (highlighting something essential to that persona, preferably related to the product)
  - Photograph or brief physical description
- Roles and tasks
  - Specific company or industry
  - Job title or role
  - Typical activities
  - Important atypical activities
  - Challenge areas or breakdowns, pain points
  - Responsibilities
  - Interactions with other personas, systems, products

- Goals
  - Short-term, long-term
  - Motivations
  - Work-related goals
  - Product-related goals
  - General (life) goals, aspirations
  - Stated and unstated desires for the product
- Segment
  - Market size and influence
  - International considerations
  - Accessibility considerations
  - General and domain-relevant demographics
    - Income and purchasing power
    - Region or city, state, country
    - Education level
    - Marital status
    - Cultural information
- Skills and knowledge
  - General computer and Internet use
  - Frequently used products, product knowledge
  - Years of experience
  - Domain knowledge
  - Training
  - Special skills
  - Competitor awareness
- Context/environment
  - Equipment (Internet connection, browser brand and version, operating system)
  - "A day in the life" description
    - Work styles
    - Timeline of a typical day
  - Specific usage locations
  - General work, household, and leisure activities
  - Relationships to other personas
- Psychographics and personal details
  - Personality traits
  - Values and attitudes (political opinions, religion)
  - Fears and obstacles, pet peeves
  - Personal artifacts (car, gadgets)

This list was partially adapted from Mike Kuniavsky's list of attributes in *Observing the User Experience: A Practitioner's Guide to User Research* (Morgan Kaufmann, 2003), where he provides detailed descriptions of these and other possible persona attributes.

STORY FROM THE FIELD

Getting the Right Goals

Kim Goodwin, VP Design, Cooper

It takes practice to create accurate, compelling personas that are useful as design tools. In all the years I've been teaching people how to do so, I've consistently seen them struggle with a handful of issues. The most obvious problems occur when people don't stick to their data (or, worse, don't have good data to begin with). One of the trickier problems people often don't expect is getting the right set of goals.

Each persona should have a few goals that shed light on his or her priorities. There's not a magic number of goals any more than there's a magic number of personas; it depends on what you see in the data. However, three or four is a typical number; I've never met a persona who didn't have more than one goal, and I've never seen a persona with half a dozen goals that were all goals and not tasks.

The most challenging part for most people is getting the goals at the right level. If they're too high level or ambitious, they won't seem relevant to the product at hand. If they're too low level, though, they won't challenge you to think beyond basic screen layout. There are two types of goals that will help you focus at the right level.

Life goals, which are generally long-term and not something your product can really influence, are only occasionally useful in design. For example, "Retire by age 45" would be of little use if you were designing a word processor, mobile phone, or PDA, but it may offer valuable insight when you're designing a financial planning tool. When you think you've found a goal for your persona, ask yourself whether the product can help them accomplish it. If not, your goals are too high level.

You may wonder whether there's any harm in including life goals anyway. While it may not be obvious at first, life goals that don't add value will only clutter up your persona description and de-emphasize the more important goals. If you're designing network management software, who cares if your system administrator persona really wants to write a rock opera? It's much more important for people to understand his goal of always knowing what's going on. People may just laugh about the rock opera thing and not take the rest of the persona seriously.

That said, in a few instances I've really needed to convey that the persona just doesn't care. This isn't something I've had to do often, but when a product team believes their product is the center of the persona's universe it can be useful to have a persona essentially say they'd rather be somewhere else. This helps set everyone's expectation that this persona is willing to exert zero effort to learn or use the tool.

Most of your persona goals should be *end goals* that focus on what the persona could get out of using your well-designed product or service. In the case of a financial planning tool, retiring at age 45 is an end goal as well as a life goal, because it's something the product could help accomplish.

The trick with end goals is to avoid getting too low level. To see whether your end goal is really a goal and not just a task, ask yourself whether it's in service of something else. For example, if you interviewed me for a digital photo organizer product, you'd see that I spend a lot of time organizing my photos and assigning keywords to them, even though it drives me crazy to spend that much time. If you took that at face value and assumed that "easily organize photos" was my goal, you'd be missing the point. Instead, ask yourself why I spend all that annoying time, and you'll see that I do it because it's the only way I can find specific photos later. Every time you think you have a good goal, ask yourself, "Why does our persona want that?" If you have an easy answer, it's probably not a goal; if your answer is "because she just *does*," then you've probably found a genuine goal.

You can also ask yourself *whether* the product can help people progress toward the goal, or whether it will accomplish it entirely. In most cases, good end goals are things the product won't entirely accomplish. For example, if a manager wants to be more proactive and spend less time dealing with emergencies, a better forecasting tool can help but won't eliminate emergencies entirely.

Experience goals are another type you may find useful for certain projects, though less frequently than end goals. They describe how the persona wants to feel when using a product; having fun and not feeling stupid are experience goals. Not every persona needs an experience goal. We usually assume that no one really wants to feel dumb; however, if you have a persona with an exceptional level of anxiety about technology, calling that out is a good idea.

Experience goals have limited usefulness for most interaction design problems, but they tend to be very helpful for branded visual design. If you're not just using the standard look of an operating system and you need to make choices about color, typography, and style, an experience goal can help guide those choices. For example, someone doing online banking wants to feel very safe about the transaction, so a lot of navy blue and a professional-looking typeface would be appropriate, but lime green, orange, and Comic Sans® would not.

Once you have the right goals, it can be helpful to articulate them in the way your personas would say them. For example, if you're describing an avid shopper's goals, which works better: buy the right thing, or find the perfect gift? The latter conveys a sense that shopping is a quest, and that there's a sense of accomplishment involved in it.

The persona's goals are, in some ways, the most fundamental part of the whole description, because they help us understand what motivates people and how they will react in a certain situation. If you watch Mr. Data, the android on Star Trek®, which gives us more insight into his behavior—what his duties on the *Enterprise* are or the fact that he not so secretly wishes he were human? Our understanding of goals is what helps us create future scenarios for successful products, since we have to understand our users' goals before we can design products that help accomplish them.

STORY FROM THE FIELD

Addressing Accessibility Issues

George Olsen, Principal, Interaction by Design

Rather than having separate personas to represent users with disabilities, I find it more useful to incorporate accessibility issues into personas as long as it doesn't distract from the persona's main purpose. This can be as simple as having personas who occasionally forget their glasses (resulting in low-vision issues) or who have color blindness. It is true that doing this will overrepresent users who actually have these issues, but personas are a design tool, so I bend reality when needed to highlight an important design issue.

START A FOUNDATION DOCUMENT (TRANSFER FACTOIDS INTO YOUR SKELETONS)

Your skeleton documents are a template you can use to create a foundation document for each persona. Each skeleton should now have a similar set of headings. For each of those headings, transfer the appropriate factoids into the related sections (as shown in Figure 4.13). It is likely that some sections will have a lot of factoids in them and others will be nearly empty.

GET SPECIFIC ABOUT EACH CORE CHARACTERISTIC

Once you have copied your factoids into your skeleton documents, evolving the skeleton into a more precise persona can be relatively easy. You will create a concrete fact, phrase, sentence, or paragraph to replace each factoid or set of factoids in the skeleton.

STORY FROM THE FIELD

Determining Just the Right Amount of Information

Damian Rees, Usability Engineer, BBC New Media

We include as much detail as we feel is necessary to be able to put that persona into any situation and know how he or she would react to it. Minimum requirements are name, photo, age, description, occupation, Internet usage, environment, trigger, ultimate goal, and current usage. We attempt to keep all information relevant where possible. All personas are collated into a one-page document, listing core components as a summary sheet. Anything we feel isn't going to help us understand the persona is stripped out but still kept for reference in a different document.

Persona Skeleton:
Boy, age 10–13

Computer use at school
- Has access to a shared computer in his classroom or a computer lab shared by the whole school
  o Factoid
  o Factoid
  o Factoid

- Has at least one computer-related assignment a week
  o Factoid
  o Factoid
  o Factoid
- Finds computer use at school boring
  o Factoid
  o ⋯

FIGURE 4.13
Transfer factoids verbatim into your skeleton document. This document will evolve to become your persona foundation document, which will be the repository for all information on each persona.

ranges of values (e.g., age = 25 to 35, parent, works full time) instead of specific values. You purposely stayed at this abstract level when considering the few attributes of your skeletons in order to stay as close as possible to the actual data during the evaluation process. Now it is time to turn most of the characteristics in your skeleton personas into very specific and more concrete values. For example:

- Works full time *becomes* a specific job, such as bank teller, department store manager, or high-school teacher.
- Parent *becomes* mother or father.
- 70% female *becomes* Laura, Dianne, Irene, and so on.
- Lives in a major metropolitan city *becomes* Chicago, Los Angeles, or Houston.

More specifically, from your skeleton (see Figure 4.14, left) transform your headings and factoids into specific, concrete details in your foundation document (Figure 4.14, right).

As you replace factoids with specific details to enrich your persona, copy the factoid or set of factoids into a comment or a footnote in your foundation document. A lofty but worthy goal is to have every statement in your foundation document supported by user data. You likely will not achieve this, but the attempt helps you to think critically about your details and highlights places where you might want to do further research. (In fact, when such research questions come up it is a good idea to make a note of them directly in the foundation document.) By the time you finish creating a description for each persona, you will have also created a very rich document that is full of direct references to data (as illustrated in Figure 4.15).

Parent (skeleton)

Demographics:
- People who make enough money to have two computers in their home tend to live in major metropolitan areas (source 3, p 1)
- etc.

Work:
- 85% of parents surveyed work full time in white-collar professions (source 5, p 2)
- etc.

Goals, fears, aspirations of parents:
- Mothers are more concerned with their child's behavior online than fathers (source 2, p 10)
- etc.

Irene Pasquez, the involved parent (1)
(foundation document)

Overview:
Irene lives in a suburb of Houston (2) with Emanuel, her husband, and her one child: Preston, who just turned 5.

Even though Irene works full time as a manager in a local branch of Bank of America (3), she is heavily involved with Preston's daily activities and has the opportunity to see him during the working day because ... etc.
- -
Data references
1. Mothers are more concerned with their child's behavior online than fathers (source 2, p 10)
2. People who make enough money to have two computers in their home tend to live in major metropolitan areas (source 3, p 1)
3. 85% of parents surveyed work full time in white-collar professions (source 5, p 2)

FIGURE 4.14
An example skeleton (left) being transformed into a foundation document (right).

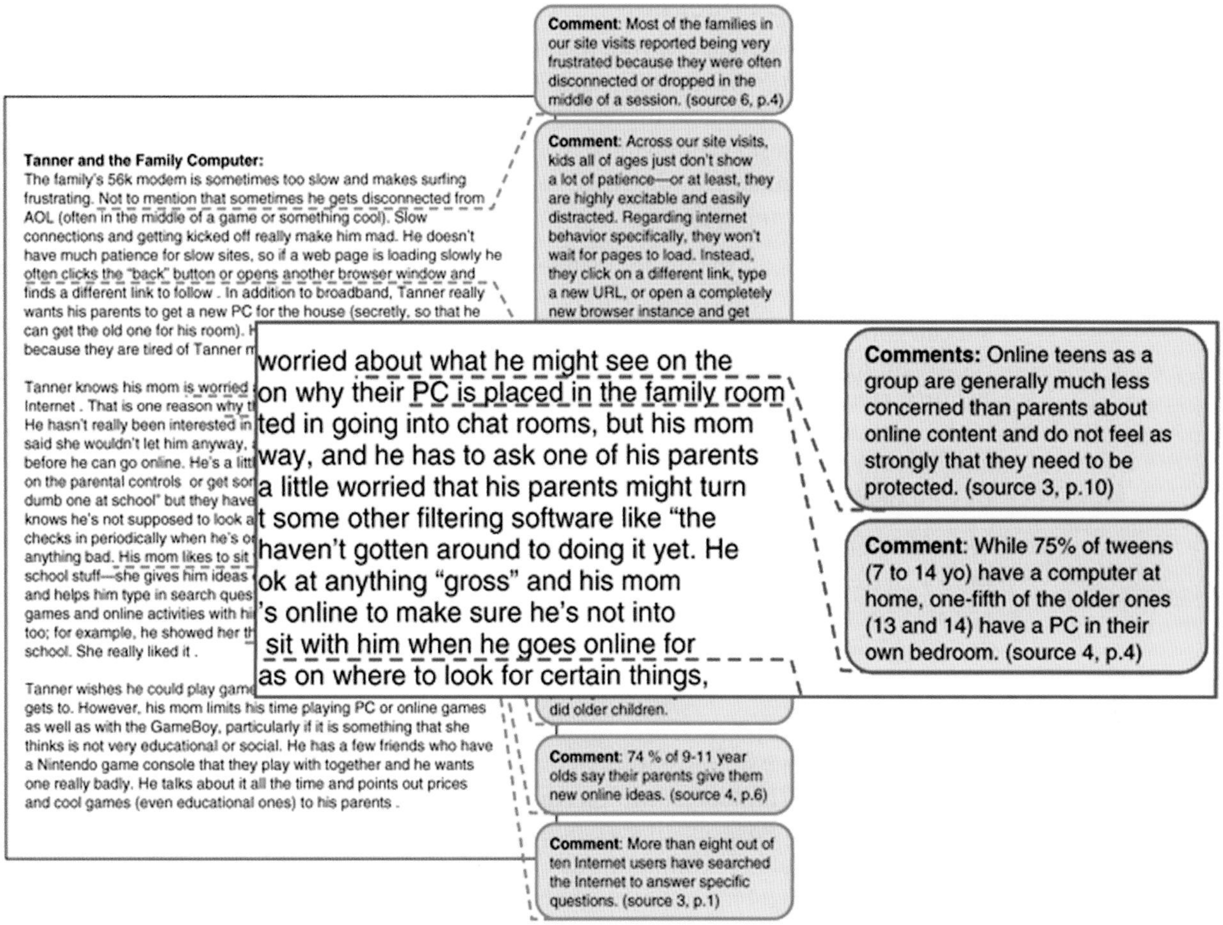

FIGURE 4.15
An example of statements in a foundation document supported by factoids using the "Insert > Comment" feature in Microsoft® Word.

HANDY DETAIL

There Are Many Ways to Include References in Your Foundation Documents

Many word processing programs and HTML editors allow you to add annotations, references, or even pop-up comments to your text. In Microsoft® Word, for example, you can use the Comment feature to do this linking and annotation. To do so, highlight a word or phrase, select Insert > Comment, and type or paste your factoid into the comment field. This makes your links not just explicit but also very salient to the reader (see Figure 4.15). If you are creating HTML foundation documents, you can create hyperlinks directly to electronic versions of data or pop-up windows containing direct quotes or summarized data from your original sources.

If you use Word to add comments in support of specific details, consider checking the Options > Security "Remove personal information" so the reader of the document will not see who inserted the comment:

- Select Tools > Options ....
- In the Options dialog box, select the User Information tab.
- Check the box to remove personal information from file properties on save.

This is a particularly good idea when multiple people are creating the foundation document. When you find yourself referencing a factoid from a data source, don't forget to include the bibliographic information for that source in the "References" area at the end of the document.

MOVING TOWARD PRECISION MEANS MOVING AWAY FROM ACCURACY

In many cases, the accuracy of your data lies in their ranges (not just central tendencies but descriptors of variance, percentages, and skew). By selecting precise descriptors you are going to lose some of that accuracy. If a category includes males and females, for example, you cannot create a single individual who represents the entire category. Rather than trying to represent every nuance of the entire category, try to pick values that are reasonable, believable, and meaningful.

As you choose specific details to include in your personas, you are zooming in on a particular person; that is, you are transitioning from rough descriptions of categories and subcategories of users to precise values and detailed depictions of a particular persona. As you build these detailed depictions, you will be making educated guesses and adding fictional elements, some of which will be directly related to the data you have collected and some of which will not. (It is a good idea to document these assumptions and to consider them possible research questions that may need answering during the validation of your personas.)

Think of your data and your categories and subcategories of users as describing *neighborhoods* of related users of your product. As you create your personas, you are describing a specific "resident" of each neighborhood. As in real life, each resident *inhabits* his or her neighborhood, but no one resident can *represent* all qualities of all people in the neighborhood.

No one who reads a persona description can understand all the intricacies of the data behind that persona; however, as design targets, personas can *stand in* for all data in your communications. Think of a town meeting. Each neighborhood might send a single representative who *stands in* for everyone else in the neighborhood, even though that one person cannot accurately communicate the particular demographics, attitudes, needs, and desires of every one of his or her neighbors. Instead, the representative communicates the *essence* of all of his or her neighbors' needs. Your personas will represent your data in the same way that a single neighbor can represent an entire neighborhood.

WHEN IN DOUBT, CHOOSE DETAILS THAT ARE PRECISE AND MEMORABLE

As you select specific characteristics for your personas, try to choose values that are clearly within the range and essence of the data and findings from which they came. You may choose to select values in the middle of the ranges described in your data, but you don't have to. Try to choose values that are reasonable, believable, and meaningful. As a rule, try to choose values that have face validity while not adding any extra baggage. Your goal is to create personas who feel real and relevant, while being memorable and even interesting.

INCORPORATE NARRATIVE AND STORYTELLING ELEMENTS

Enriching your terse skeletons into personas that are realistic and engaging requires some storytelling. To do this well, remember that you are trying to tell the story of the data in your foundation documents with narrative. What do your personas sound like and act like? What can they do or not do? Turn your factoids and specific details into a running story—that is, a sequence of actions and events with interaction and even a plot. Demonstrate their interactions with people, objects, and systems. Narratives in persona documents are typically written in third person, active voice. The following is an example of a descriptive overview for the persona Tanner written as a narrative:

> Tanner is 9 years old and is a fourth-grade student at Montgomery Elementary School. He lives with his mother and father (Laura and Shane

Thompson) in a suburb of Chicago, Illinois. Tanner has been using computers at school since kindergarten and has had a family computer at home for 2 years. He has been using the Internet in his school's computer lab for some time but only recently got Internet access at his house (6 months ago through his family's AOL account). Even though Tanner loves to be physically active (riding his skateboard and bike, playing in the yard and nearby creek, participating in organized sports, and so on), Tanner thinks computers are really, really fun and prefers the PC to the TV. He uses the PC mostly to play games and to surf the web for "stuff" but occasionally does research for school projects. His favorite computer game of the moment is *The Sims™ 2*. His uncle gave it to him for his birthday (his mom and dad usually just buy him educational games). He also really likes *RollerCoaster® Tycoon 3*. Since his dad likes computer sports games like *NBA Live 2005*, Tanner sometimes plays those with him. Tanner has a Game Boy™ Color and saves up his allowance to buy new games for it, but his parents say he can only play Game Boy for half an hour each day (they tell him "it will rot his brain").

Writing these stories can be difficult at first. This part of persona creation does take creativity and inspiration. If you have skilled writers on your persona core team, you should likely enlist them to do this part. Start writing your stories by simply expanding the bulleted factoids with context, adding situations, other characters, objects, actions, and events. If you feel blocked or awkward in writing narrative, look through the raw notes and observations from your field research and other qualitative data; that is, use anecdotes and incidents from those real people to enrich your personas. (For more ideas and a deep discussion of personas and storytelling, see Chapter 9, "Storytelling and Narrative," by Whitney Quesenbery, in *The Personal Lifecycle: Keeping People in Mind Throughout Product Design*.)

65

DERIVE SPECIFIC DETAILS AND STORIES FROM REAL OBSERVATIONS

You will notice that we are now moving from the realm of hard, accurate data, observations, and facts toward more subjective, best-guess information and particulars (i.e., toward fiction). In other words, you are starting to include details that are not solidly derived from data. This step is generally uncomfortable, but it can be fun, too. Like you had to do when you were determining what types of information (including the categories and headings) would go into your foundation document, you now have to make decisions about specific details that are based on the data, the needs of your team and product, and your knowledge of the world. Your personas need backgrounds and context to be real. Consider using specific, observed information from your site visits or other research as the exact values or characteristics of your profiles. Doing so can ease the burden of being creative, stop disagreements among your persona creation team, and add an aspect of credibility or authenticity to your resulting personas.

YOU CAN USE STEREOTYPES, BUT USE THEM WITH CARE

You may be tempted to use stereotypes and common knowledge or cultural lore in your personas. If you do, do so carefully. For example, consider this transition from abstract profile to specific details to stereotype/cultural phenomenon:

Yvonne Chandler lives in suburban Chicago with her husband, William, and their two kids, Colbi (age 7) and Austin (age 13). Yvonne works part time now that the kids are in school, but she always arranges her work schedule to accommodate a fairly complex system of carpools and after-school activities (she has become a "soccer mom"). She feels tremendously busy but wants to make sure that her kids have a lot of opportunities and learning experiences. She also feels pressure to "keep up with the Joneses" in many aspects of her life, from the activities she involves her kids in to the entertaining she does at home. Before she had kids, Yvonne was known as the neighborhood "Martha Stewart" because of the dinner parties she would host. She would like to entertain more, but right now she is just too busy with her kids.

If you are creating a persona of a user who happens to be a suburban mother, you may find yourself tempted to add details based on your own perceptions of a "typical soccer mom" or a "Martha Stewart type." In both cases, utilizing a stereotype or strong cultural icon can be dangerous. The "soccer mom" stereotype is very evocative, but perhaps in ways that work counter to the persona effort. Perhaps there is someone in your organization who has a similar set of responsibilities and recognizes herself in the persona but is put off by the reference to "soccer mom" because she does not want to think of *herself* that way. Or, there might be others in the organization who are scornful of "soccer moms" and the stereotypical suburban lifestyle. This distaste can get in the way when you ask your colleagues to use the personas in their everyday work. Similarly, Martha Stewart generally evokes a fairly strong image, at least for a North American audience—one that is either positive or fairly strongly negative.

Persona use brings sociopolitical issues to the surface. Each persona has a gender, age, race, ethnicity, family, or cohabitation arrangement; socioeconomic background; and work or home environment (even if you don't include all of these directly in the persona description, the photos you use will imply decisions on these details). This provides an effective avenue for recognizing and perhaps changing your team's assumptions about users. In his chapter, "Why Personas Work: The Psychological Evidence," in *The Persona Lifecycle: Keeping People in Mind Throughout Product Design*, Jonathan Grudin argues that stereotypes are very powerful influences that must be handled with caution because they can create a one-dimensional character—one that is not likely to be as rich and complex as most people naturally are. Furthermore, Lene Nielsen argues, in *Constructing the User* (Lawrence Erlbaum, 2003), that stereotypes are naturally formed by our teammates and can be difficult to work with in a design process. To overcome a stereotype, he suggested, "it is necessary to get access to the users' feelings and knowledge as more than one dimension of the character is needed to raise sympathy."

BEWARE ANY DETAILS THAT CAN EVOKE STRONG EMOTIONAL RESPONSES

Note that there are other types of information that can evoke strong responses. For example, if we say that Philip is a concerned dad who is recently divorced and battling for custody of his children, does this information get in the way of the more salient info about how he relates to his child as an online consumer? The information may be memorable and even be reflective of the data, but does it help your persona be effective as a design target?

So, be careful when evoking stereotypes or any information that could elicit a strong personal response. When in doubt, choose to include details that help others see your persona as a real person, with particular goals, needs, and interests that are understandable. Allow realism to win out over political correctness. Avoid casting strongly against expectations if it will undermine credibility. Break the mold if it helps get people on board with your effort. In *The Inmates Are Running the Asylum*, Cooper addressed this issue by stating, "All things being equal, I will use people of different races, genders, nationalities, and colors."

The Villain in Us

Christina Wodtke, author of *Information Architecture: Blueprints for the Web*

When a group gets together to create personas, a funny phenomenon almost always occurs. They make a bad guy. It will start innocently enough, with a set of characteristics: a male in his thirties making six figures on the east coast. Then, as your team develops him into a persona—let's call him "Fred"—he only wears gray, has a gray BMW, and is a young securities trader who works 90 +−hour weeks. Then he's suddenly a jerk who doesn't have a girlfriend because he's too selfish, and he underpays his secretary and doesn't recycle. What happened?

Perhaps it is because we know people like this. Perhaps it is our human need to create villains. They are fascinating creatures, from the wicked queen in *Snow White* to James Spader's amoral lawyer on *The Practice*. But the problem is that personas are not protagonists and antagonists; they are design targets. You have to feel for them, or you won't be trying your best to make an interface that makes consumers happy: "Yeah, that jerk, he makes twice what I do. He can figure out the navigation himself."

The solution, interestingly enough, also comes from narrative: redemption. Except that in narrative you usually wait until the end of the story to redeem your villain (if indeed you plan to do that rather than, say, drop him off a cliff). With personas, you have to redeem your villain with a bit of editing and a bit of back story before you begin your scenarios. In this example, we simply need to remove the fact that Fred underpays his secretary (it's probably the company's fault anyhow). Now we need to get into the facelift.

"He only wears gray." This could be seen in a number of ways. Let's make him colorblind. Now he's afraid to wear color for fear of being unable to match his clothes. Fred knows that if he goes into work wearing green and orange he will be mocked by his coworkers, and his boss won't take him seriously. With this change, we have both made him more humane *and* given him a useful trait for our design work. When a designer makes an interface choice, he will remember that it needs to be high contrast with redundant channels of information for Fred, who is afraid of looking stupid at work. The designer cares, because we have all been afraid of looking stupid at work.

Now we can continue. Fred is a first-generation Chinese–American, and he is saving to purchase a house for his parents. He works long hours for that. He has a gray BMW, but it's a 202 and he works on it on weekends for fun. He is a 202 enthusiast and finds it easier to talk to other car geeks than to girls, but nothing would make him happier than a girlfriend, and his parents have started to bug him about it. Obviously, if this were a car site or a dating site, one aspect or another of the back story could be played up, but we now not only feel for him but understand what motivates him.

The villain is cool, seductive, and powerful—but he's not useful. Some may argue, "Some of our users are like that," but can you really do your best work designing to make a jerk happy? Redeem your personas, and redeem your design.

DON'T OVERDO IT

Be sure to keep your stories to an appropriate length. You are not writing a novel. You will want to create interest and provide some background and context for your teammates, but keep your stories in check and don't include detail that is superfluous and highly irrelevant.

Some of the details you create will naturally be relevant to the design and development of your product, and others will seem completely irrelevant. That your persona "lives in Chicago" or "has been married for 10 years" may not inform any design decision. However, seemingly irrelevant details do have their place. Their purpose is to help make the personas

67

into people—to make them believable and memorable. Think of this "irrelevant" content as you would salt and pepper or other spices used in cooking. You are adding flavor to your meal, but too much will ruin the taste. With regard to the level of relevant and irrelevant detail, consider the following three examples written in narrative style:

- *Too little detail*

  Tanner arrives home from school at 3:15 and calls his mom to let her know that he's there. He plays a computer game and watches TV until his mom arrives home.

- *Just the right amount of detail*

  Tanner rides the bus home after school and arrives home at 3:15. Laura, his mom, is still at work, and per her requested routine Tanner gives her a phone call to let her know that he made it safely home. Tanner throws his backpack on the floor in the entryway and immediately heads to the family room. He turns on both the TV and the family PC. Within minutes, he is watching his favorite after-school shows and IMing two of his friends and playing an Internet game on his (currently) favorite site. He knows that he only has 45 minutes of "free" time before his mom arrives home.

- *Too much detail*

  Tanner rides the bus home after school and arrives home at 3:15. He likes his bus driver because he reminds him of the bus driver on the cartoon show *The Simpsons*. Laura, his mom, is still at work. Having a part-time job, she works until 4:00 p.m. three days a week. She worries about Tanner being home alone after school— particularly regarding his trip home. She worries less once he is home, and so per her requested routine Tanner gives her a phone call to let her know that he made it safely home. Tanner throws his backpack on the floor in the entryway, spilling some of its contents on the floor, and immediately heads to the family room. He turns on both the TV (a nice but old 34-inch Sony® Trinitron®) and the family PC. Within minutes, he is watching his favorite after-school shows and IMing two of his friends and playing a flash-based Internet game on his (currently) favorite site. He makes the most of this play time, because he knows that he only has 45 minutes of "free" time before his mom arrives home. Laura arrives home a little late due to traffic and gets a little irritated by the mess Tanner created in the entryway. She snaps at Tanner to get started on his homework.

HANDY DETAIL

Determine Where Personas Stop and Scenarios Begin

A foundation document as we define it is a rich and detailed description of an individual, which may include stories about how he or she approaches work, gets things done, and interacts with colleagues and products (possibly yours). The stories you include in the personas should be there to help people deeply understand who that persona is, but this doesn't mean that your foundation document will contain all possible stories for that persona.

In Chapter 6 we discuss how additional stories, specific scenarios, design maps, and use cases can be created and used outside the foundation to help your team explore and define solutions to be built into your product. Scenarios, Design Maps, and use cases are typically much more specific and focused than the stories in foundation documents. They are stories designed to specifically describe a particular person interacting with a particular part of a product in a particular situation. Your personas will become the "particular people" (or "actors") in these additional stories.

Personas are generative in nature. That is, they can drive the creation of an almost endless set of possible scenarios. When defined appropriately, your personas serve as the motivational factor and grounding requirements for future scenarios—detailed scenarios in specific domains.

KNOW WHEN TO STOP

Once you start enriching your skeleton personas into full foundation documents, you might find it difficult to stop. You and your team will discover new data sources and will want to incorporate new information into the sketches. That is fine, but it should not get in the way of sharing and "birthing" the personas into your organization. At some point, you and your core team will have to decide that you have enough information in each persona and are ready to move on to the next phase. Remember that it is likely that no one outside your core team will ever read the entire foundation document. The document need only be complete enough to support your *birth and maturation* and *adulthood* activities to the extent that you are "ready." This does not mean that you cannot keep adding information. In Chapter 5, we recommend that you assign an owner to each persona. The owner can be responsible for keeping the persona up-to-date and integrating new data and information as appropriate.

ILLUSTRATE YOUR PERSONAS

Each persona needs a face, a photo, or set of photos to make it real. We believe photos or illustrations are critical. They help your team believe in the personas and understand that each persona describes a single person. The choice of what specific photos to use is difficult. These illustrations of your personas are extremely influential and can significantly affect how your personas are perceived.

A photo is more than just a face. The model's clothing, expression, activity, and general appearance—along with the setting and background—will communicate or dictate some of the characteristics of your persona. You can either take advantage of this fact or continually fight it. The sections that follow offer some suggestions to help you with this.

FIGURE 4.16
Stock photos can look too professional.

69

DON'T USE SLICK STOCK PHOTOS

Stock photos can look too professional and slick, as the people in them tend to look like professional models (see Figure 4.16). With stock photos, you do not have control of the model's context, activity, or expression. There are also usually only one or two photos for a given model. As you'll see in the next chapter, which discusses the birth and maturation phase, it is useful to have a variety of shots of the same model. In addition, we have experienced situations in which a stock photo that was used for one team's persona was coincidentally used for a different persona for a different team in the same company. We have also seen stock photos for personas show up in magazines and on billboards ("Hey, isn't that our Dianna?").

Instead of using stock photos, locate people who look the part and hold your own photo shoot. Photos of friends of friends will look approachable and real (see Figure 4.17). Using local, known people for your models means that you will likely be able to get additional photos at a later point if the need arises. If you choose to take your own photographs (which we highly recommend), you should start looking for models the moment you decide on the primary personas. The time-consuming part of this step is finding just the right faces. Each photo session takes about an hour.

FIGURE 4.17
Photos of local people can look more real; see note above.

If you can't locate your own models or do your own photo shoot for some reason, there are other options. We recommend such websites as:

- Free photo sources
  - stock.xchng® (www.sxc.hu)
  - flickr® (flickr.com), where you can find photos that are usable under the creative commons license
  - Microsoft clip art photos (office.microsoft.com/clipart)
- Inexpensive stock photos
  - dreamstime® (www.dreamstime.com)
  - iStockphoto® (istockphoto.com)
  - Shutterstock® (www.shutterstock.com)
- High-quality photos and photo series with the same models (note that the inexpensive sites also often have series of photos with the same models)
  - Getty Images® (www.gettyone.com)
  - Corbis Images® (www.corbis.com)
  - Veer (www.veer.com)

HANDLE DETAIL

Hold Your Own Photo Shoot

To do a photo shoot, start with stock photos that have the basic look you want. Then ask your teammates and friends if they know anyone who resembles the models in the stock photos. Once you locate a few candidates, have them send a photo of themselves and have your core team evaluate which local model would work best. Then schedule 30 minutes to an hour with each model to do a quick photo shoot (preferably with a digital camera).

You will want your team to see different aspects of your personas. During your photo shoot, make sure you have the model pose in a variety of places—with different expressions and doing different things (talking on the phone, drinking a beverage, working at their desk, getting out of a car, and so on). Choose settings and activities that are core to each persona. Bring your own appropriate props to help make the right statement. Have the model bring a few changes of clothing. You can likely take 100 or more shots in an hour-long photo shoot. If possible, use a digital camera so you can immediately review your work. You will need about five to ten good shots when you are done.

Consider paying your models with gift certificates or perhaps free products or services from your company. Finally, be sure to use an image release form with these models.

Note that it is critical that you review the details of the agreement on how these photos can be used. Ignoring the terms can get you into trouble. For example, collections of clip art (with photos) might say that you cannot use more than 100 copies for a particular activity or that the use must be for educational purposes (such as passing out slides at a conference). These are normal conditions of the "fair use" clause under copyright law. It might be worth making a copy of the license for your records from whatever sources you use.

ILLUSTRATIONS CAN BE AN INTERESTING ALTERNATIVE TO PHOTOS

Consider having an artist generate sketches to represent your personas. Although sketches feel less real and may detract from credibility, they do have their place. For example, sketches can keep your personas from being interpreted too literally. Further, you have a lot of control over what the sketches look like, what the personas are doing in the sketches, and so on.

AUDITION THE PHOTOS

Hold auditions for proposed photos (or illustrations or models). Let a variety of teammates have a say as to what photos or specific models are used for your personas. Doing so will obtain buy-in and should result in more broadly acceptable images. Generally, the selected models should be attractive; not supermodels, but people that have a look that is likeable, approachable, trustworthy, nice, and engaging. In addition, the facial expressions in the photos should be pleasant. These images will likely be around for a long time—perhaps several development cycles. Choose images that are easy to look at and that inspire your team to build great products.

NAME YOUR PERSONAS

The names you give to your personas are important, perhaps on par with the importance of the illustration. In many cases, the persona's name is the one detail that everyone will know and remember. Choose names carefully. There are several simple rules of thumb for selecting persona names:

- Don't use the name of anyone on your team or in your organization.
- Avoid using the names of famous people (such as Cher or Britney).
- Avoid using names that have any negative connotation.
- Do use names that are unique and distinctive.
- Consider building a mnemonic device into the persona names to help people remember them. For example, if you create personas for segments that are already named *enthusiasts*, *ostriches*, and *neophytes*, why not select names that share the first letter of each segment? The enthusiast could be named Eddie, the ostrich Omar, and the neophyte Nanette.

If you need help in coming up with interesting and memorable names, you might refer to one of the baby-name websites (there are many to choose from). If your personas are different ages, you can also look up popular names for the years each was born.

Consider getting your larger organization involved in the naming process. This serves the purpose of both getting good, agreeable names and getting your organization engaged early with your personas (see the "Buzz Generators" section in Chapter 5). If you decide to do this, we recommend that you select a set of names for each persona and allow everyone to vote during the *birth* activities.

CREATE NAME AND TAG LINE COMBINATIONS

Generally, we recommend creating a name and tag line together, usually something alliterative. For example, you might have "Toby the Typical Teenager," "Abe the Active Administrator," or "Connie the Conscientious Consumer." Tag lines make personas easier to remember and to differentiate. Along the same line, you might consider using a simple quote or job title to bring meaning to the name. You want to highlight a key differentiator or characteristic for each persona. Be careful not to choose something potentially offensive (e.g., "Filing Goddess" or "Obsessive Organizer"). As a check, consider if it would it bug you to have these lines added to the end of your name.

Step 6. Validate your personas

You have just spent a lot of time crafting personas to stand in for the users you researched and the embedded knowledge of your stakeholders. Your personas should now be looking and sounding great—full of solid information and complete with illustrative photos and meaningful names. Your stakeholders have reviewed them and you now seem to have the right set of target customers in your focus. But how can you be sure your personas embody the data you worked so hard to collect?

TREAT VALIDATION AS AN OPPORTUNITY FOR DATA GATHERING

You may have created your personas based almost completely on existing data sources. If this is the case, you are probably missing some of the qualitative information that can inform the narrative surrounding your persona. If you utilized only qualitative information, you might need to understand aspects of your personas related to market size, spending, or other quantitative or domain-specific information. You can organize your validation efforts to serve two purposes: (1) validate the persona details you have developed from your data sources and (2) collect the additional information that will help complete the personas.

As you finished your assimilation exercises and moved on to create skeletons and full personas, you probably noticed some categories of information missing. For example, you may have collected tremendous amounts of data related to a teenager's schoolwork and entertainment interests but may find yourself with virtually no information about typical family activities and concerns. When you create the narrative for your teen persona, you can:

- Fill in this information based on assumptions.
- Return to your clusters, or even your original data sources, to see if there was relevant information you simply didn't use.
- Take the opportunity to look for more details as you conduct your validation activities.

Before you recruit people to survey or observe to refine your personas, create a list of the types of information you still need and use this additional data to inform targeted content areas or to create the narratives and storyline. It is perfectly reasonable to create the data-driven persona details and wait to build additional narrative until you have completed most of your validation activities.

VALIDATING AD HOC PERSONAS

If you are using ad hoc personas, it is important to validate them to make sure that the personas you created really do fall into the neighborhood of your actual target users. The validation process can be quick and dirty, or you can treat it as an opportunity to gather data about your current and target users.

We recommend starting with ad hoc personas no matter which type of persona you intend to finish with. This step helps in several ways, including getting everyone on the same page *and* identifying what key questions you have to answer in order for everyone to feel comfortable that the personas are appropriate for the project.

Quick validation of ad hoc personas

At the very least, show the ad hoc personas to other members of your organization who were not part of the persona creation process. See the "Have Subject-Matter Experts Review Your Personas" section, below.

Using data to validate ad hoc personas

Some companies have tons of data, and starting with ad hoc personas can help you and your core team get organized before you dig into a huge mountain of factoids. In this case, the ad hoc validation process can include finding data points that support the details you have included in your ad hoc personas.

In cases where the company or team does *not* have a lot of data to work with, the validation process might include collecting new data. The benefit of creating the ad hoc personas before embarking on a data collection project is that you'll know the questions you really need to answer through the data you collect. This can often provide some much-needed structure to any research effort and ensure that you don't end up with just another pile of data you don't know how to apply.

We suggest you also review the validation methods provided in the next section. If you have the time and resources, these methods are equally valuable for ad hoc persona validation.

VALIDATING DATA-DRIVEN PERSONAS

Your personas were likely created from a variety of data sources (primary and secondary sources; some older, some newer, some quantitative, some qualitative) all stitched together by educated guesses, assumptions, and business strategy. You have pieced together data points that may or may not actually fit together—some of which may not be directly comparable or inherently compatible.

Your goal during validation is to ensure that you did not stray too far away from your data when you made their characteristics specific and concrete and added elements of storytelling. Although it is true that personas cannot and do not need to be completely accurate, you do want to ensure that they reflect the essential information about your target users that you found in your data. If you built assumption personas, you want to ensure that the personas you created really do capture the assumptions in your organization. We discuss five approaches to validating your resulting personas (presented in order of increasing cost and rigor):

1. Review your personas against the original data sources.
2. Have experts (those closest to your users) review your personas.
3. Have representative users of each persona review "their" persona.
4. Conduct reality-check site visits.
5. Conduct large-sample surveys or interviews.

These five approaches are not mutually exclusive nor are they the only means of validating your personas.

CHECK BACK IN WITH YOUR DATA

Now that you have enhanced your personas with details and narrative, schedule a short meeting with your persona core team. Ask everyone to skim back over the data sources from which the key factoids were derived. If you have transcripts or profiles from qualitative research, we suggest that you focus your review on these. As you skim the original data, ask each core team member to identify any ways in which the completed personas seem to contradict the data sources and decide together whether these contradictions are acceptable. Make appropriate revisions to your personas to ensure they are as representative of the data as possible.

STORY FROM THE FIELD

Personas at zylom.com

Erik Goossens and J. Vanzandbeek, Zylom.com

At Zylom.com, we make interactive word and puzzle games. Our target audience is mostly women, age 30 and over, who typically like to play games at home when they "have a little break during the day." We saw a presentation on personas at Shop.org and decided we wanted to try using them. Our goal was to redesign our corporate website from an information source for our advertising business to a try-and-buy storefront for our games. We wanted to get started right away, so we came back to the office and created assumption personas. To do this, we created a core team of five people which included colleagues from management, market research, games development, and process experts. The core team brainstormed to capture our existing assumptions about our users on a whiteboard; these assumptions were based on our experience in this business and some market research data from a survey done to profile our audience for our advertisers (completed last year). We initially created three assumption personas to represent older women, younger women, and men: Maria, age 51; Sophie, age 31; and Michael, age 29.

Our resulting personas felt right to us, but we wanted make sure we were on target. To validate our assumptions, we bought a survey tool and created questionnaires for various groups of users. We put together a representative sample of users to survey, based on our analysis of "typical" usage patterns we found in our data. After we collected and cross-tabbed the data from the surveys, we cross-referenced our findings with other data sources, such as transactional data from our site, user characteristics collected during registration, time spent on the site, etc.

We concluded that all of our data made sense and was presenting us with a very clear picture of our actual users and how they were similar to (and different from) our assumptions. For example, through our data, we realized that women approach and use online games differently depending on their ages, so we revised our definitions of Maria and Sophie to comply with these findings. We also found that men comprised only 15% of our market. After this realization, we decided to focus or redesign efforts on Maria (our most profitable target) and Sophie, using Michael as a secondary target when appropriate.

Once we had our personas firmly in place, we:

● Defined Maria's and Sophie's goals for the site
● Created mockups of the site
● Brought in "Marias" and "Sophies" so we could watch (and videotape) them using the functional mockups
● Iterated the mockups
● Built and deployed the site

From start to finish, this entire process took 3 weeks, and the new site was up and running less than 4 months after the presentation on personas that we had attended.

BRIGHT IDEA

Collect New Data

If you did not have time to collect qualitative and quantitative data before you started creating the personas or find that you need additional information to create good narratives for your personas, you can stop your persona creation efforts now and embark on your validation exercise before continuing (discussed in the following text). As you do the footwork necessary to validate your developing personas, you can collect the missing qualitative information that will allow you to add narratives to your personas based on observations rather than assumptions.

HAVE SUBJECT MATTER EXPERTS REVIEW YOUR PERSONAS

Consider taking your personas to people who know your target audience. Look for domain experts who have direct contact with your users (or proposed users) and who were not involved in the creation of your personas. These may be sales personnel, product support engineers, trainers or educators, or people who have directly conducted research with your audience (focus group moderators, usability engineers, ethnographers, and so on). If you built your personas to help redesign an existing product, you might have access to people in your company who are very close to your existing user base and can help you validate your personas. If you have a customer service or sales team, these are the perfect people to validate your personas with. Basically, you want them to answer the following questions:

● Are these the people you interact with (or, in the cases where the personas represent target versus current users or customers, the people you *want* to interact with)?
● Is anyone missing?
● Are these really all separate people? Have we captured "differences that make a difference"?

Avoid Confusion: Design Personas are Not the Same as Marketing Personas

When you talk to members of the marketing organization, remember to explain that you are validating *product* personas and not *marketing* personas. Here is a great way to explain the difference:

- Marketing personas would capture important psychographics and demographics that help us *target* people and *get them to* our product. In this case, a user who is male and 22 is very different from a female who is 65, and you would advertise in very different ways to them.
- Product personas are intended to capture differences in goals, prior experiences, assumptions, and behaviors that impact the way people will *use* the product. In this case, people managing their finances on their own for the very first time (e.g., a 22-year-old guy who is newly graduated from college and a newly divorced 65-year-old woman) are more similar than they are different.

In simple terms:

Marketing is about getting eyeballs to our product. Personas are about moving those eyeballs around within the product.

Ask these experts to read the foundation documents and point out things that don't match their experience with these users. Again, make revisions as appropriate to the personas so they best fit the original data and your experts' observations.

SHOW YOUR PERSONAS TO REAL USERS

Another simple but slightly more demanding way to validate your personas is to show them to the actual people they are designed to represent. For example, if you created a bank teller persona, show your persona to several bank tellers. Tell the real bank tellers that your goal was to create a profile of a typical bank teller and you would like to know if your persona looks right, as such (see the following "Story from the Field"). You want to know what aspects of the persona resonate with real people that fall into that category of users.

In our experience, you only need to do this with a handful of people per persona. You will likely find that comments start to significantly overlap after the first three or four reviews. You might consider doing minor revisions after each review so the next real person sees only the most accurate persona. As you do these reviews and revisions, make sure you are not violating your original data. If there are major conflicts, choose the characteristic you trust the most and note the need to do further research if the discrepancy falls within an area important to your product domain.

CONDUCT "REALITY CHECK" SITE VISITS

A more involved way of approaching persona validation (if you have the time and budget) is to visit people who are very similar to your personas and attempt to ascertain if your personas match your observations. The goal here is to visit users who match the personas on high-level characteristics to see how well they match on low-level characteristics. This goal is the same as with the previous validation technique, but here you are relying on your ability to see how real users actually are and how they behave, not just what they think about themselves and their reflection on their actions. We call these *reality-check site visits*. To do this, you will take the steps described in the following sections.

Create persona profile screeners

Work backward from your rich persona to a set of characteristics that are essential to that persona. The sketches you started from are likely to be useful here. From this set of characteristics, you will develop questions that can be used to evaluate whether or not any

Sharing the Persona with the Personae

Debby Catton, Technical Writing Consultant, and Jennifer Dunne, Technical Writer, Sun Life Financial

Gaining approval to create personas wasn't an easy task. We were either too busy or people just didn't see the value. Finally, after two years of persistence, our assistant vice president (AVP) gave us permission to proceed. Because we had a number of different personas to create and were new to the process of creating a persona, we decided to first create the persona on our smallest but perhaps most significant user type—our financial center trainers.

We were somewhat shy during our first interviews with the trainers, but soon every interview was a completely successful and passionate experience! As the time drew near to present our persona to our AVP group, a twinge of doubt crept in. What if they didn't see the value in our work? What if they told us we couldn't proceed with the other personas?

We decided that if we presented the completed persona to the trainers we interviewed and got their opinion on how this work would benefit them, our leaders couldn't dispute the effectiveness of this tool. And we were right. The trainers loved the concept and provided the following statements:

- "Wow! You have done an excellent job at capturing our persona in my opinion. I like the perspective you took and how you personalized it. Good write-up. Hoping that the powers that be are able to get a better grasp of the role and how it works out here in the financial center."
- "It is a good generalization of the role as I am sure that each of us trainers has a broad and varied role. No two are exactly the same."
- "I like Sandra! Sounds like you have captured us—mood, job, etc. Great job. Now I hope that others who influence and affect our position and the tasks we undertake have a real good read and get to know Sandra intimately."

Having the blessing and acceptance of our personas made a huge impact at our presentation to our leaders, as we received unconditional approval to proceed with the rest. We know what a great communication and decision-making tool a persona can be. As the creators of personas, we have found that the process is an invaluable exercise in truly understanding our audience.

candidate participant is a good representative of one of your personas. For more information on doing screeners (including an example), see the "Use Personas as a Recruiting Profile for Usability Testing and Market Research" section in Chapter 6.

Recruit representative people and visit them

Using your new persona screeners, locate several people who are good representatives of each persona. Three to five people per persona should be adequate. Visit those people and conduct a brief observational study and interview in an attempt to determine how well the low-level and peripheral characteristics of your personas match these people. Alternatively, hold focus group sessions with groups of representatives of each persona. Use the outline of the foundation document as a rough script for your discussion sessions. In either of these cases, and in addition to your direct observations, you can also show them personas and get their feedback as you would using the previous validation technique. With these observations and feedback, revise and refine your personas, being careful not to violate the original research findings that made up your personas. You will likely find that you are simply tweaking bits and pieces of the design-irrelevant details or fictional components of your personas in order to fit your validation findings.

CONDUCT LARGE-SAMPLE SURVEYS OR INTERVIEWS

If you have even more time and resources, you can consider doing a more sophisticated validation effort. Using surveys, you can determine how pervasive your personas are in addition to the existence and coexistence of their attributes. To conduct this research, you will need to identify individual characteristics per persona and translate them into a form that real users can respond to as part of a questionnaire or survey. For example, you might generate a series of statements that respondents can rate (examples A and B following) or check as appropriate (example C).

Example A

Rate the following after-school activity statements regarding your own behaviors:

a. I usually watch television after school. (strongly agree, agree, disagree, strongly disagree)
b. I usually play computer video games after school. (strongly agree, agree, disagree, strongly disagree)
c. I usually play outside at home after school. (strongly agree, agree, disagree, strongly disagree)
d. I usually talk on the phone with friends after school. (strongly agree, agree, disagree, strongly disagree)

Example B

Indicate the frequency with which you engage in the following activities after school:

a. Watching television (frequently, sometimes, never)
b. Playing computer video games (frequently, sometimes, never)
c. Playing outside at home (frequently, sometimes, never)
d. Talking on the phone with friends (frequently, sometimes, never)

Example C

Indicate which of the following activities you engage in regularly after school (check all that apply):

a. Watch television.
b. Play computer video games.
c. Play outside.
d. Talk on the phone with friends.

Analysis of such data can take many forms and can be quite complicated. This can be similar to segmentation or cluster analysis, which you might have started your persona effort from, only now you have target profiles to evaluate the responses against. Your goal is to understand how the characteristics of a broad sample of users relate to the known (or proposed) characteristics of your personas. The details of doing such an analysis are beyond the scope of this book. We recommend that you do not undertake such a validation effort without the involvement of a trained statistician or researcher. Keep in mind, however, that this approach can be greatly simplified by focusing on only a few of the key attributes of your personas. The analysis for this simplified approach can be as basic as comparing a few descriptive statistics (e.g., averages or a series of frequency counts) or doing a correlation analysis. For an example of this, see the "Story from the Field" by Colin Hynes regarding putting real values on your personas.

The invitation started with a subject line explaining, "Get $10 off your next purchase by filling out a quick survey." We sent the link out to 15,000 customers from our database. On the survey page, each respondent was presented with the seven defining quotes and an "Other" option for those who did not feel they bucketed neatly into any of the persona statements. After scrubbing the data, we ended up with 1048 valid responses.

Upon our initial high-level analysis of the data we were somewhat disappointed that respondents were fairly evenly distributed across the seven personas. There were some slightly heavier buckets, but all personas garnered between 10 and 20% of the overall

Putting Real Values on Your Personas

Colin Hynes, Director of Usability, Staples.com

After a lot of effort went into creating meaningful and valid personas for our development team, and when our final personas were presented to the senior executives, our VP of Marketing commented, "I wish we knew how much each of these personas was worth in bottom-line dollars." This kicked off our "persona valuation project."

The main thrust of the persona valuation project was a joint effort between the Usability and Marketing teams. After several meetings between the two groups, we decided that data would be gathered through a survey with one simple question tied to the defining quote of each persona. This, of course, put much pressure on the defining quotes to fully encapsulate the essence of the persona. Our hope was that a user would read one of the quotes and immediately see himself in the statement.

Then we decided on the criteria for distributing the survey, which was simplified: people who had purchased from Staples (any channel) in the last six months, had visited Staples.com in the last six months, and had an e-mail address. We also decided to offer an incentive ($10 off) to participants, even though the survey was only going to be two questions. One requirement was that we had to be able to link responses to other info in the database for calculation of value regarding each respondent (see Figure 4.18).

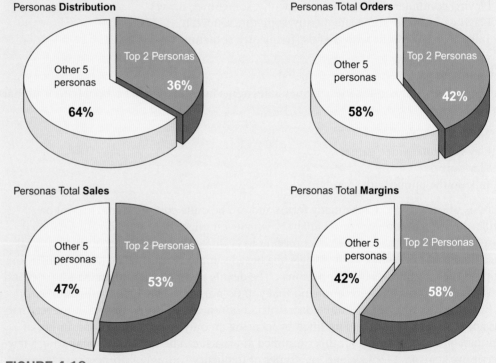

FIGURE 4.18
Staples was able to attribute spending per persona by matching survey respondents to purchases in their transaction database. As they looked at the data across different purchase metrics, a clear picture of the most valuable personas emerged.

distribution. The usability hypotheses that two particular personas would dominate the distribution was not supported. We feared that without one or two clear-cut leaders we would be left trying to serve all personas. Our ultimate concern was that this would manifest itself in a website design that tried to be everything to everyone, instead of having focus.

One highly encouraging data point was that only 8 of the more than 1000 respondents bucketed themselves as "Other." This made us feel confident we had nailed the original persona descriptions.

Although the distribution did not give us the clarity we were hoping for, when we matched the responses against 12-month sales figures the picture became crystal clear. We calculated the percentage of orders, sales, and margin generated for each persona. The figures were an aggregate of all purchases made through any channel. Strikingly, the data showed that two personas that made up a combined 36% of the distribution also made up 42% of the orders, 53% of sales, and 58% of the margin (see Figure 4.19). Further, if we were to map the personas out in a Venn diagram to illustrate overlap in goals, these two personas would have the greatest overlap. *Note:* We tried to have as little overlap as possible overall in the personas. If we deemed that there was a significant overlap between personas we combined the personas in the creation process.

It is difficult to overestimate the impact this data had on the future design direction of Staples.com. To ensure accuracy, we reanalyzed the data and obtained the same results. At that point, we knew we had lightning in a bottle. With the inclusive nature of the study and the airtight research design, the results were difficult to dispute.

COMPLETED PERSONAS DO NOT MARK THE END OF USER RESEARCH

At the point you finish the creation of your personas, you may be tempted to think that you do not need to further understand (do research) or involve real users in the development of your product. From our perspective, this couldn't be further from the truth. We believe personas are a great starting point for understanding and incorporating user information in the development cycle.

As you will find in Chapter 6, personas can (among other things) be used to create excellent recruiting profiles for further testing and insight. User testing, focus groups, beta testing, and other methods of involving real users in the process should continue as long as possible throughout the entire development cycle. Personas can serve not only as recruiting targets for these activities but also as a communication device and a repository for new findings. You may find that you need to update your completed personas every six months to a year as your target audience changes, though you must be thoughtful about how you approach this (for more discussion of this, see Chapter 7). In other words, even though other activities are now in focus, the validation of your personas should continue throughout the persona lifecycle.

HOW TO KNOW YOU ARE READY FOR BIRTH AND MATURATION

You should now have a set of rich, meaningful personas that have been validated against real users. Still, you may be tempted to keep refining your personas until they seem perfect. You may feel hesitant about putting them "out there" for people to see and use. How do you know when you are ready to begin introducing them to your broader team? There are signs that will indicate you are ready. You will notice that the amount of tweaking and reexamination slows down or stops. You may still have some open questions, but you shouldn't have any blank sections in your foundation document that are truly critical to your product domain. The personas will just *feel* right to you and your core team. In addition, your stakeholders should have signed off on your work. They now agree that no critical audience is missing and that the personas are robust, credible, and in line with your business objectives.

If your creation process took several weeks to several months, it may be that your product planning and design are now under way—or, worse, coding has begun. If so, it is likely that your broader team is becoming eager to obtain information about your target audience. They may be asking for you to deliver your personas ASAP. All of these things tell you that you are ready to deliver—that the *birth and maturation* phase should start. This is the phase in which you not only introduce your personas to the team but also begin a persona communication campaign. At this time you introduce the persona method and other UCD techniques, many of which will directly employ your personas (possibly changing the team's design and development process forever).

SUMMARY

The *conception and gestation* phase of the persona lifecycle involves a great deal of activity, teamwork, and decision making. You have become an alchemist, combining data, assumptions, and your understanding of what will and will not work in your company to create a rich set of design targets. You have translated raw data into information and that information into prioritized categories and subcategories of users. You have created a set of personas that combines fact and fiction to reflect your business priorities and convey the essential information about your target users you found in the data. As much as possible, you have with explicit links to the original data supported every important characteristic and statement found in your foundation documents. Last, you have done validation work before finalizing your personas.

As we have stated several times previously, we believe that, whenever possible, personas should be based on data. Even the *perception* that the personas are not based on data can damage their credibility and utility. However, we've also shown you how to create ad hoc personas, which can be incredibly helpful despite their lack of hard data. No matter how you create your personas, it is practically unavoidable that some elements of personas are generated from educated guesses or are simply made up. Your job in the *conception and gestation* phase is to make informed decisions about how much fiction and storytelling are needed to make your personas feel real and be truly engaging. Creating personas involves straightforward fact gathering, but there is also an art to it. Be inventive, but also be practical and stay as close to your data as possible.

Once your personas are complete, substantive, and stable, you have only just begun. You are now ready to begin the education process. Communicating your personas will take time and effort. You will have to be strategic, persistent, and patient. Once your personas are out there, they will need to actively participate in the design and development process (the *adulthood* phase of personas). Your personas are ready to be born. Labor can be painful.

HANDY DETAIL

Get Ready for the Birth and Maturation Phase by Cleaning Up

Once you have your personas fully created—pared down, prioritized, with perfect images in place, and details of profiles substantiated and revised with a quick user study—you probably need to do some cleanup work. Make sure you have solid, cleaned-up foundation documents before moving to the next phase (*birth and maturation*). Make sure you have copies of the reference research materials, including local copies of data you found on the Internet (i.e., material that might move or otherwise disappear). Take notes about your specific process, including who did what, when, and how. You will want to have notes on the problems you encountered and the reasoning behind critical decisions made. You might even want to keep records of how long certain activities took. This could be useful for return on investment (ROI) measures in the final lifecycle stage.

Persona birth and maturation

> Giving people the wrong information at the wrong time is like trying to teach a pig to sing. It wastes your time and it annoys the pig.
>
> **— adapted from Paul Dickson**

WHAT IS BIRTH AND MATURATION FOR PERSONAS?

The *birth and maturation* phase is perhaps one of the trickiest phases of the persona lifecycle. It marks the transition from persona creation to persona use. During the birth and maturation phase, information about your complete personas is sent off into your organization to interact with other people. Your personas are fully formed but will now begin to develop in the minds of your product team. Although introducing personas to your organization may seem straightforward, it usually isn't.

The most important thing to remember during birth and maturation is that personas are effective only if you can make them come alive for your colleagues. You just spent a lot of time creating rich, detailed foundation documents with a fully bought-in persona core team, and now you and your core team must understand that almost no one else in your organization will ever read the foundation documents from end to end (and at most they will read them only once). So, you will need to progressively (and strategically) disclose information about each persona in small, highly digestible chunks. You will educate your colleagues on the very specific ways they can (and should) use the persona information in their day-to-day work.

The birth and maturation phase of the persona lifecycle consists of three distinct activities:

1. *Enrich your communication strategy (prepare for birth and beyond)*. During family planning, you created a communication strategy to help you communicate the basic value of personas to a possibly less than interested audience (see Chapter 3). During step 1 of birth and maturation, you must transition from a relatively heads-down period of hard work and creativity, with a core team that is already convinced of the usefulness of personas, to a period of heads-up, active evangelism.
2. *Introduce the persona method and your personas (birth)*. During birth, you and your core team will put your communication strategy to work as you embark on a communication campaign. You will introduce the persona method, your reasons for creating the personas, and basic information about the personas you have created and how you expect them to be used.
3. *Progressively educate and maintain focus on your personas (maturation)*. During maturation, you will progressively disclose persona details, persona uses, and persona benefits. Your personas really come to life during this phase. During maturation, your job is to help your colleagues as they prepare to incorporate the personas into their design and development processes.

We recommend that you read about all three steps before you complete your own communication strategy. During steps 2 and 3, you and your team will create and distribute persona artifacts. For easy reference and comparison, we have included information about all artifacts in support of birth and maturation activities later in this chapter.

In the next section, we discuss the work you will do to prepare your core team and stakeholders for the birth of your personas. In step 2, we include suggestions for introducing the persona method and the personas into your organization. In step 3, we provide recommendations for progressively disclosing information about your personas to bring them to life in your organization.

STEP 1. PREPARE FOR BIRTH AND BEYOND

The key to success during the birth and maturation phase is a willingness on your part to step back, look around, and remember that people outside your core team are going to need a lot of help with the personas you have created. Your colleagues need to understand what personas are, why you are asking them to use personas, and how to integrate personas into their already packed work schedules. In an organization with existing user-centered design (UCD) processes, your strategy may be quick and fairly straightforward. In an organization new to the idea of UCD, your tasks during the birth and maturation phase may be more onerous.

It is time to create a persona communication campaign. Your communication strategy should address who, what, when, and how:

- Who you need to communicate the personas to
- What information each audience will need
- When you will present each type of information
- How you will convey the information

Create your communication strategy

Think of your communication campaign as the work you do to create a set of ever-widening concentric circles of buy-in. The more top-down (or, in the concentric-circle metaphor, the more center-out) involvement you get, the better. The more your stakeholders treat the persona information as familiar and useful, the more likely it is that the rest of your organization will as well. Attempt to align your goals with the business goals so stakeholders see something familiar or something they can relate to.

Your communication strategy is your plan for your communication campaign. In your communication strategy, include a specific schedule of the activities, presentations, and distribution of materials you will use to achieve your goals. Your plan should be fully dependent on the schedule of milestones in your product development cycle. Your communication strategy should include the following:

1. Goals for the communication campaign:
   - Introduce the persona method, help colleagues understand the reason we are using personas for this project, and provide the right amount of background on how we created the personas we are about to introduce.
   - Bring the personas to life in the minds of all colleagues who influence the design and development of the product (or whichever subset of these people you decide to focus on).
   - Progressively disclose the right information to the right people at the right time to ensure that the user data embedded in the personas is understood and absorbed.
   - Ensure that the personas are used during the decision-making process in whatever ways you and your core team determine (see Chapter 6).
2. Communication strategy (who, what, when, and how):
   - *Who*—Who are the audiences for your personas? Are there different audiences with different needs?
3. For each audience, identify:
   - *What*—What specific information about the personas do these individuals need? Identify the subsets of the persona-related information you believe will be most helpful to each audience.
   - *When*—When should you introduce the various types of information to this audience? After you have introduced the persona basics, when is the best time to introduce *new* or *enriched* information about the personas into your development cycle?
   - *How*—How should you and your core team communicate various aspects of the personas and the ways they can be used? What are the best ways to deliver persona-related information so it will actually be consumed?

Creating your communication strategy and realizing the strategy in a communication campaign don't have to take a long time. Your plan can be as short as a few notes on which

83

topics you need to address or as long as a detailed set of presentations you will deliver to various audiences. You can choose to cover all four of the important topics listed previously in a single meeting if that is appropriate for your situation.

Keep stakeholders "in the know"

The best way to ensure top-down involvement is to make sure that key stakeholders are well aware of your goals and how you plan to pursue those goals. Although stakeholders may like the idea of personas in the abstract, they may be dismayed to hear that you want to change, for example, the way product design documents are written. Make sure stakeholders are aware of what you are trying to do, why you are trying to do it, and what measurable goals you have set and the plans you have to see those goals to fruition. Create a draft communication plan—complete with goals, possible measures of return on investment, etc.—and obtain feedback from stakeholders. You will be surprised by how many political landmines stakeholders can help you avoid with their view of the big picture and an understanding of the pressures being exerted on the various teams you will be talking to.

Remember that clarifying your own goals is important. Making sure that your goals jive with the current business or product goals is critical.

Evaluate your audiences and determine who needs what information

During family planning, you thought about your organization and what problems you want to solve with the personas. You identified obstacles to your persona effort, including people you thought would resist the personas, the inertia of various work habits and processes, and other environmental factors. Now it is time to take a close look at your insights and to get creative. It is time to enhance your communication strategy to account for all of the obstacles you have identified and your best guesses about what types of information different people in your organization will respond to. First, evaluate how many different audiences and needs really exist in your organization:

- What are the major divisions, roles, and disciplines of your product team? Do these people and groups already understand anything at all about users and UCD? What are their work goals and challenges?
- Which parts of the product development process do they have ownership over?
- What types of information about the personas would help them in their job?
- When do you think they will have time and mental energy to devote to learning about personas?

You will probably find that the answers to these questions can vary quite radically from group to group and role to role and that it makes sense to create slightly different strategies for communicating the personas to different sets of colleagues. You will probably deliver some of your education on a broad level—to everyone at once—but you might want to follow up with smaller meetings involving people with shared interests.

The agenda for product managers may be quite different from the agenda for developers. Product managers will understand the value of the personas quite quickly, but will be interested in how much buy-in you have on the persona process throughout the organization. Developers are more likely to ask a lot of questions about how and why you created the personas and how they relate to data, how you expect them to use the personas, and the dangers of designing for the wrong persona. Create a schedule for the delivery of persona-related information appropriate to the various teams and key team members in your organization.

Birth can be a private event if necessary

If the answers to the questions in the previous section lead you to believe that no one in your organization is going to be receptive to any persona-related information and that nothing

Who Is the Primary Audience for Personas?

We asked 25 experienced persona practitioners, a mix of user-experience consultants, and in-house specialists who they thought the primary audience was for their persona efforts. The following is a list of the audiences identified, in order of priority:

1. Designers
2. Program/product managers
3. Developers/engineers
4. Executives, business strategists, and "clients"
5. Marketing

Many of these practitioners noted that these audiences were important at different times in the development cycle (executives early on for funding and go-ahead approval, product managers throughout, developers starting in the middle onward, and marketing later). Of course, there are plenty of other audiences for your efforts, and we strongly believe you should strategically seek those out (e.g., quality assurance testing, user assistance/documentation, market research, product planning, product support). The following are quotes from practitioners on this subject:

> *In our experience, developers tend to use the names for communication purposes. Other users—such as QA, usability, and tech writers—seem to use more of the persona characteristics in writing tests, user guides, and creating application user interfaces.*
> **—Holly Jamesen Carr, GreenShape LLC, formerly Usability Specialist, *Attenex Corporation***

> *The developers refer to the persona most, so it is mostly geared to them. I included QA and documentation because they might refer to it.*
> **—Lori Landesman, *The MathWorks***

Aside from the usual things people need from personas, here are some differences I've observed:

- Marketing folks are more interested in purchase motivators and the context in which the decision to buy is made.
- Executives use the personas in road shows as evidence "that our organization actually knows how to walk the walk of being customer centered."
- QA looks for the core tasks that people perform, so they can build robust test cases early in the project.
- Usability specialists use them to create task descriptions and scenarios and to determine criteria for recruiting test participants.
- Project managers look for clues to help them prioritize work and to ideally remove work entirely from the project schedule.
> **—Bob Barlow-Busch, *Quarry***

> *From what we've seen so far, the executives don't tend to read the profiles, they just want to know that they are there. Marketing tends to focus on the demographic and buying pattern related information. However, in general, everyone is focusing on the overall picture of the user so tailoring the persona to the different audiences is currently less of a concern.*
> **—Bob Murata, *Adobe***

As you can imagine, each audience will have its own needs and interests related to the personas. Product planners and marketing are interested in purchasing behavior, desired features, and influence. Designers are interested in effect, style, brands, and preferences. Usability and market research need participant screeners (high-level must-have characteristics) for recruiting in studies, interviews, and focus groups. Executives want the market characteristics, revenue projections, and demographic data related to these personas as customer segments. Moreover, and as you will see in the next chapter, each will need to have specific ways of using your personas spelled out for them.

85

you can do will change this, you may decide not to publicly announce your personas. There are many reasons to keep personas visible to only select people, even if you have spent a great deal of time creating and perfecting them and are antsy to put them to work. The fact that you have put so much effort into your personas is a great reason to be cautious before sharing them with others.

In Chapter 3, we talked about the importance of the first impression the personas make. If you are sure your organization as a whole will simply not welcome the personas into your development processes no matter what you do, you do have other options. There are always obstacles to introducing personas as a new method, and you shouldn't balk at the challenges these obstacles produce. However, remember that your goal during birth is to introduce the personas in order for them to help your colleagues in their work. If you really believe that the obstacles you face in introducing the personas to your organization are currently insurmountable, consider alternatives so the personas can live to emerge another day.

Planning for limited exposure is an alternative when the timing for launching personas to everyone just feels wrong. Launching your personas to select individuals, people who will be able to use them right now to make important decisions, will help you argue the benefits of personas to a larger group later.

Be realistic about your timing

While you were working on the first two persona lifecycle phases, a lot may have changed. The overall vision might have evolved, tactical plans may have solidified, and coding may have already started. Now that you are ready to introduce the personas, is your organization really ready for them? Where exactly are you in your development cycle? If you find that the development cycle is already pretty far along before you start communicating anything, don't create a long and complicated communication strategy. Instead, create a "just-in-time" education approach. Instead of planning to carefully introduce each group to the personas in the order they will use them, approach the specific owners of the *next* document or artifact in the product development cycle. For example, if the product vision or technical specification documents have already been written, talk to the designers and try to convince them to incorporate the personas' names into wireframes, storyboards, and visual prototypes.

More generally, you don't want to lose your window of opportunity to contribute the personas at a time when they will be useful and used in the overall development process. If you take too long in creating them, the rest of the team will be so far ahead that your work will not be useful or used. You have to stay very much in tune with where the rest of the project is and with all that is happening politically. You may even need to introduce your skeletons (or brief sketches based on them) before enriching them into full personas.

Prepare the core persona team for their new roles in birth and beyond

When you have a plan, you and your core team need to switch gears from analysis to action. You need to transition from *creation* mode to *communication* mode. Even teams who do manage the transition are often unprepared for the ongoing responsibilities related to supporting and promoting personas.

TRANSITION PERSONA CORE TEAM MEMBERS INTO PERSONA WRANGLERS

Until now, your team's ownership of the persona process and the personas has been complete and insular. As the persona creators, you and your core team made all decisions (with some input or approval from your stakeholders)—from what data to use to how many personas to create to how to structure the foundation documents. For personas to flourish in your organization, you must allow your other colleagues to take some ownership of the personas and the processes surrounding their use. As you launch into birth and maturation activities, you also have to be prepared to share ownership of the personas and take on the role of persona wrangler.

We use the term *wrangler* here purposefully. Like the InfoWranglers that Saul Carliner described in his 1998 article [Carliner 1998], persona wranglers must "act as messengers in the communication process…. The work of the InfoWrangler solves a business problem; it does not merely document the system." In his discussion of sharing user profiles, Kuniavsky (2003, p. 153) also recommends creating the role of wrangler:

> Although you can share a lot of information, there is always going to be more information than everyone can remember. A profile wrangler (or profile keeper) position can be useful for centralizing the information. The wrangler is present during the profile creation process and is responsible for keeping profiles updated. He or she also serves as a resource for interpreting profiles to the development team ("What would Jeff think about a Palm Pilot download option?")

As persona wranglers, your core team will be responsible for maintaining the integrity of the personas (and their underlying data) without standing in the way of their acceptance and use by your colleagues. You will need to ensure that your personas are known, accepted, and utilized. It is not an easy task.

ASSIGN A WRANGLER FOR EACH PERSONA

Assign ownership (really, "wranglership") of each persona to a single team member. If you don't have enough core team members to assign every persona to a different individual, you can assign more than one persona to each team member, or you can consider enlisting people outside the persona core team. The fewer personas each team member has to wrangle the better. Each wrangler should become the absolute expert and identified go-to person for the persona he or she owns. The team member should assume responsibility for fully knowing and maintaining the foundation document for his or her assigned persona. This is not to say that each wrangler will make all decisions related to updates and revisions, but that person will bring the need for a correction or update to the attention of the core team and will make the eventual alteration to the official version of the foundation document.

Why assign a wrangler to each persona? Why not let the core team as a group maintain all personas? Because the transition into birth requires that you, the overall persona champion/owner, shift your attention from the details of each persona to the grand challenges of communication and facilitation with your colleagues. It will become more and more difficult to keep track of all details incorporated into all personas. Assigning individual wranglers ensures that each persona will have at least one team member who maintains a deep understanding of that persona's details and data. This frees you to take care of broader issues. The wrangler's job is to:

- Field questions regarding the persona from the organization.
- Track down the answers to these questions (in collaboration with the core team).
- Communicate the answers as needed.
- Revise foundation documents or other materials as applicable.

For example, if someone asks, "Does Laura have a wireless network? I didn't see the answer to that in the materials," Laura's wrangler should be ready to reply: "Good question! Let me find some data on that" (and follow up). Note that not all questions and issues with your personas need to be immediately addressed. So that such issues do not become overwhelming, you might want to have a weekly or monthly meeting to collectively prioritize and discuss such issues.

AGREE ON WHICH PERSONA CHARACTERISTICS MUST BE PROTECTED

Although you must maintain the integrity of the data, you must also invite your colleagues to adopt the personas as resources. Your carefully crafted personas may change a bit during the birth and maturation process and throughout adulthood. In fact, one of the powerful aspects of personas is that they are generative and extendable. Your personas will be put into new contexts, complete new tasks, and accomplish their goals in new ways as they are applied to the design of your product. Your team members will push the boundaries of your personas to fit the needs of the domain they are working in and to answer the questions that arise about their specific areas.

This extension is good—and dangerous. You must be ready to decide which changes and extensions are acceptable and which are not. Without assigned wranglers, foundation documents can easily become dated and lose some of their utility as reference materials. As your team focuses on communication, education, and the creation of new persona artifacts, you will all have less and less time to concentrate as a group on the foundation documents. Because each wrangler is fully responsible for maintaining and revising the foundation document as new data surfaces, you will not have to worry about important details falling through the cracks.

STEP 2. BIRTH

Birth is the introduction of your personas to the product team; it's when you put your communication campaign into action. Birth should include an organized and ongoing series of educational, political, and tactical activities that help your colleagues understand what you have been doing, what the personas are and how they enable UCD, how they fit into your existing processes, and how you will continue to support the use of personas as the product development efforts gear up and proceed. You must fully convince colleagues who may never have heard of personas or their benefits, and you must do so relatively quickly. Problems during the birth and maturation phase can lead to lack of acceptance and to personas that die on the vine. Worse, a single failed persona effort can sour your organization on the whole idea of using personas, and therefore make your job a lot more difficult in future persona efforts and even in regard to other UCD techniques.

Introduce user-centered design, the persona method, and your persona project

You will need to communicate three related yet distinct topics before finally introducing your specific personas:

- The benefits and methods of user-centered product design (UCD evangelism)
- Basic information about the persona method (persona method evangelism)
- How the persona method will fit into and enhance your existing processes (your persona method in context)

These can be covered together in a single kickoff meeting to your entire product team or in separate meetings over time. Your communication challenges with each of these topics will depend on several factors, including:

- Your specific goals
- Differences in your colleagues' current level of knowledge and interest
- The timing of the communication relative to the progress of your product development cycle

Similarly, the types of materials and communication strategies that will work best for you will vary. In the following sections, we include a variety of suggestions for you to choose from.

COMMUNICATE THE BENEFITS OF USER-CENTERED PRODUCT DESIGN

Birth can be a golden opportunity to educate your colleagues on the benefits and methods of UCD. Consider spending some time describing and discussing your organization's current commitment to and understanding of UCD. Is your organization already committed to

UCD? If so, your personas will be just one of many user-centered methodologies in your development process. Does your organization talk about being user or customer centered but lack concrete processes to back this up? Or is the entire concept of user-centered product design relatively new for your organization?

We recommended in Chapter 3 that you surface assumptions about target users of your products. Now take time to understand how much your colleagues really know (and don't know) about creating user-centered products. Talk to colleagues and find out exactly how much each group knows and does not know about the UCD process. The results of this investigation might surprise you. It is an unusual company or product development group that does not call itself "dedicated to our users/customers" or "user/customer focused"—but it is also an unusual company that truly walks the walk with embedded and supported UCD processes.

If there are already other user-centered methods incorporated into your development process—such as field research, contextual inquiry, user testing, surveys, and focus groups (see the UsabilityNet site at www.usabilitynet.org/tools/methods.htm for a complete list)—your challenge will be to help people understand how personas will enhance and in some cases alter the existing processes. It is your job to evaluate when and how (within the overall development process) current UCD methods are employed and to propose changes to integrate the personas. (See Chapter 6 for examples of how personas can be used in conjunction with other UCD methods.)

If your organization talks about being user centered but doesn't currently have any user-centered methods integrated into the development process, or if the entire concept of user-centered product design is relatively new to your organization, you have a bigger challenge. In these cases, you may want to educate your organization on practical UCD and why you think UCD methods will make good business sense for your company. There are several books on the market that make a strong case for UCD. For example, see the books by Donahue (2002), Garrett (2002), Hackos and Redish (1998), Kuniavsky (2003), Mayhew (1999), Preece et al. (2002), and Vredenburg et al. (2001). Although you and your core team might want to read these books cover to cover, remember that the rest of your colleagues will only have the time and patience to read summaries or listen to a short presentation.

It is also possible that broaching the subject of UCD is too much for your organization at this point. The success of your persona effort does not necessarily depend on broad UCD commitment from your organization. This is a topic you may want to start pursuing either very early on (e.g., during *family planning*) or even after the current development cycle is complete (i.e., after your personas have provided some utility and user focus for your team). Again, an understanding of your organizational culture and the potential acceptance of UCD should influence your decisions here—whether UCD is overt or covert ("stealth" usability/UCD), whether a champion needs to participate, or whether it should be labeled something different (such as "continuous improvement" or "market-driven design") to meet with better acceptance.

COMMUNICATE THE BENEFITS OF USING PERSONAS

During family planning, when you created a communication strategy to include in your action plan, you prepared yourself and your team to answer the following questions:

- What is the persona method, and why does it work?
- Who are your personas?
- How were your personas built, and why did you build them that way?
- How should your personas be used during the design and development of your product?

Why take the time to evangelize the persona method in general? Why not dive in and talk about the ways personas can be used in your organization and for your products? One reason for evangelizing is that the persona method is still quite young and even controversial in some circles. There are some (very predictable) questions your colleagues will have. It is not easy to tackle these general questions and the specifics of how you would like to see personas used in your organization at the same time.

Return to the work you did during *family planning* to predict the particular benefits personas would bring to your organization. It is likely that questions you and your core team discussed and debated during your conception and gestation work will be the same questions you are faced with as you introduce the persona method to the rest of your organization.

COMMUNICATE THE SPECIFICS OF YOUR PERSONA EFFORT

After you have educated your organization on the principles of UCD and have introduced the persona method, you will want to talk more specifically about how you see personas fitting in to your organization's processes. Your colleagues will want to know how you developed the personas for your organization, and they will want to know what process changes you expect them to make to accommodate the personas.

Explain where the personas came from

Before you introduce the personas and encourage people to use them, you should open up the books and tell people about your persona effort thus far. Let them know the following things:

- Who is on the persona core team and why you invited these particular people to participate as members (as opposed to other individuals or a large group)
- The process you used to identify data sources, gather data, and analyze data (or the process you used to identify and evaluate assumptions) and what those data sources are; offer to share the data
- How you validated, or plan to validate, the personas
- How you plan to measure the internal ROI of the persona process (and impact on the costs of development)

In other words, help everyone understand where the personas came from before you introduce the personas themselves. This will help preempt questions related to the credibility of your work or process and the validity of your resulting personas.

Explain how your personas will fit into your existing development cycle

If you are trying to create a more user-centered organization, you probably have a lot of ideas related to improving the product development cycle. You probably wish that UCD professionals were involved earlier, that visits to customers were funded, that usability testing was accepted and scheduled early enough to make a real difference, and so on. Although many of these methods are linked, and successfully introducing one may increase the likelihood of introducing more, it is helpful to maintain focus and to not try to change too much all at once. Even if you think the current development process is riddled with problems, you should still try to communicate the value of personas in the context of the development process as is. If you try to make too many changes at once, you will run the risk of alienating the very people critical to the success of the persona effort.

Simply introducing personas can—and should—have fairly significant effects on your development process, and you should take the time to envision all of its potential effects. (See Chapter 6 for an array of examples showing how personas can be directly used in design and development.) Once you have the big picture and a list of all possible changes the persona effort could engender, you need to take a close look at the list and decide which changes could have the most significant effect on the quality of the product.

Describe the everyday benefits of personas

If you can prove that personas will make their lives easier, your colleagues will be much more likely to accept the personas into their everyday work. By citing examples of the daily benefits of personas your colleagues can easily identify with, you can start to prove that personas make things easier even before you introduce them:

- *It will become easier to communicate.* At the simplest level, the persona names will replace the word *user*. When we talk about the features and functions of our product, we will be able to use the persona names to communicate unambiguously about who we are building things for.
- *Decisions will be based on data, not opinions.* How many times have you been in meetings in which someone has said, "The user is never going to want this" or "Let's put our user hat on now?" Let's face it: When we argue about what the "user" wants we end up making decisions based on who in the room is loudest, the best arguer, the most powerful, or the most annoying. Personas will help us stop this pattern. Instead, we will be able to refer back to the data that served as the source of the personas. Sometimes we like to say "user is a four-letter word!"
- *You will understand the goals of the executive team.* Properly prioritized personas reflect prioritized business, brand, and user experience goals, which reflect the intentions of the executive team. Many people in your organization will be relieved to have this kind of top-down clarity.
- *Data will be a lot easier to use.* Personas are memorable digests of data, and they help us remember to access relevant data at the right times. As we continue to gather new data and revisit old data sources, the personas will serve as the equalizers and homogenizers of disparate data sources. Old and new data will stay accessible and relevant as facets of the persona descriptions.
- *You will find new sources of inspiration.* Personas are deep and detailed descriptions of your target users. Just like real people, they have habits and personalities, and you can get to know them well. Innovation can come from the combination of your technical knowledge and your observations related to unmet needs of real people.

91

Introduce your personas

Once your product team is properly prepared, you will be ready to introduce the actual personas you have worked so hard to create. As you introduce the personas to your colleagues, you should embrace the notion of "progressive disclosure." The trick is to give everyone just the right amount of information to ignite their imaginations, enable them to continue doing their work (perhaps more easily than they did it before), and inspire them to come back for more information when they are ready for it. With that in mind, the real work of educating your teammates about the details of your personas really happens during step 3 (*maturation*) and runs through the end of persona *adulthood*.

In Chapter 4, we recommended that you create detailed foundation documents for all of your main personas. These foundation documents capture all the information you have about your personas, including links to the data sources from which that information arose. Completed foundation documents are likely to be rich and complex, and as such do not make for light reading. You probably cannot expect everyone on your product team to read and remember every detail in these documents. You will have to prioritize and target the information you want your broad team to really know about your personas. Your personas live in the minds of your product team, not in some document or communication artifact. You will have to be strategic about how you make that happen effectively and efficiently.

The material following in this chapter describes three categories of persona artifacts you and your core team can create (buzz generators, comparison facilitators, and enrichers). For birth, select a subset of these artifacts—primarily buzz generators and perhaps one or two comparison facilitators—according to the communication strategy you have created; for example:

- If your organization is not very user centered and people are potentially going to be resistant to the persona effort, create several buzz generators that introduce your personas and express the value of personas in general. After these have been posted for a while, create some introduction posters that include important data points on them. Build a presentation that conveys how much data were used to create the personas, perhaps by including a slide that shows the long list of data sources you and your core team used. More generally, be sure to make the link between the personas and the data as clear as possible. The fact that you have used data as the foundation for the personas will speak volumes and will defuse most push-back related to the validity of the personas. Consider making a fact sheet to hand out with critical factoids about your target audience. Finally, make sure that copies of the original research reports are available to anyone who is interested.
- If your organization is likely to pick up on personas quickly and be eager to learn more, start with more modest introduction posters and perhaps a few basic comparison facilitators. A little while after you introduce the personas, plan to use enrichers to communicate additional details centered on data points.

However you decide to introduce your personas, focus on the key attributes that define them, and make sure to highlight the main differences among them. Plan to explain why these particular personas were chosen, reviewing the highlights of your evaluation and prioritization work in the *conception and gestation* phase. Consider discussing a few of the user categories, skeletons, or sketch personas that didn't make the cut (and explain why).

WHAT IF BIRTH MAKES YOU REALIZE SOMETHING IS WRONG WITH THE PERSONAS?

As you introduce your personas to the product team, the questions will start flying. For many of them, you will have solid answers. Others will be worth noting and will lead you to further research as you realize you need data to fill in some key persona characteristic. Still others will leave you dumbfounded, perhaps pointing out some flaw in your collective thinking. Ideally, you found most of the major issues as you reviewed the personas with your core team and stakeholders during the *conception and gestation* phase, or perhaps during your reality-check site visits. If there are now new small changes that need to be made, just make them; however, be sure you are thoughtful and careful about it. Reconvene the core team and discuss the changes before you make a final decision. If a major change does have to be made, our experience is that if you do it early in the process it won't be as much of a step backward as it might seem. Don't wait. It is good to just bite the bullet, make the necessary revision, and move on. Also, remember to plan for reintroduction of the personas after any major changes are made. Don't assume that you can simply revise your communication artifacts with new information after a major change without announcing that the revisions have taken place.

In some cases, the changes required might be too large to integrate into the existing personas. Remember to respect the "personhood" of the personas. If you discover that you have created the wrong persona, it is a good idea to shelve the old persona completely—particularly the personal details that make him or her seem real—and create a new one based on existing and new information.

WHAT IF BIRTH JUST DOESN'T WORK?

There is a slight but very real possibility that your personas and the persona method will be rejected by your broader product team. It may not happen overtly, but then again it may. Either way, you will need to adjust your plans, refocus your management's expectations, and mitigate your losses to maximize your existing investments. At the very least, you can use the personas in a small circle of colleagues—the smallest being just you and the core persona team. Our own experience with personas has led us to believe that our personas have been valuable toward our own job responsibilities, and that alone has been worth the effort (see the "Birth Can Be a Private Event if Necessary" section, above).

If you get an extremely negative response at your kickoff, talk to a few trusted colleagues on the product team and ask why it didn't work. They should be able to tell you. From our collective experience, it is probably due to one or more of the following:

- The team didn't really understand exactly what personas were for, how they would be beneficial, or how they were created from and related to data (i.e., the personas themselves didn't seem rigorous or right).
- The timing was wrong. If they were under too much pressure to get "real" work done, they were likely not open to any new method that would impact their familiar process, especially one that can feel as loose and improvised as personas can (if they are not communicated well).
- Individuals were not clear on exactly how personas would help in their specific jobs. A gut reaction is that "these things are for marketing people, designers, or usability people—not for me."

Knowing the specifics of their reactions can help you to fix the problem. Remember that you can always just scope the effort down to specific uses and roles. Seek out those individuals who do find the personas interesting and potentially useful, and help them to make real use of the personas in their work. We have seen situations in which, after introducing personas and failing to get engagement, product team members became more aware of the differences among users. Ultimately, through repeated exposure, they began to meet or see customers similar to the personas they were first introduced to. That experience made it more real for them, and the personas began to have a sense of credibility they didn't have initially.

STEP 3. MATURATION

Birth is an event. *Maturation* is an ongoing process of personas being adopted into the culture and vocabulary of your organization. As your colleagues come to understand what personas are, why they are valuable, and the particulars of the personas you have built, they will move past the need for basic education. Your colleagues will need time to digest the new information about the persona process you have introduced. Once they fully understand the purpose of personas, they will be ready for more details about the personas you have created.

Progressively educate and maintain focus on your personas

Remember that personas live in the minds of your teammates. This doesn't happen overnight. It is an ongoing process that carries through from birth to the end of adulthood and perhaps beyond. You will facilitate this process by creating a series of communication artifacts and engaging in communication activities—the variety of which is described in material to follow. As we said earlier in this chapter, *maturation* should be built on the notion of progressive disclosure of information and consideration of keeping the personas fresh, updated, and interesting. Depending on duration and current progress in your development cycle, you will need to spread your communication activities out appropriately.

Send your personas out into the world, but maintain ownership

Whatever artifacts and activities you choose to pursue, you and your core team should focus on maintaining your roles as persona wranglers. Remember that maturation continues through to the end of the next phase, adulthood. So continue meeting with your core team regularly to discuss how maturation is progressing and to reevaluate the artifacts you are using to progressively disclose persona details.

Although it is important to keep a close eye on your personas as they are adopted and used by your colleagues, it is also important to stay open to suggestions and be willing to make some changes if necessary. It is possible that small changes in the persona descriptions, or in the way you present the personas, could make a big difference in your colleagues' willingness to use them. You already identified influential people in the organization during *family planning*. Ask these people for candid feedback on the progress of your communication campaign as it is undertaken. If you discover that changes would help, reconvene the core team, discuss the changes, and create a plan to reintroduce the new and improved personas.

Work to build credibility

In many organizations, you are likely to get push-back related to the validity and reliability of your personas, where the personas came from, their accuracy, and their value. As you create the variety of communication artifacts appropriate for your team, product, and process, you will want to incorporate information that builds up the credibility of your personas. Credibility is created by building trust and demonstrating expertise and rigor. Your product team might be wondering if the creation process was rigorous, if the personas were based on research, if the management team has bought into them, and if other companies have used them successfully.

As we discussed in Chapter 4, foundation documents should contain explicit links to the underlying data from which personas were derived. This is recommended for exactly the same reason here: to build credibility (though it also enables and encourages your teammates to explore the data directly). Your communication artifacts probably should not contain the specific supporting data on the personas—at least not in large quantities (the artifacts would lose their ability to communicate effectively). However, they should point people to the foundation documents or provide references to relevant studies or reports.

Conduct persona-based user research

Now that you have introduced the personas and are helping your colleagues learn more about them, you and your core team can plan your next steps for the personas. If you have time, it is a good idea to conduct ongoing user research (as possible) to continuously enrich your understanding of the personas.

In Chapter 6 we describe how your personas can be used as recruiting targets for usability testing, field studies, and market research. As you continue to research your target users, and bring them in to test mockups and prototypes, you are gathering more and more data relevant to the personas. A very strong credibility builder is to report your research findings in relation to your personas—for example, "The 'Lauras' we tested had difficulty using the Sign-up Wizard, whereas the "Tanners' whizzed right through it." An even stronger communication device is to invite your teammates to examine these studies as they are in progress. Alternatively, you can consider using video to really engage your team. Showing a variety of short clips from your site visits or user tests can go a long way toward communicating that you observed real users who are represented by your personas. Seeing a few "Tanners" in the lab or "Lauras" in a focus group can be a dramatic, eye-opening, and highly enriching experience. We have had teammates come to our studios and walk away saying, "That was such a 'Laura'!" These teammates now know Laura on a direct and personal level.

Focus on more than getting the personas known; focus on getting them used

As the maturation process ensues, your product team (and perhaps your entire organization) will become familiar with the names, images, and more critical details of your personas. They have begun to discuss and understand the meaningful characteristics of your personas. In fact, a bit of "persona mania" is not uncommon. Your next task is to get your personas actually integrated into your team's design and development activities. If your team's immediate response wasn't to inquire about how they should actually use the personas in their jobs, you can trust that they will be asking about that within a short period.

Persona *adulthood* is all about getting explicit use and utility from your personas. Every job role on the team can incorporate some level of user focus into development activities. Your job is to find those appropriate uses of the personas and push them into action. As we said earlier, persona maturation (i.e., the communication campaign) continues all the way through adulthood. In fact, successful adulthood depends on a relentless maturation of your product team's awareness and understanding of (and intense focus on) your personas—and more importantly on your target users.

PERSONA ARTIFACTS (THE WHAT AND HOW OF COMMUNICATING YOUR PERSONAS)

You should now have a good top-level understanding of the three basic steps involved in the birth and maturation phase. In the following sections, we provide many examples of artifacts you and your core team can use to make birth and maturation happen. Once you have created your persona foundation documents, which include all links between the data and the persona details, you can pick and choose which additional materials and artifacts you want to create. There are many different ways to communicate your personas to your team, including different types of documents, posters, handouts, activities, and other materials. Keep in mind, however, that these materials don't have to be fancy, expensive, or time consuming to create in order to be useful.

The persona artifact design process: things to consider whatever materials or format you use

Remember that the artifacts and materials you create to communicate information about personas are very important. They are the user interface for your personas and the data behind them. Persona materials that are well thought out and well designed can add credibility to your entire persona effort and help enormously with your persona communication campaign. Note that it doesn't take a lot of these artifacts to make an effective communication campaign. We present numerous examples in the material that follows to help illustrate the possibilities. Be very strategic and frugal in your choices. In approaching the creation of any persona artifacts thoughtfully, consider the following.

AGREE ON THE SPECIFIC GOAL OF THE ARTIFACT

Why are you creating this specific artifact? The goal will probably be related to one of the three categories of artifacts (buzz generators, comparison facilitators, and enrichers) described later.

AGREE ON THE AUDIENCE, TIMING, AND DISTRIBUTION METHOD FOR THE ARTIFACT

Your persona artifacts should eventually be everywhere around your office (on doors, in hallways, coffee rooms, meeting rooms, stakeholders' or leaders' offices, and so on), but they should appear progressively. For every artifact, consider who is going to see it, when (in the development cycle) they are going to see it, and how the environment will affect their ability to digest the information. You might, for example, decide to create different buzz generator posters for the developer's hallway versus the marketer's hallway. If you work in a place that doesn't allow posters and such to be displayed around the building, create artifacts that can be handed out to individuals, carried around, or placed on desktops.

AGREE ON THE INFORMATION ELEMENTS THAT SHOULD AND SHOULD NOT BE INCLUDED ON THE ARTIFACT

By the time you are ready to create persona artifacts, you will have quite a bit of information about each persona at your disposal. The information you have will all seem highly relevant and deeply interrelated, and it can therefore be difficult to comb out small snippets to include on individual artifacts. Remember that the easiest way to create a useless persona artifact is to overload it with information. Suppose you decide to create "wanted" posters to create buzz and to convey the name, role, and picture for each of your primary personas. It will be tempting to include a quote and maybe a few bulleted details with additional information, but remember your priorities. If you really do want to build buzz and interest, consider limiting the poster to just a photo, a name, and a role. When in doubt, always opt for less information and leave your audience craving more.

AGREE ON THE RELATIVE PRIORITIES OF THE INFORMATION ELEMENTS ON THE ARTIFACT

Once you decide which information elements should be included on an artifact, prioritize these elements according to how important it is that the element is read and understood. On a "wanted" poster, the photo and name should probably be very large and eye catching. In contrast, a comparison poster you distribute a few weeks or months later should include names and roles, but these are probably not as important as comparative information about each persona's goals, abilities, desires, and so on.

Don't use up your entire budget on birth and maturation. If you have limited resources (e.g., very little money to use on persona artifacts), think carefully about the artifacts you will need now and try to predict what you will need later. Don't use your entire budget on artifacts distributed early. Remember that you still face the challenge of keeping the personas alive and useful throughout the *adulthood* phase.

Select the best communication tool for the job: three categories of persona artifacts

We have separated the persona communication materials into three basic categories that describe the goals the materials support: buzz generators, comparison facilitators, and enrichers. Within these categories, we describe which types of materials tend to work best early in your communication campaign (closer to *birth*) and which work best later, when the personas are fairly well known and you are working to keep them alive in the product development process. You will probably create one or more artifacts from each of these categories. Throughout this section is a discussion of printed posters to be hung on walls around your building and offices. Posters can be easy and inexpensive to generate, but don't let our inclination toward posters distract you or lead you to create artifacts that are inappropriate for your corporate culture. Keep in mind that there is no right way to communicate your personas and that it is important to continue to stay alert to the needs and difficulties arising in your organization.

BUZZ GENERATORS

Buzz generator artifacts are materials that get people talking and interested. Although they may include some small amount of practical information, their purpose is *not* to convey detailed information about what personas are or how your personas should be used. Rather, their purpose is to generate excitement and interest in the *idea* of personas. They should be eye catching and encourage people to think that something new, fresh, and exciting is happening in the product design process. They should leave people wanting more information and asking questions. Buzz generators foster a sense of anticipation and a bit of mystery. You can enhance this by posting new buzz generators only after everyone has gone home so your team is greeted first thing in the morning with new posters and questions that seem to have appeared magically overnight (or over the weekend).

Early buzz generators

Many buzz generators work best early in the development process. These tend to be artifacts that let people know that the personas are coming and that things are going to change. They *can* capitalize on and enhance the ramp-up of excitement and energy that marks the start of work on a new product. As posters or other physical artifacts, buzz generators should be visually interesting, bright, easy to read, and very light on information. As such, they tend to be at home almost anywhere in office spaces.

"Do you know who our users are?" posters. Before you introduce the idea of using personas to stand in for users, why not get people thinking about how much they do (or, for the most part, don't) know about your user population? "Do you know who our users are?" posters don't mention personas and don't include any data. Instead, they should plant interesting questions in the minds of your colleagues. These posters can be very inexpensive and easy to create (see Figure 5.1). Remember the "Got Milk?" advertising campaign that featured large billboards with just those words? Your "Do you know who our users are?" posters can be similar. You can print single questions in a large font size on tabloid-sized paper and post them all over your offices. Think of questions that will stick and will inspire some curiosity and discussion.

"The personas are coming" posters. "The personas are coming" posters (see Figure 5.2) generate buzz around the idea of using personas as design targets. They are useful if

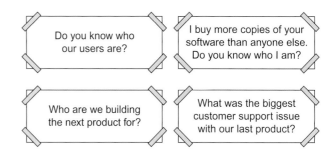

FIGURE 5.1
"Do you know who our users are?" early buzz generators.

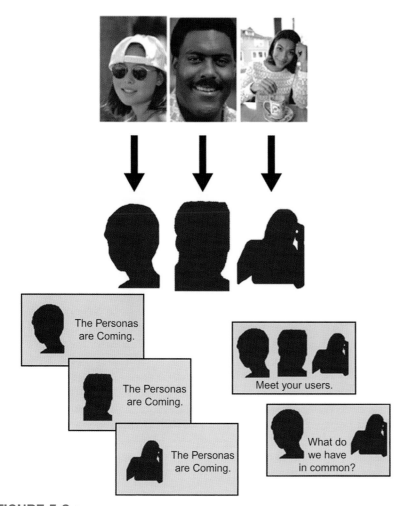

FIGURE 5.2
"The personas are coming" early buzz generators.

your company has never used personas before (to get people wondering what personas are and what it means that "they're coming") and if you are introducing a new set of personas to colleagues who already have experience using personas ("Oh! We're getting new ones! I wonder who they are this time?"). These posters can also be very easy and inexpensive to create. Simply take the persona photos you have and create back silhouettes of the faces. Print these (black and white is fine) on large sheets of paper with a simple statement that lets people know that more information is on its way.

Introduction posters. Introduction posters are very popular among persona practitioners. They are usually the first public artifacts that include the names, roles, and photographs of your primary personas. Unlike "Do you know who our users are?" and "The personas are coming" posters, introduction posters often stay on the walls throughout the project. They are worth spending some money and time on. Introduction posters work well when hung in public places with a lot of foot traffic, such as hallways and lobbies.

These posters, examples of which are shown in Figure 5.3, should definitely include the persona's name and a photograph. They might also include quotes that express the persona's interests or point of view, the market share related to the persona, photographs of the persona's environment, and so on. Introduction posters should not require more than ten seconds of directed attention to comprehend. It is a good idea to include directions on how to obtain more information—either the name and contact information for that persona's wrangler or perhaps a link to your persona website.

Later buzz generators

Later buzz generators are a great way to revive interest and encourage people to refocus their attention on the personas. Like early buzz generators, they should be light on information but packed with as much of a punch as possible. If you have additional photographs of your

FIGURE 5.3
Two very simple persona introduction posters for the persona named Tanner. Note that these posters intentionally communicate little more than the name of the persona and a few characteristics. Although they do contain a few tidbits of key information, they are designed to be taken in within a few seconds. The goal is to help the team learn the names and faces first, before providing more detailed information. (Illustration created by Craig Hally.)

personas you have not shared with the team, use them in your buzz generators. You might even consider getting your persona models to come back so you can take photos of them interacting with product mock-ups or prototypes as they are developed, subsequently using these new photos in the artifacts you produce.

As the development process progresses, people on the development teams will become overwhelmed with their daily responsibilities and will be less and less open to new ideas and methods. Respect this, and make later buzz generators fun and, if possible, a relief from the everyday grind. Remember that once the development process starts in earnest, documents will be flying everywhere. Stacks of them will have appeared on people's desks, whiteboards will be full of words and diagrams, and there will be project scheduling charts on the walls. Don't add to the paper nightmare, or especially to the reading-related workload. Later buzz generators work best if they are intrinsically interesting and in a format different from other product-related information sources. Toward this end, use new photographs of your personas, fresh information, and attractive artifacts. Consider a range of media and formats, such as video, physical objects (custom key chains, laminated placemats, mouse pads, coffee mugs, stickers, magnets, and so on), and e-mail (newsletters, updates, persona fact of the week).

Trinkets and gizmos (if you have a budget). If you have a budget and need to generate some buzz, consider outsourcing the production of a custom persona collectible. Trinkets and gizmos create desire ("Hey! Where'd you get that? I want one!"). If they take up residence on people's desks, gizmos can successfully transmit information for a long time. There are hundreds of companies that specialize in creating the customized "trash and trinkets" we have all picked up at trade shows and conferences. You can get virtually anything printed on anything, if you have the budget. Most custom printing companies have very large catalogs and offer custom-printed items at a wide variety of price points, so even if you need only a few items you will probably find something that will fit your budget. The following are examples of professionally printed trinkets and gizmos:

- *Coffee cups, beer glasses, squeeze toys, tumblers, yo-yos, magnet sets*—You can't print much on any of these types of trinkets (see Figure 5.4), but you can certainly include the names and roles of the personas, which can help to embed the personas more deeply into the corporate culture and conversation. Consider including a drawing or cartoon of the persona instead of a photograph. Illustrations tend to print and look better on the finished product. Also, illustrations can be printed in one color. The more colors you include in the printing process the more expensive the trinkets will be.
- *Persona T-shirts*—Customized clothing bearing logos or slogans is almost always a hot item. You could create a design per persona or a single shirt that advertises some aspect of all of them. You might give the shirts out as prizes (e.g., teammates who go out on site visits or participate in some other UCD activity get an "I really know my user" T-shirt). You will need to keep the information to a minimum on these items. They are more about engagement and awareness than education.
- *Mouse pads*—Due to their size, mouse pads can include more information than the previously discussed trinkets. You might want to have one printed that includes the photos, names, and roles of all of your primary personas, as well as the persona website (which is a good item to include on all persona-related materials).

Trinkets and gizmos (if money is scarce). Even if you don't have much money (or just want to be resourceful), you can still create effective persona trinkets. These artifacts just require

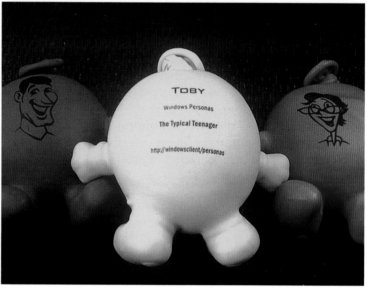

FIGURE 5.4
Persona beer glasses and squeeze toys.

creativity and time to produce. The following are examples of inexpensive, hand-made trinkets and information sources:

● *Laminated summary sheets*—Instead of investing in a professionally produced mouse pad, you can create and print placemats that include summary information about your personas. It is relatively inexpensive to print these mats in color and have them laminated at your local print shop. The fact that these mats are in color and laminated will make them seem less disposable to the product development teams, and they will be more likely to take up permanent residence on desks, bulletin boards, and walls than nonlaminated printouts.

● *Custom candy wrappers*—It is not difficult to find, or even create, a custom candy-wrapper template. To create your own template, carefully remove a wrapper from a chocolate bar. Measure the entire wrapper and the areas that appear on the front and back of the candy bar. Use whatever software you are comfortable with to create a template using the measurements of the bar. Include a photo and a small amount of interesting or important information

about the persona. For example, the "Tanner Bar" might include information on the type of homework Tanner does. Print the wrappers on a color printer using glossy paper. Cut out the wrappers and glue them *over* the existing candy wrappers (to avoid any unlikely, but possible, liability issues). Create a series of candy bars with the primary personas and encourage people to collect them all. You can even use different types of chocolate bars for the various personas. Leave the candy bars on people's desks after everyone has left the office.

Bring the personas to life (or life size!). As the product development process continues, you might find that people are so busy that trinkets won't be enough to get their attention and refocus them on the personas. In this case, consider more drastic buzz-generating activities that really bring the personas to life for the development staff. Consider bringing in live actors and stage some role-playing activities in which the actors (who could be talented friends of yours) play the personas. The kickoff meeting might be one good time to do this, but also consider bringing in persona actors for spec or mock-up reviews. Prepare the persona actors so they feel comfortable walking through whatever design materials exist from the perspective of the persona they represent.

Comparison facilitators

Comparison facilitators are artifacts that help people understand important differences between personas. Comparison facilitators are especially useful for anyone working on or making decisions related to more than one interface. Product managers, documentation specialists, trainers, and user interface designers and developers are great target audiences for comparison facilitator artifacts. By their nature, comparison facilitators contain different details from most buzz generators and enricher artifacts (covered later in this chapter). Enrichers provide deep details, whereas comparison facilitators provide a broader context. They work best when created in a form that enhances examination and reflection and are posted in places where people have the time and inclination to examine details. In other words, don't post comparison facilitators in busy hallways, but do consider posting them near the microwave or coffee maker, on meeting room walls, in bathroom stalls, or anywhere you have a captive audience.

EARLY COMPARISON FACILITATORS

Early in your communication campaign you can use comparison facilitators to help everyone understand the collection of personas you have created and the roles they have with respect to your product. Comparison facilitators will help you convey information basics about more than one persona at a time.

Persona rosters

You have probably already created individual information posters for your personas, which might include the persona's photo, name, role, and perhaps even a quote. Consider creating a roster poster (see Figure 5.5) that shows this basic information for all of the personas (not just one at a time). We mentioned earlier that you could put such comparison information on a mouse pad or other artifact that has a little more space.

Persona communication constellations

A communication constellation shows the "use community" represented by your personas. Communication constellations show how your personas are linked to or interact with one another through your product. This is much like the model for roles, except that it is simpler and is created as part of the contextual design process (Beyer and Holtzblatt, 1998). To create a communication constellation (see Figure 5.6), generate an image that expresses the (highly simplified) relationships among the personas. Include all personas and the product you are creating, and draw lines between these images to show the connections and the relative "proximity" of each persona to your product. You can also include

101

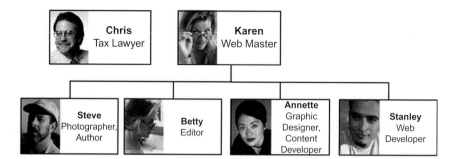

FIGURE 5.5

Persona roster in the form of an organizational chart overview from 2006 (http://ccmredhat.com/user-centered/personas.html).

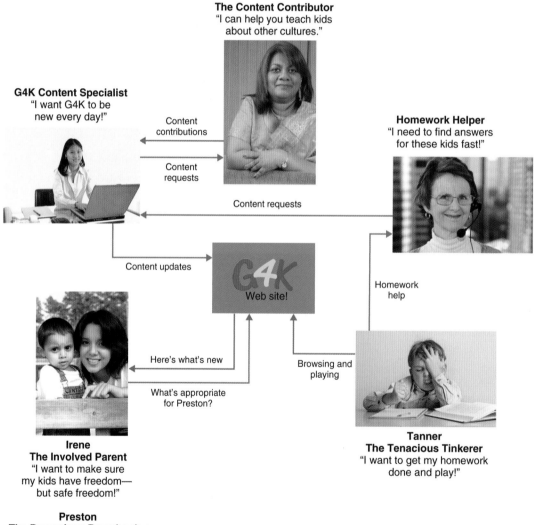

FIGURE 5.6

A persona communication constellation. Designed to show the "use community" created by your personas, a communication constellation is light on persona details. Instead, it should show relative proximity to the product. These constellations can help your team understand who the personas are, what their roles are with respect to the product, and how they interact (or don't interact) with one another (or even other relevant systems).

other users (roles), artifacts, systems, or products that will affect the use of your product. Communication constellations are highly useful early in the communication campaign to help people understand why you created your particular personas and the fact that the personas will have different levels of interaction with the product.

Executive summary slides

The product development team is not the only group that needs your focus! Create an executive summary slide (see Figure 5.7) in a program such as PowerPoint® so that anyone (including VPs, managers, and even salespeople) who needs to speak about your target audience can include it in any slide presentation. The executive summary slide should include only very basic information about the personas—just enough so that anyone looking at it can understand who the personas are. You may also want to create a few slides that describe your basic development process, including how the personas fit into this process. It is a good idea to have these materials on hand and readily available to distribute for inclusion in presentations. If you don't, at best you will be asked to create them at the last minute. In the worst case, you will not be asked to create them because someone else will have—and you may find that your personas and the persona effort are misrepresented.

Remember that many different people in your organization will be talking about development progress and process and should likely be referring to the intended audience for the product. Make sure you provide good, high-level materials that accurately represent your personas (and how you are using them, if you think this information will be useful).

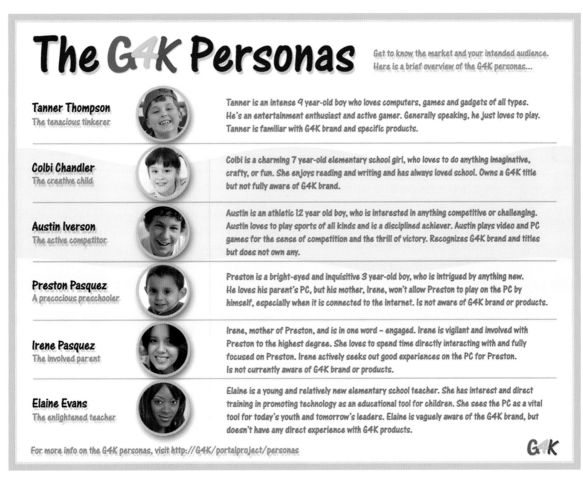

FIGURE 5.7
An example of an executive summary slide for the G4K personas. (Illustration created by Craig Hally.)

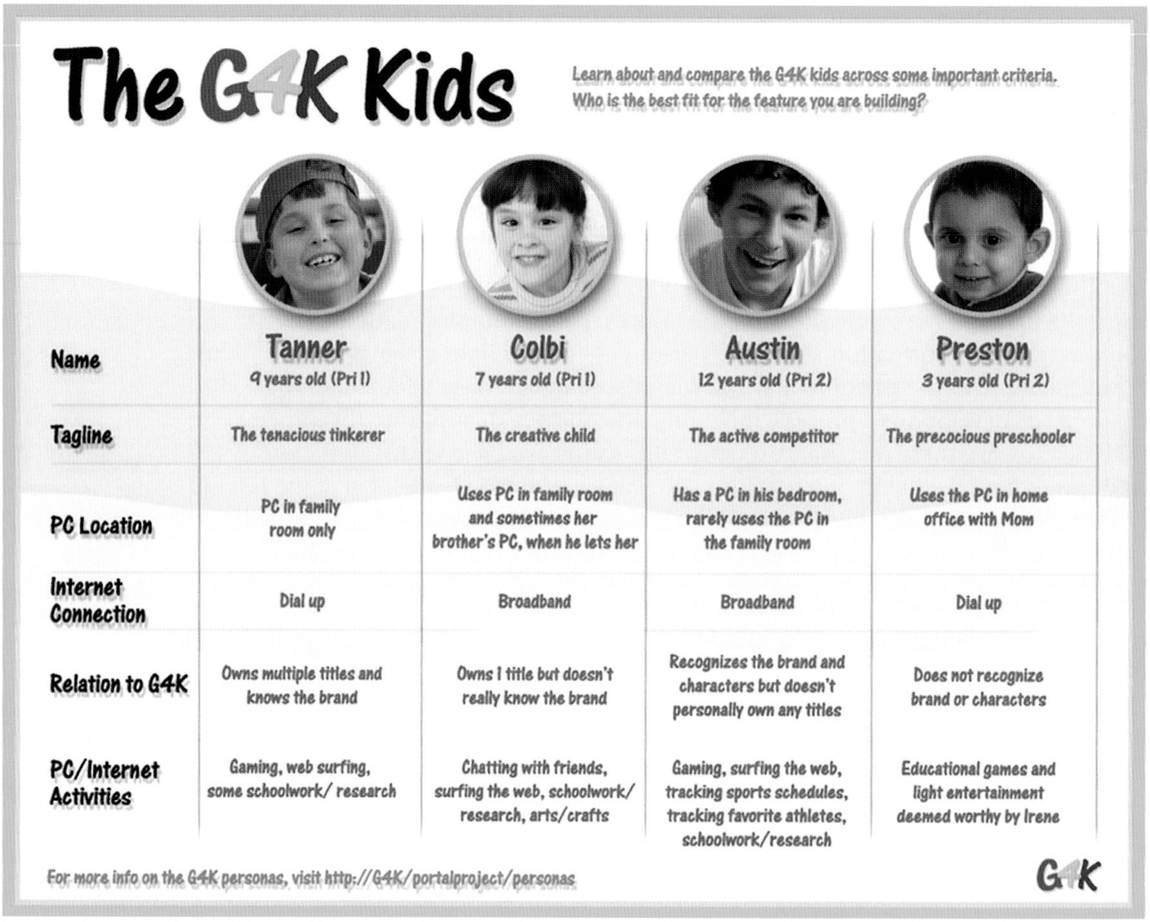

The G4K Kids

Learn about and compare the G4K kids across some important criteria. Who is the best fit for the feature you are building?

	Tanner	Colbi	Austin	Preston
Name	9 years old (Pri 1)	7 years old (Pri 1)	12 years old (Pri 2)	3 years old (Pri 2)
Tagline	The tenacious tinkerer	The creative child	The active competitor	The precocious preschooler
PC Location	PC in family room only	Uses PC in family room and sometimes her brother's PC, when he lets her	Has a PC in his bedroom, rarely uses the PC in the family room	Uses the PC in home office with Mom
Internet Connection	Dial up	Broadband	Broadband	Dial up
Relation to G4K	Owns multiple titles and knows the brand	Owns 1 title but doesn't really know the brand	Recognizes the brand and characters but doesn't personally own any titles	Does not recognize brand or characters
PC/Internet Activities	Gaming, web surfing, some schoolwork/ research	Chatting with friends, surfing the web, schoolwork/ research, arts/crafts	Gaming, surfing the web, tracking sports schedules, tracking favorite athletes, schoolwork/research	Educational games and light entertainment deemed worthy by Irene

For more info on the G4K personas, visit http://G4K/portalproject/personas

G4K

FIGURE 5.8

A detailed comparison poster showing the G4K kids. Note that this poster does not compare all of the G4K personas along every possible dimension. Rather, in this case it shows the differences among the primary personas across important characteristics for the G4K portal project. (Illustration created by Craig Hally.)

LATER COMPARISON FACILITATORS

As your project progresses, you will probably notice that many people in your organization will begin to ask similar questions about the personas and their different needs related to specific parts of the product. Comparison facilitator artifacts are a great way to answer these questions. They can be designed to convey parallel information about any set of relevant personas. Showing both the details and the big picture of how the personas differ from one another (with respect to these details) can be incredibly helpful. The main difference between early and later comparison facilitators is the level of detail. As projects progress, team members tend to need much more specific information in particular domains.

Detailed comparison posters

Detailed comparison posters (see Figure 5.8) are similar to the brief persona rosters described earlier, except that they contain more information. On these posters, detailed information is provided in several domains—key domains important to your product. These posters can be created so they are broadly interesting, highlighting key information that won't change or become less important over time. Like the enricher artifacts described in the next section, they can also be created to answer specific questions or domain issues known to be critical to your product's development (see Figure 5.9). The specific details in this comparison artifact are probably only interesting while certain decisions (related to those

Human Resources   ORGANIZATIONAL MANAGEMENT PERSONAS

Primary Persona   Secondary Persona

Elena Montgomery	Carl Stephens Ph.D.	Gillian Winters	Martin Schwartz	Otto Bauer
Human Resources Coordinator, Amino Pharmaceuticals	Laboratory Manager, Amino Pharmaceuticals	Human Resources Manager, Lacy's Department Store	Dir. of Manufacturing, Sunny Electronics, USA	Organizational Planner, Volksmotorwerks AG

"This form requires the manager's signature." — "Didn't we just do reviews?" — "People are our number one asset." — "Can you get me those numbers by Tuesday?" — "Let's start thinking about your succession planning."

Elena spends most of her day processing all the forms required to hire, transfer and terminate employees in the R&D division of Amino Pharmaceuticals. When something's incomplete or unclear, she takes the time to track down the answer. She's an expert on all the necessary forms and procedures

Elena's Goals
Move up in HR
Excellence through accuracy
Be helpful
Don't fall behind

Although his main job is research, Carl also creates budgets, hires and trains employees, writes reviews and distributes bonuses. Carl wants to make sure his employees and his manager are happy, but he regards HR paperwork as a distraction from his real work.

Carl's Goals
Focus on his experiments
Keep his people happy
Keep his management happy
Grow his department

Gillian wants to help build strong teams by improving communication between managers and employees and watching for "hot spots" that require her attention. She needs context to help her quickly find and solve problems.

Gillian's Goals
People not paperwork
Partner with management to build healthy departments
Be proactive
Build relationships within the corporate-wide HR departments

Sunny Electronics has manufacturing divisions all over the world. Martin needs access to headcount and salary information to help him understand the performance of his divisions and projects and plan for the future.

Martin's Goals
On time, under budget
Understand the bottom line
Maximize productivity
Controlled growth

Otto helps VP's and Directors structure their organizations for best productivity. He wants access to HR statistics about employees so he can understand historical performance of projects and forecast future changes to the company.

Otto's Goals
Build a healthy organization
Partner with divisions and upper management
Find danger and opportunity in the workforce
Set the vision, chart the course

COOPER (INTERACTION DESIGN   HR Organizational Management   November 23, 1998
PAGE 1 of 1

FIGURE 5.9

A persona summary matrix from Cooper Interaction Design (as posted on http://advance.aiga.org/timeline/artifacts/Matrix.PDF in 2006).

details) are being made. Thus, like many of the artifacts we have suggested, these posters may have a limited shelf life (although probably longer than buzz generators).

There are other artifacts you can use to facilitate comparison among the personas, including the following:

- *Persona trading cards*—If you have a lot of personas for your team to learn about and keep track of, you might consider creating trading cards (see Figure 5.10). With fewer personas, you can get the same effect by creating playing cards with persona info on the backs of the cards. These are a cross between buzz generators (because they are cool and interesting) and comparison facilitators (because they include more information than most buzz generators and allow easy comparison across personas). One valuable aspect of these cards is that they can be brought along to a design meeting or other activity for which having a quick reference to your target customers is useful.
- *Persona reference booklet*—You can very inexpensively create a little reference booklet (e.g., in a 5 × 7-inch ring binder) that teammates can carry with them to meetings. Like trading cards, while providing mobile access and utility for your persona information they will serve to make others aware and perhaps even promote learning and usage. With this artifact you can cram a lot of information into a small space. Even so, the information should still be well designed (but not completely exhaustive).

ENRICHERS

Enricher artifacts allow you to communicate very detailed information about your personas. Unlike buzz generators, these artifacts do not necessarily need to be fancy or eye catching,

FIGURE 5.10
Persona trading cards.

but they do need to be very well designed, and, more important, their content must be very well thought out and highly relevant. Enrichers are any artifacts or activities that tie the personas to more information, especially data or detailed descriptions of the persona with respect to a particular information domain (such as a persona's activities, knowledge level, behaviors, biases, and so on).

Enrichers don't necessarily need to stick around. They may not need to take up residence on everyone's desks and even may not be relevant after a particular set of decisions has been made. Rather, their purpose is to enhance your team's understanding of the personas, usually with respect to a particular domain or set of questions. The information in enricher artifacts should enable the product development staff to make persona-driven (and therefore data-driven) choices for specific aspects of the product. In many cases, simply pointing the development team to particular areas of the persona website over time is all you need to do.

Enricher artifacts tend to contain more information than other artifacts. They are designed to enrich understanding of the personas in a deep way in some domain, probably one that hasn't been on the beaten path so far. For example, an enricher could describe every little thing about how a persona goes about printing or what she does with books once she gets home. Many of the buzz generators described previously also have enriching elements in that they contain some detailed information in a particular domain, enhancing the understanding of your personas. Persona trading cards, for example, include selected persona details in addition to photographs, names, and job descriptions or roles.

Persona one-pagers

After the bare-bones persona basics have taken hold in your organization (that is, when you start to hear people talking about the personas by name), you might want to distribute persona one-pagers. These résumé-like documents are probably what most people think of when they envision "personas." Examples of one-pagers can be seen all over the Internet. Similar to résumés, persona one-pagers should include only the most pertinent information (as compared to, for example, a *curriculum vitae*)—information you think will be of particular interest to your product team.

Meet... Tanner Thompson

Summary:

Tanner is an intense 9 year-old boy who loves computers, games and gadgets of all types. He's an entertainment enthusiast and active gamer. Generally speaking, he just loves to play.

Tanner is familiar with G4K game titles and is a likely frequent visitor to the G4K site – seeking out new ways to entertain himself. Tanner has significant influence over his parent's spending towards family fun.

Description:

Tanner is a 4th grade student at Montgomery Elementary School, a public school. He lives with his mother & father (Laura & Shane Thompson) in a suburb of Chicago, Illinois.

Even though Tanner loves to be physically active (riding his skateboard and bike, participating in organized sports), Tanner thinks computers are really really fun and prefers the PC to the TV.

Tanner has been using computers at school since kindergarten and has had a family computer at home for two years.

He uses the PC mostly to play games and surf the web for "stuff" but occasionally does research for school projects. His favorite computer game of the moment is The Sims 2. He also really likes Roller Coaster Tycoon 3.

for more info on Tanner, visit http://G4K/portalproject/personas

G4K

FIGURE 5.11
A persona one-pager for G4K's Tanner persona. (Illustration created by Craig Hally.)

If you have the time and resources, you might consider creating different one-pagers for different groups in your organization, highlighting somewhat different information from your foundation documentation as appropriate. For example, the details interesting to the marketing group are probably quite different from the information that will be useful for developers. Because you have all of the persona information at your fingertips (in the persona foundation documents), you can be selective about which information elements you put together in the one-pagers depending on the audience for each. However, we highly recommend that the one-pagers be consistently formatted. In other words, if you create a set of one-pagers for the marketing team, make sure the format is the same for each persona, so readers can easily find the information they are looking for. If you create one-pagers for each persona, you can take them to a copy shop and have them bound into a reference booklet or provide easy-to-access direct links to online versions. An example of a one-pager is shown in Figure 5.11.

Targeted detail posters

Targeted detail posters can be created to help you communicate specific information about your personas. These should be created in relation to hot topics or current needs of the development cycle. They can help create organizational focus, putting everyone in the same frame of mind about the same domain or topic. Figure 5.12 shows an example of a targeted detail poster. In this example, the team is very interested in PC and Internet use, as well as entertainment and gaming activities.

Tanner has already been using computers for years

Computer use begins at an early age. About three-quarters of 5-year-olds use computers, and over 90 percent of teens (ages 13–17) do so.

About 25 percent of 5-year-olds use the internet, and this number rises to over 50 percent by age 9 and to at least 75 percent by ages 15–17. (28)

Tanner uses the PC for gaming, surfing the web, and schoolwork

A majority (59 percent) of 5- through 17-year-olds use home computers to play games, and over 40 percent use computers to connect to the Internet (46 percent) and to complete school assignments (44 percent).

Tanner
the tenacious tinkerer
is a great target for G4k..

Tanner considers the PC as entertainment

The number of children age 12 and under going online for entertainment and games more than tripled between 1998 and 1999, reaching 9.2 million and surpassing homework as the most popular activity in this age bracket.

Growth has been exceptionally fast among boys age 12 and under. (1) Sixty-three percent of those surveyed prefer going online to watching television, and 55% choose online over talking on the telephone. (11)

Tanner is picky, easily distracted, and a multi-tasker

41% of tweens say they do other things while surfing the net. Some split their attention between surfing and talking on the phone, eating or listening to music. Still others say they watch TV while working at their computer. (4)

for more info on Tanner, visit http://G4K/portalproject/personas

G4K

FIGURE 5.12
This targeted detail poster targets specific information about Tanner's PC and Internet use. (Illustration created by Craig Hally.)

Targeted detail handouts (candy, gizmos, and so on)

Many of the buzz generator artifacts discussed earlier can also serve as enrichers, depending on the amount and type of information you include. Like the persona flip-card set described previously, candy wrappers can only hold a small amount of information, but you have a lot of choices when it comes to which information you decide to include. Remember that trinkets and other giveaways never lose their appeal. Consider using different types of artifacts to convey different types of information (e.g., a key chain for targeted information about mobility, a mouse pad for PC activities, or a coffee mug for leisure activities). Remember, though, that it is always a good idea to include the basics, including the persona's photo, name, and job or role. You may also identify other information elements you want to consistently include on all persona artifacts, such as the persona's goals or a defining quote.

Persona e-mail campaigns

Persona e-mail campaigns can be extremely valuable. They can help very naturally roll out more and more information about your personas over time. A well-crafted e-mail campaign can be fun and interesting and can help you communicate details quickly and effectively. However, people tend to be highly sensitive to getting too much e-mail and are very quick to label certain types of e-mail as spam. The last thing you want is to associate your persona effort with spam. As you plan a persona e-mail campaign, plan to keep e-mails as short and sweet as possible and build in checkpoints to evaluate how your colleagues are reacting. In

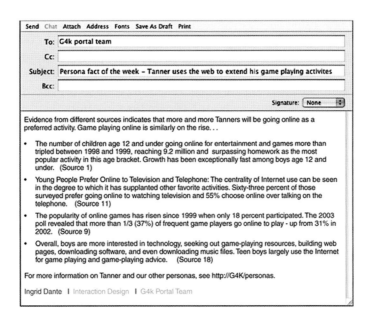

Send Chat Attach Address Fonts Save As Draft Print

To: G4k portal team
Cc:
Subject: Persona fact of the week – Tanner uses the web to extend his game playing activites
Bcc:

Signature: [None]

Evidence from different sources indicates that more and more Tanners will be going online as a preferred activity. Game playing online is similarly on the rise. . .

- The number of children age 12 and under going online for entertainment and games more than tripled between 1998 and 1999, reaching 9.2 million and surpassing homework as the most popular activity in this age bracket. Growth has been exceptionally fast among boys age 12 and under. (Source 1)

- Young People Prefer Online to Television and Telephone: The centrality of Internet use can be seen in the degree to which it has supplanted other favorite activities. Sixty-three percent of those surveyed prefer going online to watching television and 55% choose online over talking on the telephone. (Source 11)

- The popularity of online games has risen since 1999 when only 18 percent participated. The 2003 poll revealed that more than 1/3 (37%) of frequent game players go online to play - up from 31% in 2002. (Source 9)

- Overall, boys are more interested in technology, seeking out game-playing resources, building web pages, downloading software, and even downloading music files. Teen boys largely use the Internet for game playing and game-playing advice. (Source 18)

For more information on Tanner and our other personas, see http://G4K/personas.

Ingrid Dante | Interaction Design | G4k Portal Team

FIGURE 5.13
An example of a "fact of the week" e-mail. This example describes Tanner's web and gaming behaviors.

some cases, you may want to allow people to opt in or out of the e-mail campaign, and it is a good idea to post the e-mail messages on your persona website so that those who opt out or miss the e-mails still have access to the information.

- *Monthly persona newsletters*—Once a month or less frequently, you can create a short newsletter to communicate specific information across all of your personas. The following are sample newsletter headlines: "What Preston and Irene Do in Their Leisure Time," "Why Elaine Is Afraid to Upgrade," and "What Austin, Tanner, and Colbi Think About Our Competitors." Various topics or domains will become important to your developing product over time. Focus your newsletter on those topics (e.g., setup/installation, security, internationalization, mobility, checkout or purchase, and so on). To create a newsletter, simply write a small blurb for each of your personas regarding the topic at hand; add a few photos, data charts, or other illustrations; and include links for obtaining further information (e.g., a link to your persona website, links to your persona foundation documents, or direct links to supporting research reports). Alternatively, you might use your personas as an organizing scheme for reporting progress and other developments on your product. Through the eyes of your target audience, report important design decisions or feature changes that have occurred. Report the various activities or ways in which your personas have been utilized. If you have engaged in ongoing research and other UCD efforts, you might consider lumping all of your "user" information highlights into one coordinated report.

- *"Fact of the week" e-mail*—You don't have to create a full newsletter to convey persona-related information via e-mail. Create a "fact of the week" (see Figure 5.13) to send out to the organization, and choose facts based on the type of information you think will be most welcome. This can be a great opportunity to reconnect with the core team. A "fact of the week" meeting is an opportunity for all of the persona wranglers to get together and talk about how the personas are, and are not, being used. The weekly fact e-mail should be very brief—short enough to read in total in the area of the viewing window (i.e., a few sentences or one paragraph). To help keep it short, be sure to include a link to further information.

- *Persona e-mail addresses*—Ask your e-mail administrator to create an internal e-mail address for each persona (or, if you get resistance to this idea, you can create an e-mail address using one of the free Internet e-mail services, such as Hotmail or Yahoo!). If possible within your organization, e-mail sent to this alias should be automatically redirected to the wrangler for the persona campaign. There are several ways you can use the persona e-mail accounts. Consider sending kudos and "thank you" messages to team members who have done something good to benefit your end users (perhaps sent from the one persona who will benefit the most from their efforts). Doing so serves two purposes, in that it promotes the existence of the personas and encourages team members to be pursuing user-focused work. Advertise the existence of the accounts to your organization and invite people to send persona-related questions to the e-mail addresses. The individual persona wranglers can then research and address these questions and reply from the persona.

Although sending e-mail messages from your personas may sound extreme, we have actually tried this technique. Most of our team thought it was fun and interesting. There are considerable benefits and risks of using persona e-mail aliases. If you receive many e-mails, you can collect them and evaluate them at the end of the project to help in the measurement of return on investment. You can argue and show examples indicating that the personas were a well-used and effective means of conveying important user data. On the downside, in some cases, e-mail from personas can seem silly and possibly annoying.

Anti-personas

One way to enrich the understanding of your personas is to show your team who they are *not* targeting by creating anti-personas (or negative personas, as Alan Cooper originally defined them in *The Inmates are Running the Asylum*, p. 136). As described in Chapter 4, anti-personas are brief persona sketches that exemplify people you do *not* want to build the product for. If many people in your organization have strong but incorrect ideas about your target audience, you *might* want to consider creating anti-persona communication materials.

This happens many times where the product team members are users of the product you are developing or are intensely engaged in your product's domain area. The core team might find, for example, that the development team is very engaged in gaming. Perhaps many people on that product team are parents of young children. The people on the development team may relate to the target audience in significant ways. What they don't realize is that they may be different from the target in significant ways, as well. For example, your development team is likely to be much more technical and technologically inclined than your target audience. Anti-personas help convey these differences and strengthen the notion that "you are not the typical user."

Anti-personas don't have to represent "bad" people or users with inherently negative connotations. They are simply used to surface misguided assumptions about target users that are circulating in your organization and to clearly express that this is *not* the persona everyone should be designing for. As an example, an anti-persona for a website targeting elementary-aged children interested in video games might be an older teen or adult who is an "extreme gamer"—someone who takes gaming very seriously. They own multiple gaming consoles or platforms, purchase every new game that comes out, subscribe to gaming magazines, and even compete in local and online game tournaments. Perhaps many of the people that work at the company actually fall into this category. Clearly, that type of person is not a central target for the project.

Create real people posters

Finally, you might create a few artifacts that are more about building credibility than providing useful information. For example, consider creating a poster that simply has real quotes from real users that fit a specific persona. Figure 5.14 shows one such poster with a variety of Tanner-like kids talking about themselves and computers. These posters show that the personas are made up of data about real users who have real needs.

FIGURE 5.14
A real people poster showing quotes from real kids who fit the Tanner profile. (Illustration created by Craig Hally.)

Create a central repository for your persona artifacts

No matter how many (and which) materials you choose to create, it is a good idea to keep a centralized storehouse of all of your materials. This will help your core team keep track of which materials exist and monitor how they are being used, and it will enable people throughout your organization to come to one location for all of the information they need. There are several ways to accomplish this.

First, consider simply making a specific room (e.g., a meeting room) or work area (a table in a common room) your persona headquarters. Place copies of your foundation documents, research reports, and communication artifacts in this space. Post a FAQ sheet and create a suggestion box or announcement board to encourage interaction. Keep this area organized and up-to-date.

In addition, if your company has a broadly accessible (but private) network or intranet, set up a shared folder or website. We have found that creating an internal persona website enables you to really structure your content and easily focus your team's attention on important materials.

THE PERSONA WEBSITE

If you have the resources available to do so, we think it is a good idea to create an internal website to serve as a central repository for all of your persona data, descriptions, and materials. Of course, you can create your persona website in any way you see fit; however, we suggest that your website be designed to progressively disclose the large amount of information your personas might contain. At the topmost level (your persona home page), you will want to provide three basic things:

- A list of the primary and secondary personas, with links to more information for each persona (*Who is our target audience?*)
- Links to information and tools or templates for specific uses of the personas (*How do I use these personas?*)
- Links to information about the persona method and your persona creation process (*What are personas and why should I care?*)

Ironically, the first materials that are ready to be included in your website are those that should reside deepest in the information hierarchy: your foundation documents and the raw data sources (or links to them). The materials you want to provide easiest access to should be those designed for buzz generation, summaries or sketches that include the most fundamental or critical qualities of your personas, and any navigational elements designed to help visitors find any deeper information they need.

Rather than simply linking the foundation documents directly from the home page, we recommend that, for each persona, you include an interstitial summary page with basic information. Include roles and goals and any primary description information that helps progressively disclose the persona definition without overloading the reader with too much detail. You might also consider including a simple comparison page that presents the most basic and key characteristics of your personas (formatted to be easily scannable) to visitors so they can quickly understand how the personas are different. More generally, try to include easy-to-access materials that will answer most of the questions visitors will have, and bury potentially overwhelming details.

Your persona website is the one artifact that allows you endless depth and breadth as well as technology to help bolster your team's faith in your personas. You can use your website to increase awareness of seemingly peripheral information (your data and the process) as people casually browse primary information about your personas. Make sure that the relationship between your personas and their underlying data is clear. By using hover-over effects and hyperlinks, you can easily connect characteristics to data points. The original data reports can be linked from your home page or from the foundation documents that should also be available on your site. Sometimes people just want proof that you have looked at data and don't need the details. If you created a data source index, as discussed in Chapter 3, you should make that available on your site. You may want to post links to information on the persona method itself, such as case studies, examples of use, and so on. Your persona website should be an ever-growing source of information about target users and your UCD activities.

IF YOU ARE A CONSULTANT

Persona birth and maturation can be quite difficult for the outside consultant to promote. Your client may not be receptive to or understand the importance of broad education and ongoing persona communication. Getting funding for artifacts or billing for time related to creating them may be a difficult endeavor. Moreover, you simply won't be able to hang around throughout your client's development cycle to promote and monitor the proper use of your personas. Unless you can find an "insider" champion for the campaign, your personas may die on the vine and the likelihood of repeat business for your service may be diminished. We offer a couple of suggestions to help you along in this regard.

First, encourage participation from the client in any and all of your persona creation and communication activities. It is likely that if the client team is involved in the persona creation process you will need less of a direct evangelism effort yourself. You will want their input on appropriate artifacts. Our advice is to stay on the inexpensive side here. If you can make it happen, have client team members run the kickoff meeting and do the presenting. This will garner ownership but could possibly decrease credibility (that is, as a consultant your input is often taken as gold, as you are viewed as a guru). Be vigilant in your meetings with the client so you can find and target an influential team member as your persona champion. Spend extra time to personally convince them of the value and need for an ongoing persona wrangler.

Second, if personas are a major part of your deliverable to a client, make sure your client has very explicit knowledge, instructions, and expectations regarding the personas. Moreover, provide them with tools to help them manage the personas and the ongoing campaign (e.g., Photoshop® templates, spec templates, example documents, and communication campaign ideas). Not only will you need to convince your client of the need for ongoing persona communication, but you will also have to convince them to spend the money on good artifacts (and not just rely on the persona documentation to do the communication). At the very least, make sure they have big posters mounted on posterboard that they can bring into the meetings and actually set up on the chairs. Include a lot of data on these posters so the information is always right there and doesn't have to be hunted for. Chapter 6 explores some specific tools (e.g., the scenario spreadsheet) you can prepare and hand over to the client that will aid in persona management and persona usage.

Finally, make it a point to check back with your client several times throughout their development cycle and product launch after your consultancy has ended. If nothing else, you will remind them that it is important to keep referring back to their target audience after the initial design phase is complete.

In the end, it may be difficult to explain the amount of work that has been done to create personas and not give the client the feeling that you have been wasting time. It may also be difficult to convince them to invest more time and effort into their continued evangelism. Remember that what your client really wants to see is good design, not good personas. Invest your efforts where they will have the most impact and value.

SUMMARY

The *birth and maturation* phase is a period of strategic communication and determined execution of plans. It may not seem like it, but it is a time when you and your core team must redouble your dedication and effort toward the persona method. During this phase, you analyzed your internal audience (your teammates) and created communication devices tuned to their needs, styles, and environment. You educated your broader team about UCD, the persona method, your particular persona creation process, and your resulting personas. You have planned a progressive disclosure of information about your personas, starting with the creation of "buzz"—a general awareness and excitement that something interesting is coming. Ideally, this will have the result that your team will be enlightened about its users to a degree never before achieved in your company. You will continue with various forms of knowledge enrichment, making sure that the personas are easily differentiated from one another and that your process and personas are seen as credible, important, and useful. In the end, if *birth and maturation* activities are executed appropriately your team will be primed for and even enthusiastic about incorporating your personas into their design and development activities. Your next job is to show them how that is done.

Persona adulthood

WHAT IS ADULTHOOD FOR PERSONAS?

Adulthood is the phase of the persona lifecycle when you put your personas to use. To ensure that your personas are used, you must provide your teammates with persona-related procedures, instructions, guidelines, templates, and tools they can easily weave in with their other tasks. We think adulthood is one of the most exciting aspects of the persona lifecycle model. Until now, there have been very few documented methods for *using* personas beyond suggestions to include the personas in design discussions.

In this chapter, we provide sections on how to wrangle and promote personas as they are used by your product design and development organization. We then break the chapter into sections dedicated to specific persona methods you can use to help plan, design, evaluate, and release your product. Each section provides structured activities, tools, and in most cases several case studies from other persona practitioners. We have also included many examples in the detailed G4K case study, which you'll find in Appendix C.

WHAT TO EXPECT DURING PERSONA ADULTHOOD

When you start promoting and using personas around your organization, you might get a bit carried away. Everyone does. Personas are charming. They are fun, creative, interesting, and new. Personas highlight interesting issues that are engaging and feel important. Such issues are probably considerably more intriguing than most others you are dealing with. However, personas also raise complex questions that may require deeper analysis and other techniques to truly understand and solve problems. Personas can't do everything.

Keep your wits about you. Do not let yourself—or your organization—get swept up in persona mania. Remember that personas are most effective when they augment existing design processes. They can't solve every problem in your organization or inform every design decision. Persona mania happens when all anyone in the organization can talk about are the personas, when no other UCD techniques are being employed, and when all you want to do in your own job is work on the personas and related materials. When you feel yourself slipping into persona mania (and we bet you will), come back to this page and reread some of our persona caveats.

Personas are not a panacea, and other methods do work

Again, personas should augment, not replace, existing design processes and user-centered design (UCD) methods. They can help you maintain focus on your target audience and answer certain types of questions. Remember that many decisions need to be based on competitive strategy, technological constraints and feasibility, or simple economic or political reasons. When your personas do not provide an appropriate or reasonable answer, it is an indication that some other UCD technique or market research is needed. Don't abandon the other tools in your toolbox.

On the other hand, you do not necessarily have to abandon the methods in this chapter if your personas do not quite catch on. Maybe the data-driven personas have not caught on, but you do find your organization talking about simple user classes, market segments, delineated roles, profiles of real users, or loosely defined ad hoc personas. If you find yourself in this situation, you can still try the tools and techniques we provide in the following sections. Of course, we believe that these techniques are all done best when using rich and rigorously defined personas, but any user representation is better than nothing.

Personas are not "golden"

Although we do argue that personas should be derived from data, we do not believe it is possible to create perfect, infallible personas. Persona use requires decision making. They are a useful method and tool, but not a science. If not used appropriately, personas can be as dangerous as any other powerful tool. Powerful tools can easily lead you down the wrong path if you are not careful. (We are all familiar with the hazards of showing nonrepresentative video examples, overcuing participants in usability tests, and presenting misleading statistics or graphics.) Always use common sense, gather information and requirements from many sources, and validate your decisions with real users and other data.

Personas are not your company's product

You were most likely hired to help your company create excellent products and services, not personas *per se*. Your company does not sell personas. Personas are a means to an end, not an end in themselves. Your real product is what generates revenue for your company. So be judicious with the time and effort you put into personas. If you cannot find the time to work on personas and maintain your other responsibilities, scale back the persona effort.

Personas will never be universally loved and respected

Although your personas can capture the attention and imagination of your organization, some of your teammates are going to resist them. Personas simply will not appeal to nor be useful to everyone. Even colleagues who completely buy in to the persona effort will not focus on the personas all of the time, and they are likely to forget why and how the personas can help them do their jobs. When team members do use the personas, many of them will try to twist the personas just a little to align them with pet technologies and features or strongly held beliefs. To add insult to injury, after the product is complete no one will be certain if your personas did anything for the team or the project. That is just the way it is. Be comforted by the fact that many a persona practitioner has been there before you, and we have done our best throughout this book to give you practical advice for spotting and solving these problems.

JOB 1: HELP YOUR PERSONAS SETTLE IN

Your personas are like new employees in your organization: they could be embraced as invaluable resources your team can't imagine living without or they could be marginalized and deemed useless. It is your job to help these "new employees" settle in. Personas can bring fresh insights and new energy, but they will also need to be trained a bit to suit the work habits of the rest of the organization. In Chapter 5, we recommended that you assign a wrangler to each of your personas. Each wrangler should be responsible for keeping an eye on the use (and misuse) of the personas during *adulthood*.

117

Each wrangler should think of himself as the persona's boss. You have prepared your organization for their arrival, you have introduced them, and you have provided them with high-level goals or tasks. Now you have to let go enough to allow the personas to do their jobs. Just like a boss, each persona wrangler will have to check in with the personas and to a certain extent manage and even police the way they are working in the organization. In other words, you have to allow your colleagues to engage with and use the personas fairly freely, but you have to ensure that the personas are not being misused, dying on the vine, or becoming feral.

In general, the key to keeping personas in *adulthood* present and alive throughout the churn and chaos of a long product development cycle is to assign them jobs to do that are specific to the disciplines and roles of your teammates.

START WITH THE BASICS: INVITE PERSONAS INTO YOUR OFFICES AND INTO YOUR MEETINGS

Adult personas are ready to be put to work in a variety of ways. We provide some very specific (and structured) ways of using personas in the four main sections of this chapter; however, personas can be used more generally (in nonstructured ways) across your entire organization and throughout the entire development cycle. They can help by answering difficult questions and by focusing activities in a way that takes the guesswork out of making customer-driven decisions. Adult personas can participate in your product planning, design, and development process by:

- Being present at your meetings and representing the voice of your customer throughout the development cycle
- Providing consistency by serving as a common reference point across your organization, even in a highly chaotic, fast-moving, ever-changing environment
- Providing a way for all of the product teams to touch base using a common language and by serving as a means of assurance that everyone is staying focused on creating a good experience for the right audiences

Personas can only be involved and helpful in these ways if they inhabit your workplace and attend your meetings. Even though they are not real people, personas can become the most powerful voices in the room. You will need to expend considerable effort on creating communication devices for your personas, many of which you can use to help your personas move into your workplace and conversations (see Chapter 5).

Beyond bringing the personas into the team spaces, you can and should *specifically* invite your personas to meetings. During any meeting, start looking for opportunities to use the personas to help answer issues that come up. If a disagreement about features or priorities comes up during a meeting, one of the personas will likely offer a fresh perspective. Refer often to the persona details listed on the posters or other artifacts and consider recording decisions directly on them; for example, add notes to the persona posters with sticky notes if the personas help with a decision: "Frank says we don't need support for high-resolution graphics, because he never needs to print things out!" or "Sarah reminded us that she uses a dial-up connection—and she's going to leave if the page size takes too long to load." Include the date these decisions were made, the rationale, and by whom. Doing so will help others not attending that meeting understand why certain decisions were made (although note that the rationale for the decision is in part embedded in the persona and in part based on other considerations). This also makes clear that your personas are actually being used. Your persona posters and other artifacts will become important records of team decisions.

Although having personas participate in discussions may feel a bit forced and awkward at first, this technique ensures that you never stray too far from the customer data that serve as the lifeblood of good decisions. After everyone becomes comfortable asking personas for input, your team will probably find that the personas' presence is a relief. Decisions can be attributed to (and blamed on) personas. They are happy to take the heat—as long as their opinions are not misrepresented.

PLAN, DESIGN, EVALUATE, RELEASE: HOW TO USE PERSONAS DURING THE STAGES OF PRODUCT DEVELOPMENT

Let's look back at the traditional waterfall model of product development we briefly discussed in Chapter 2 (see Figure 6.1). You will note that in an ideal situation persona *adulthood* extends over the majority of the development process. In fact, persona *adulthood* may even continue after development is complete, beyond the release phase, providing help to marketing, sales, operations, and support. For this chapter, we have further simplified the waterfall model into four distinct development stages (see Figure 6.2). The rest of this chapter is organized according to these four stages. For each stage, we provide several usage techniques and tools that engage your personas to the benefit of your team and product.

- Stage 1—Plan your product (system requirements, software requirements, analysis)
  - Determining the product vision and functional requirements
  - Competitive reviews
  - Feature brainstorming, prioritization, and work planning

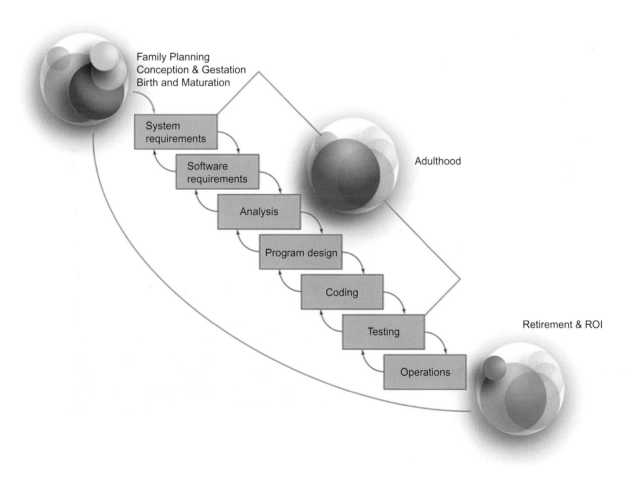

FIGURE 6.1
The classic waterfall model of software development with persona lifecycle phases added. (Adapted from www.maxwideman.com/papers/plcmodels/1990s.htm.)

119

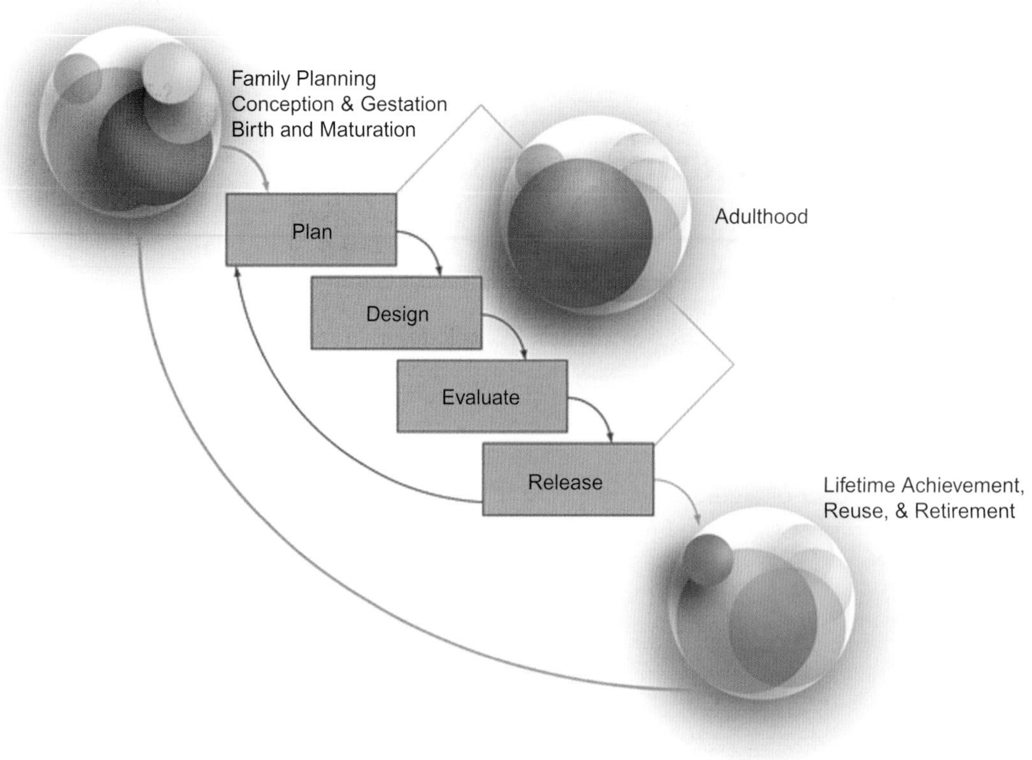

Family Planning
Conception & Gestation
Birth and Maturation

Plan

Design

Evaluate

Release

Adulthood

Lifetime Achievement,
Reuse, & Retirement

FIGURE 6.2
Plan, design, evaluate, release. We have further simplified the waterfall process model into four stages: plan your product, design your product, evaluate your designs, and release your product.

- Stage 2—Explore design solutions (product design)
  - ○ Scenario-based design and mapping
  - ○ Design explorations and mood boards
- Stage 3—Evaluate your design solutions (coding and testing)
  - ○ Design reviews and cognitive walkthroughs
  - ○ User testing and ongoing user research
  - ○ Quality assurance testing and bug bashes
- Stage 4—Support the release (operations)
  - ○ Documentation and product support
  - ○ Marketing and sales

Finally, note that this chapter covers only a handful of uses of personas, and we believe that personas can be used in many more ways than we have explored. Also note that the waterfall model of development is not the only model in use. Personas can be applied to any development model and design approach that lends itself to understanding users.

STAGE 1. USE PERSONAS TO PLAN YOUR PRODUCT

Before delving into the real work of development, your organization needs to create a vision and generate an overall development plan for your product. To do this, your leaders will want to understand both industry and market trends, customer requirements, and more technical system requirements for your product's domain. You will need to develop a big picture for your product: what it will do, how it will fit into the market, what problems it will solve, how you will approach building it, and so on.

Now that you have created your personas, you can ask the personas to tell you their stories. The needs, goals, and contexts you so carefully included in your persona descriptions will now allow you to generate helpful stories about the way your product will be used and the actions (and reactions) it should elicit.

In this section, we explain how personas can help during this planning process, both by helping you discover important features and by helping you evaluate the relative values of each feature. You can use personas to help you understand and capture your user and system requirements through:

- Persona narratives and storytelling
- Persona-focused competitive reviews
- Persona-focused feature brainstorming
- Persona-focused evaluation of proposed features

Use persona-based approaches to understand user requirements and envision your product

The personas' presence around your workplace can help you define an appropriate product for your target audience in a general fashion. The personas can also participate more directly by helping to identify specific user requirements and desires in terms of particular features and functionality.

How does your development team generate the high-level vision and then determine the key functionality and distinct features to build into your product? These decisions are often made by high-level leaders and executives in your company and are typically based on the availability of certain technologies, system architectures, and business plans or strategy ("We have the technology to do X, so let's build a product around it" or "No one has a product that does Y, so we should create it"). In other cases, your team members promote pet features, sometimes thinking of themselves as the ultimate user ("Well, I like to do Y, so the product should support doing that"). The basic requirements, functionality, and feature ideas for your product may come from any or all of the following sources:

- Executive directive
- Technological maturity (it's already built)
- Pet features ("I know what I'd like it to do")
- Team brainstorming of ideas
- Technical or feature-based competitive reviews (keeping up with the Joneses)
- Customer requests
- Support issues/costs
- Strategic partnership, key client request ("make the sale" feature)
- Demand from key industry influencers (e.g., John Dvorak, noted PC industry guru)

We believe it is important for you to let your target audience play a role in this process. Toward this, we examine storytelling, feature brainstorming, and competitive review using personas to help your team explore requirements and generate feature ideas. However feature ideas are generated, it is not uncommon for a product team to end up with a long list of features they are considering for the product release. We describe a two-part approach that helps bring the personas' voices (and the data they encompass) into the evaluation process—the decision-making process that determines which features and functionality end up being pursued.

Invite personas to tell you their stories

In Chapter 9 of our original book, *The Persona Lifecycle: Keeping People in Mind Throughout Product Design*, Whitney Quesenbery includes a rich exploration of the value of stories in product design and their relationship to personas. As she says, stories:

- Communicate culture.
- Organize and transmit information.

121

- Explore new ideas.
- Put personas in motion.

Putting personas into motion helps us understand behaviors, reactions, and expectations which in turn helps us design the best possible features and functionality for our products. The first stories you need to understand are the stories about the way things are done today. You can use your personas to capture and understand the problems, challenges, and pain points people encounter as they work within your product's domain *without* the help of the product you are building. Once you understand these stories, you can create new stories (scenarios, flows, use cases, and narratives) that describe the way things could work once your product is built. Whitney describes many types of stories in her chapter, each of which conveys a different level of detail and scope of context. These include:

- Springboard stories
- "Points of pain" stories
- Key scenarios
- Design maps
- Narrative scenarios
- Flow diagrams
- Use cases

During your product planning work, we recommend that you focus on springboard stories, "points of pain" stories, and reality maps (for more on reality maps, see Chapter 10 of the original *Persona Lifecycle* book). These "big picture" stories will set the context and motivation for your product. They will expose pain points and highlight design opportunities to your team. They can call out possible new features and clarify needed redesigns of current implementations. They show you where improvements and innovation can occur. Later, as you explore design solutions, you can use design maps, scenarios, flow diagrams, and use cases to design the features you have prioritized. For an interesting example of using stories to understand the big picture and identify opportunities, see "Story from the Field: Lifestyle Snapshots Help You Envision Design Opportunities," below, by David Anderson of Microsoft Corporation.

STORY FROM THE FIELD

Lifestyle Snapshots Help You Envision Design Opportunities

David Anderson, Visual Studio Enterprise Systems, Microsoft Corporation

With ubiquitous mobile computing devices and applications that can be accessed from Internet terminals almost anywhere, it has become increasingly difficult to know in advance the context of use for an application. Without a firm context, the designer's job is difficult. Anticipation of the user's needs in any given situation is much more difficult.

This gap in contextual information can be filled by expanding the definition for each persona with a detailed "lifestyle snapshot" of how that persona lives and works for important time periods, situations, or events. A lifestyle snapshot describes a simple period in which the proposed application may be useful to that persona. It must be a sufficiently long period to provide a context for usage. Multiple lifestyle snapshots are typically generated for a given persona, though if appropriate a single snapshot could describe an entire "day in the life" of a persona.

Usage Opportunities

Lifestyle snapshots describe how the persona lives now—today—without any new technology. They come before usage scenarios, which describe how the persona might use a new application. Like anthropology, lifestyle snapshots provide insight into the life of the persona and allow us to see the opportunities for the new application to add real value for that persona. Value might be saved time, saved money, better communication, quality improvements such as improved accuracy of information, or style improvements such as improved presentation, access to previously unknown information, or faster access to stored information.

An Example

Cascade Air is a new premier service carrier operating out of SeaTac International airport near Seattle. They are determined to steal business from low-cost carriers by providing a range of personal services and quasi-luxury accoutrements. Imagine that they have asked you (as designer) to participate in the creation of a new messaging service that could enhance sales and customer satisfaction.

One of your personas is Ferdinand "Ferdie" Mosler, a 48-year-old son of German immigrants. He is fluent in German and English. He holds a degree in economics from the University of Washington and an MBA in international business affairs from IMD in Geneva, Switzerland. He works as a venture capitalist for a secretive Seattle-based firm. He lives on Mercer Island in the middle of Lake Washington.

He is a frequent flyer who travels business class. He is a very desirable catch for Cascade Air, and they want his business badly. The following is a lifestyle snapshot of a typical day in his life when he is traveling.

Ferdie rises at 4:45 a.m., when his alarm clock rudely awakens him earlier than it would on a normal, non-travel day. He is traveling to San Francisco today to meet with a promising medical technology start-up company, Genogeek Incorporated. He gets up and makes coffee. On his way to the shower, he checks his mobile phone to make sure it is charged and to see if there are any new overnight or early-morning messages. (Because his company does East Coast and international business, it is not unusual to have plenty of things waiting for him.) He also fires up his laptop and starts it synchronizing his e-mail and calendar. He then showers and dresses. Before packing up his laptop, he finds a few new e-mail messages and makes sure that he has the reference material for Genogeek that he will read on the plane. He packs his laptop bag with a clean shirt and his toothbrush, just in case. He heads out, driving his Mercedes out into the darkness of the Northwestern winter. It is wet and 36 degrees outside.

Ferdie pulls on to the I-90 express lanes and heads for downtown Seattle, the I-5 highway, and the road to the airport. Traffic flows smoothly despite the rain, though it is heavier on I-5 and Ferdie is denied the HOV lane. His Mercer Island privileges end at exit 1 on I-90.

At the airport he pulls in to the long-term terminal parking lot, parks, and crosses the skywalk to the main terminal. He walks to the business class check-in desk. As he approaches, he sees a board to his right. Flight CC003 to San Francisco is delayed by two hours.

With each lifestyle snapshot, we identify a number of candidate usage scenarios. In this example, several things pop out as interesting opportunities for innovation. Not only would Ferdie benefit from flight schedule updates, but he could also use traffic and weather information. Even given his morning routine of proactively looking for information, he might not think to check traffic conditions until he is already on the road. Ferdie uses both a cell phone and a laptop, and the service could capitalize on that fact (but might need to be wary of overdoing it). The service should likely consider both push and pull technologies. Now armed with the contextual information from the lifestyle snapshot, you as the designer can determine the value proposition and develop more detailed usage scenarios.

Summary

Lifestyle snapshots work from the same assumption as personas. Rather than try to design an application that probably works most of the time, design it to be compelling for at least one specific context of use, relevant to a given persona. That way, we as designers ensure that the application is at least compelling for the user group represented by the persona on at least one real occasion in their life. The application delivers real tangible value. By identifying these opportunities to deliver value, it helps us communicate the value proposition for the application and communicate better with the target audience.

123

Analyze your competition through the eyes of your personas

You can use the personas to evaluate the competitive landscape into which you are going to introduce your product. You have used stories to understand your personas "in motion." Now that you know how to do that, you can project your personas into just about any situation.

Find out which existing products your new product will compete with. Your marketing team has probably already done this, and they are a good source for help with this exercise. If you can, purchase each of the competing products. (If the products are prohibitively expensive, you can do this exercise using the marketing or collateral materials instead of the actual products. This will give you insight into the reaction of your potential customers to the messages your competitors have deemed important.) Once you have access to the products, it is relatively easy to look at them from your personas' perspectives. To conduct a competitive review using your personas:

1. Ask at least one colleague per persona—and preferably more—to help you with your competitive review. You will probably need at least one or two hours to review each product from the perspective of each persona (although you can do quicker reviews if you are extremely time pressed).
2. Convene in a meeting space and make the competitor's product as visible as possible (if it is a software product, project the interface on a wall).
3. Ask everyone to carefully review the persona and then assign a colleague to be the persona (in this example, let's call the persona "Sandra the Scared Shopper").
4. Conduct a simple walkthrough (or cognitive walkthrough) of the competitive product, with your colleague assuming the point of view of the persona. Ask Sandra to talk about what she wants to do (her goal or task). Then ask her to look at the product and to talk about what she is seeing, how she feels about what she is seeing, and how she would approach her goals or tasks. Ask her what she would do (or click), and before she takes that action ask her what she would expect to happen once she does take that action.
5. Ask observers to record their ideas and observations during the walkthrough (or after, if you are recording it). Ask the persona (the colleague assigned to be Sandra) to try to stay in character as much as possible during the session, even if she has ideas she wants to convey.

As you observe this persona walking through the product, you will find aspects of the product that work well and some that do not. If members of your product design team are present, they will come up with ideas for functionality you must address in your product, as well as ideas for brand new features. From this walkthrough, you will be able to answer some interesting questions that will give you a unique insight into your competitors' businesses—and you will be able to avoid some customer experience mistakes they've already made.

As you do the review, ask yourself:

- Which of your personas do the competitive products seem to focus on? Do your competitors try to appeal to a persona who is missing from your "cast of characters"?
- Which of your competitors' features appeal to which of the personas? If you decide to do a persona-weighted feature matrix (see material following), this information will be very helpful.
- How do your personas react to your competitors' branding and marketing messaging?

Note that this is a great exercise to do with your marketing team. The result might be a superb new strategy for marketing your product based on differentiators from your competitors. How will you want to highlight the differences between your product and your competitors' based on the things you now know about your personas? If you decide to do persona mood boards later (see material following), you will want to find creative ways of presenting these differentiators that to appeal to your perspective customers. Later in the development cycle, you can use similar methods to conduct design reviews and cognitive walkthroughs of the features and experiences you decide to incorporate into your own product (for more information, see stage 3 later in this chapter).

Brainstorm possible features using your personas

Personas can help you understand user requirements and explore possible features by using them in collaborative brainstorming sessions. To conduct a persona feature brainstorm, first arrange a two-hour meeting with no more than ten key stakeholders from your product team. Be sure to schedule the meeting in a room that has ample space for interaction and easels or whiteboards. Then, before the meeting, prime the room with any and all of the communication artifacts you have created to date and make copies of your persona foundation documents. If you don't have whiteboards and persona artifacts, put large sheets of paper around the room with the names of each persona written on them.

1. At the beginning of the meeting, have everyone browse through the persona materials to refamiliarize themselves with the personas. Remind them of the basic rules of a brainstorming session:
   - Don't evaluate the ideas that are being explored. Evaluation will happen later.
   - Document every idea that is expressed. At this point there are no bad ideas.
   - Do not spend much time considering the specific implementation of any idea.
2. Before you start generating ideas, ask the participants to summarize motivations, goals, and behaviors for one primary persona (you can do this as a discussion or use sticky notes to post these on the large sheets of paper).
3. Ask the participants to think about opportunities you have for your product, given these motivations, goals, and behaviors. Ask them to think of ways your product can help each persona.
4. Repeat steps 2 and 3, spending about 15 minutes per persona.

Ideas will come in the form of new features or functionality, the acknowledgment of unnecessary or unpleasant experiences, high-level redesigns of existing solutions, and new content or domain areas that seem relevant, useful, or desirable to your personas. The meeting should end with a long list of possible features and product ideas for your team to further explore and evaluate.

Prioritize features using the persona-weighted feature matrix

If you did the previous two exercises and asked your personas to tell you their stories, you likely have a long list of possible features or services, perhaps some coming from other sources (e.g., a VP's wish list). Your team will now need to determine which are best to pursue. The process of honing in on the best features can be difficult and can sometimes feel haphazard.

There are a lot of forces weighing in on the decision making for your product. The persona-weighted feature matrix is a tool that will help your team make decisions based on the needs of your personas and, through them, your target customers and users. It will help you determine which features should not be included in your product—or at least which ones your team should focus attention on—based on the needs of your users. The persona-weighted feature matrix can also help when you (inevitably) have to triage which features you do and do not have time to include in your product. Figure 6.3 shows an abstract version of the persona-weighted feature matrix, and we've included a completed feature matrix in the G4K case study in Appendix C.

To create a persona-weighted feature matrix, create a spreadsheet as follows:

1. List one feature per row and one persona per column.
2. Assign a weight to each persona (beneath each persona name) according to the relative importance of the persona. These weights represent the relative importance of each persona and the audience he or she represents; for example, you can assign weights that

	Persona 1	Persona 2	Persona 3	
Weight:	50	35	15	Weighted Sum
Feature A:	0	1	2	65
Feature B:	2	1	1	150
Feature C:	−1	1	0	−15
Feature D:	1	1	1	100
Etc.	–	–	–	–

FIGURE 6.3

An abstract persona-weighted feature matrix. The features are listed in rows, the personas in columns. Each persona has a weight to identify its relative importance. Scores (2, 1, 0, or −1) are assigned for each feature according to how valuable or attractive it is to each persona. The weighted sums are the product of multiplying each score by each weight and then adding across the rows. For a detailed example of a completed persona-weighted feature matrix, see the G4K case study in Appendix C.

add up to 100 (see Figure 6.3). For detailed instructions on how and when to prioritize personas according to business goals, see Chapter 4, step 4.

3. Assign a score for each feature to describe the value or impact of that feature on the persona:

   2 The persona loves this feature or the feature does something wonderful for the persona (even if they don't realize it).

   1 The persona receives some value, perceived or not, from the feature.

   0 The persona doesn't care about the feature one way or another.

   −1 The persona is confused, annoyed, or in some way harmed by the feature.

4. Calculate a weighted sum for each proposed feature by multiplying the score by the weight and then adding all results across each feature's row. In the example shown in Figure 6.3, the weighted sum for feature A is calculated as $(0 \times 50) + (1 \times 35) + (2 \times 15) = 65$.

5. Once the scores are derived and the weighted sums are calculated for each feature, sort the rows according to the weighted sum to create a prioritized list. In the example, features B and D would sort to the top of the matrix because of their high weighted sums. These features should be made a high priority for the development team. Feature C should probably be dropped.

Note that it is a good idea to leave features that *must* be included in your product out of the matrix. For example, if you are creating a transactional website, you really can't leave out privacy and security features. Do not include these in the matrix.

The basic concept of feature-by-audience evaluation is not a new one. Geoffrey Moore, in his book *Crossing the Chasm*, described the creation of a target customer value matrix that employs the use of his persona-like representations (called "target customer characterizations") to evaluate the value propositions of a product in development (Moore, 1991, p. 101). Mikkelson and Lee (2000) extended this basic idea toward product development by evaluating scenarios against a prioritized (weighted) set of user archetypes, much like personas. We have pushed it one step further by employing personas to evaluate product features or customer services. To create a persona-weighted feature matrix, you and your team must be able to:

- Assign meaningful weights to each persona that communicate their relative importance to your product.
- Score each feature according to the value of that feature to each persona.

Each of these activities can be accomplished in either a rigorous scientific fashion or in a more casual fashion. The weighting scheme can involve real measures of market size and historic revenue, or, alternatively, the weighting scheme could be derived from estimates of size and predicted revenue or aligned with some notion of competitive strategy toward your target markets (e.g., your competitor doesn't attract certain audiences). At its simplest, the weighting scheme could be a simple priority rating (say, from 1 to 5, with 5 being the most important audience, or a distribution of points that total 100 across all of your personas) generated from an educated guess by your executives or market research team. You likely discussed some of this information during the prioritization of skeletons while creating personas (see Chapter 4, Step 4).

It is a good idea to ask business stakeholders to participate in—or completely own—the process of assigning value ratings to the personas. Once you have these values, and once you have agreement that the values really do reflect business goals, the matrix can become a very powerful communication tool. If the values assigned to the personas really do reflect core business goals, the weighted sums in your matrix will allow your organization to discuss the merit of features according to these goals.

Scoring the features per persona within the matrix is another matter altogether. It is the more difficult of the two steps. Again, the process can range from rigorous to casual. The more rigorous approach involves recruiting groups of people that match your personas on certain critical characteristics (a topic discussed more thoroughly later in this chapter in the section on using personas in user testing and marketing research) and then having those persona representatives evaluate your features relative to one another. This can be done in focus groups, in individual interviews, or through remote methods such as online surveys. The participants can provide rating scores or you can have them allocate sums from a fixed amount of "money" to choose the features of highest value. (Note that one very important aspect of collecting this type of data is to ensure that your participants truly understand the features they are evaluating.) Once evaluations of your features are collected, it is a relatively simple process to collate, collapse, and transform your data into scores for the persona-weighted feature matrix.

On the less rigorous side, the scoring can be accomplished by committee or by individuals. When doing so, care must be taken to ensure that the scoring is done with stakeholders being fully aware of their own biases toward certain favored features. (Of course, this is not easy for any of us.) When a feature is not fully understood by the group, mark it to be reviewed later and move on to the next feature (we recommend changing the cell color to yellow to indicate that there's an issue and remind everyone to return to the discussion later.). When the group is uncertain about how a particular persona would value a feature, make note of this; it represents an area your user research team could further investigate. Whether done by committee or by individuals, we recommend the 2, 1, 0, −1 scoring scheme (see above) for the persona-weighted feature matrix because it is simple yet compelling and is fairly easy to apply.

Completing the persona-weighted feature matrix almost always results in surprises. "Our top feature fell to the bottom of the list! And who had any idea that feature X would be that important?" When this happens, it is important to remember that this matrix is simply one tool that can be used to analyze your product offering and target market. Don't allow it to dictate your feature decisions without thorough analysis and examination. The value of the tool rests in its ability to bring implicit assumptions into team consciousness, providing a common understanding of your product and audience.

Treat each surprise in the matrix as a flag for further investigation. When a feature that was supposed to be your product's killer feature is shown as low priority in the matrix, begin to ask questions about the matrix itself and about that specific feature. Do you have the right audience? Why was that feature determined to be a killer feature? Perhaps your killer feature is simply the one feature your competition has over you. In that case, including the feature is a no-brainer, but the matrix can offer guidance as to how rich and complete the competitive feature needs to be. That is, if the feature simply completes a competitive checklist but your audience doesn't derive value from it, don't spend monumental development resources building all the bells and whistles into it. Allocate the most time to features that are the most valuable to your target audience.

HANDY DETAIL

Consider Your Business Strategy and Broader Market

When creating the persona-weighted feature matrix, you might consider the broader audience your product has to answer to. This may go beyond your persona set. For example, is there a buyer or business decision maker, independent of the end user, who determines whether or not your product will be purchased? Is there a highly revered magazine editor or consumer advocate organization that will be reviewing your product, giving it a thumbs-up or thumbs-down? If so, consider adding a column for that person or organization to reflect their reaction, actual or estimated, to your feature set. If you have a clear non-target or anti-persona, you might experiment with what happens to your feature set when their scores are added to the equation.

Take the matrix one step further: plot feature value versus technical feasibility

As illustrated by Dilbert and friends (Figure 6.4), determining what features are included in your product is not merely an exercise in what pleases your target audience. There are other factors you must consider; however, these need not be considered in isolation. The weighted sums generated in the persona-weighted feature matrix can be plotted against other key dimensions to help your team know how to best proceed. For example, technical feasibility (or, rather, the amount of difficulty or effort required to build a feature) is an important factor to consider. Feasibility affects overall development cost, time to market, and general risk. Your team can make more precise decisions to help your overall development plan when they consider both customer value and technical feasibility. Other key dimensions might include competitive or strategic importance, or some other characteristic related to the domain or business you are in (e.g., deployability, scalability, support cost, or international appeal).

This approach was first introduced to us by one of our persona practitioner workshop participants, Damian Rees, from BBC New Media, in 2002. Rees suggested a color-coding method to evaluate the value of each feature versus the technical difficulty. He pointed out that this would be a great way to quickly arrive at and explain to those charged with technical scoping and to making executive decisions which features are worth development resources. We have created a variation of Rees' idea to incorporate the values generated in the persona-weighted feature matrix.

FIGURE 6.4
Product features may come and go for a variety of reasons. (Copyright © Scott Adams/Distributed by United Feature Syndicate, Inc.)

Generating a user-value versus feasibility plot is fairly simple. We have found that it is best accomplished collaboratively with your more technical staff: your development manager, system architect, or lead developers. It is also useful to have key stakeholders present. Schedule a one- to two-hour meeting with the appropriate people in a room that has a whiteboard or a large easel and bring along copies of the persona documentation and the final version of the persona-weighted feature matrix. To create a feature-value versus technical feasibility plot:

1. Label the *y*-axis "Benefit to Personas" (or "User Value" or "Target Audience Need") and the *x*-axis "Technical Feasibility" (or some other dimension important to your product domain or organization).
2. Assign a color or symbol to each feature listed in your persona-weighted feature matrix (or write the name of each feature on its own sticky note, particularly if you have a lot of features to plot).
3. Place a colored dot (or sticky note) on the *y*-axis in accordance with the weighted sum of the corresponding feature (see Figure 6.5). Note that the features will probably not be evenly distributed along the *y*-axis, which is fine. Also, note that the position of the *x*-axis does not have to coincide with a score of zero in the matrix.

Now have the more technical folks in the meeting begin to arrange the features along the *x*-axis (without changing their positions on the *y*-axis; see Figure 6.5) according to the technical feasibility of the feature:

- Will that feature be difficult to build?
- Will it take a long time?
- Will highly skilled developers be required to tackle the work?
- Is it something that has never been attempted?

You will probably have a lively discussion as you evaluate every proposed feature for your product. Make sure someone in the room is taking notes regarding the reasoning behind the placement of each feature. Use your completed plot to further evaluate and triage the proposed feature list (see Figure 6.6):

- *Top right-hand quadrant* (high benefit to users, easy to create)—These are features your team should consider high priority. Tackle these features first.

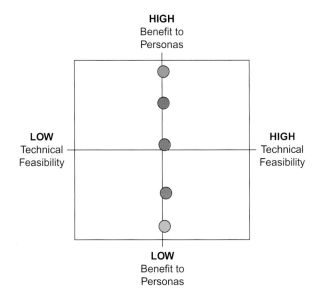

FIGURE 6.5
The first step in a feature-value versus technical feasibility plot is to assign a color to each feature and plot the weighted sum value for each along the *y*-axis.

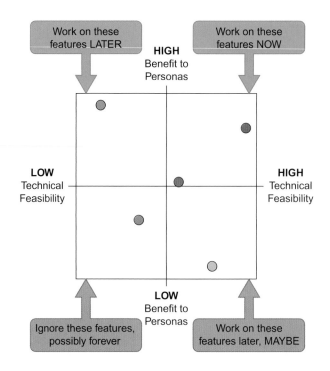

FIGURE 6.6
Completed feature-value versus technical feasibility plot. Collaboratively arrange the features along the second axis (technical feasibility) without altering the value on the first axis (value to your target users).

- *Top left-hand quadrant* (high benefit to users, not so easy to create)—These features are more difficult to assess. These are features that may require more resources or time committed to them if you want to ship them with your product.
- *Bottom right-hand quadrant* (lower benefit to users, easy to create)—These are low-hanging fruit, but they are probably not that tasty to your users. We suggest that you postpone any work on these features until after the first version of your product goes out the door.
- *Bottom left-hand quadrant* (lower benefit to users, not so easy to create)—You should completely ignore these unless there are other very strong reasons to include them (e.g., a vocal and well-respected industry expert is always complaining about the lack of this feature). Generally, you will be better off spending your development dollars elsewhere.

We've also had a lot of success using this technique with teams other than the development team. For example, you could work with the marketing team on a version of the graph labeled "competitive advantage" on the x-axis. Like most tools, this one can be adapted to solve various problems. When you find yourself having a hard time working with another team in your organization, create your own variation to help internal teams translate their concerns and ideas, while maintaining focus on the needs of the personas.

Note that this process has not represented the fact that some features are must-have features (i.e., you can't ship your product without them). These might be required by law, a direct request by the customer or client, or an essential function in a higher level process. For a related method of feature analysis, prioritization, and selection, see Walden's (1993) description of the Kano method.

STAGE 2. USE PERSONAS TO EXPLORE DESIGN SOLUTIONS

Once your organization has a vision and overall development plan in place, it is time to design the elements of your product. Your personas helped you understand the big picture, and now they can help you make decisions about specific features and design elements. That is, your personas can help you decide what these features should look like and how they

should behave. There are several methods you can use to integrate your personas into your design efforts. In this section, we discuss several of these methods:

- Scenarios and design mapping (a form of storyboarding)
- Mood boards and visual design explorations

Personas and scenario-based design

> The persona is static, but the figure becomes dynamic when it is inserted into the actions of the scenario. In the scenario, the persona will be in a context, in a specific situation and have a specific goal.
>
> **—Lene Nielsen (2003a, p. 1)**

Your personas can stand in for the people who are going to use your completed product to accomplish their tasks. You have gathered a great deal of information about the people themselves, and your persona descriptions include important social and cultural contexts for each person. You have created stories to help understand the current experiences and pain points of your personas. Now it is time to design the features that will go into your new product. Your personas will help you explore the experiences, behaviors, and reactions your designs will elicit. These details are typically captured and illustrated in tightly scoped stories. Earlier, we referenced Whitney Quesenbery's chapter "Storytelling and Narrative" in *The Persona Lifecycle* and the broadly scoped stories that are most effective during product planning. Now that you have moved on to product design, you will need more specific stories to guide the design process.

Generally speaking, more specific stories that are to be used in guiding the design process are called *scenarios*. Scenarios can be long descriptions of specific tasks your personas undertake to achieve a goal or short snippets describing activities related to a specific tool. They typically refer to very specific elements of a product and an experience with that product.

As Lene Nielsen (2002) pointed out, "A scenario is a written story that describes the future use of a system or a Web site from a specific, and often fictitious, user's point-of-view." That is, scenarios describe in detail how your product will be used once it is built from the point of view of your personas. Traditional scenario-based design techniques can benefit greatly from the inclusion of personas as replacements for actors and agents. Because personas themselves include information about behaviors, skills, and expectations, these do not have to be repeated in persona-based scenarios. Scenarios written around personas tend to clearly highlight the impact of your design on your target users. Scenarios usually include:

- A specified user
- A particular task or situation
- Clearly defined desired outcome or goal for that task
- Procedure or task-flow information
- A time period
- References to specific features or functionality the user will need or use

There are many good books and other reference materials on doing scenario-based design. John Carroll (1995, 2000a,b) has championed the concept and has provided much of the thinking and application of it toward product design.

You will find that there are a number of types of and uses for scenarios. For our purposes here, we will focus briefly on one: walkthrough scenarios. Feature specification documents (feature specs) are detailed descriptions of what the system is supposed to do and how it is supposed to do it. The feature spec tells the developer what to program in sufficient detail so that it is possible to proceed with coding. We believe that feature specs should always reference your personas, and this is best done by including scenarios.

A walkthrough scenario communicates and clarifies what, exactly, the feature is and does. Walkthrough scenarios are probably the most common and well-known type of scenario.

131

They demonstrate the feature in use by the personas in a step-by-step fashion. They provide the context and actions taken to achieve a goal. Walkthrough scenarios can be written in detail or at a fairly high level. Following is an example of a walkthrough scenario at a high level:

> Colbi is checking a shared calendar before purchasing concert tickets. She wants to go to a concert with three of her friends and is online at the G4Ksite, has her mom's credit card in hand, and is eager to purchase three tickets with prime seating. The only problem is that she knows that one of her friends is going on an overnight family outing sometime that same week. Fortunately, Colbi's group of close friends have shared their G4K buddy calendars with her. Colbi clicks on the Calendar tab and selects her friend from the shared calendar pull-down menu. Her friend's overnight trip shows up in a different color on the calendar. Colbi instantly knows she can purchase the tickets for the concert that night.

Keep in mind that scenarios do not have to be static text descriptions of actions and events. You can use the design mapping techniques described later in this chapter. Design maps depict the personas' experiences using your yet-to-be-built product. They are essentially long, detailed scenarios built out of sticky notes, created to depict an end-to-end experience from the point of view of a persona. These maps can be broken down into shorter scenarios and augmented with wireframe design elements that deeply illustrate and complement walkthrough scenarios. Design mapping can be a great way to create scenarios interactively with your design team.

Scenarios can also be illustrated graphically or even acted out live or on video. Consider creating storyboards starring your personas. This can be a great way to make your product plans and your personas come to life and to communicate the end result you are planning with your executive team and other key stakeholders. Many practitioners have recommended acting out scenarios to help make them real and comprehensible. For example, Lynn Upshaw, in *Building Brand Identity* (1995, p. 105) , suggested "acting it out in the 'purchase theater'." Here, his user representations ("indivisualizations" of customers, which are analogous to personas) are employed to inspire dramatic enactments of users making a purchase decision. Salvador and Howells (1998) described an interesting and related concept they refer to as a "focus troupe," which relies on short dramatic vignettes presented to potential end users and other stakeholders for evaluation.

Of course, scenarios for your product and its features can and will be created in various forms apart from those described here. The persona can, and likely will, be used to create scenarios that do not exist in the original persona foundation documents. To create an effective scenario based on the persona, the scenario writer needs simply to read through your persona description materials (focusing on the persona's goals, fears, aspirations, behaviors, and other core characteristics) and then apply that information toward the feature or domain of interest—stepping through the actions and dialog between the user and the system.

CREATE A SCENARIO COLLECTION SPREADSHEET

It is likely that there are already many usage scenarios of various types and quality floating around your organization. Your core team members are probably not the only ones writing and thinking about scenarios. Others across your organization may already be drafting and including scenarios in specs, vision documents, marketing plans, or other materials designed to support product development. These scenarios, all created for slightly different purposes, will differ considerably in length, content, and clarity. Some of them will reference users and perhaps your personas; some may not.

As your organization creates new scenarios, we recommend that you make an effort to collect and evaluate those scenarios. Collecting these scenarios into a single repository (preferably a spreadsheet or simple database) will help you make sense of them and allow you to do some quality control. To create a scenario collection spreadsheet, ask all of the teams working on your product to send you any scenarios they have created or to send you the documents they have created so you can identify the scenarios they contain. Copy and paste each scenario into a spreadsheet (however long the scenario turns out to be). In another column, list the ways users or personas are referenced in each of the scenarios (we show an example of this in the G4K case study in Appendix C). Once you have created the scenario collection spreadsheet, you can use it to do several things:

- Look for the word *user* or any other reference to the eventual users of your product.
- Look across scenarios for a single persona to make sure that the scenarios utilize the personas appropriately and consistently.
- Do a simple count of the scenarios written for each persona.

If you find references to users that are not stated in terms of the personas, you can contact the scenarios' owners and educate them on the personas. Consider rewriting the scenario for the document owner to demonstrate the value of using the persona names and information. When you find references to the persona names in existing scenarios, check to make sure that the personas are described consistently and accurately with respect to your persona foundation documents and other materials. Make sure, for example, that Tanner isn't described differently from scenario to scenario.

Finally, count the number of scenarios that refer to each of your personas. Doing this frequency count will shed light on your team's actions and focus (and this can be compared and contrasted to the overall product vision). There should be a proportional number of scenarios relative to the importance of each persona. If you find that a secondary persona appears in more scenarios than a primary persona, follow up with the scenarios' authors to make sure they understand the needs and value of the primary persona.

This scenario collection exercise highlights a tough question that many persona practitioners have come across. When you are creating scenarios for a particular feature, how do you decide which persona to use as the main user (a.k.a., actor/agent) in that scenario? Many times, any one of your personas could reasonably serve as the actor in a scenario. If it is not clear which to use based on the goals, activities, and behaviors of your personas, the best choice is to use the primary persona (or the persona with the highest weighting in the priority matrix tool discussed previously). We have seen practitioners use the reference "all personas" in scenario descriptions in place of a single persona. We suggest that this is not a good solution, as it relinquishes the specificity and focus personas attempt to add.

Use design maps to create new experiences for your personas

Design maps tell stories that look into the future. These stories describe how your personas will behave once your new product is built. Those familiar with scenario-based design will recognize that design maps have a distinct similarity to scenarios. Scenarios are short prose stories that describe how aspects of your product will be—or should be—used. Design maps are a special type of scenario, a collection of related scenarios and a process by which to create scenarios and modify them. Design maps are flowchart versions of many scenarios strung together to create a big picture of the experience your product will support. They are inexpensive (both in terms of time and materials) and are most helpful when built before paper prototypes and certainly before any code is written.

WHAT EXACTLY ARE MAPS?

Maps help you visualize and comprehend end-to-end user experiences. Mapping is the process of creating flow charts in collaboration with the users and members of your product design and development team.

Maps show steps in a process or experience sequentially, with any questions, comments, or ideas regarding these steps arrayed underneath (see Figure 6.7). Finished maps are large

133

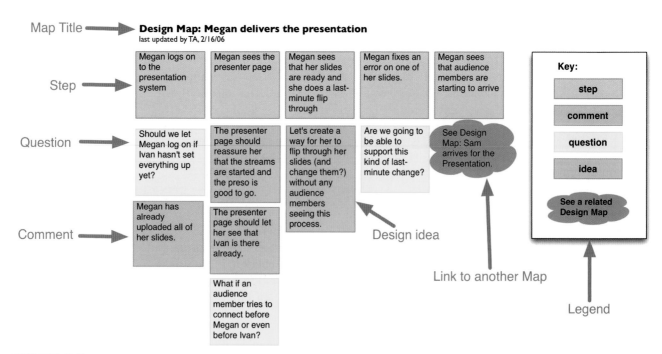

FIGURE 6.7

Steps, questions, comments, and design ideas in a design map.

sheets of paper covered with color-coded sticky notes that describe the use experiences related to your product.

There are two types of maps: reality maps and design maps. Reality maps are created in collaboration with current users of a product or service; they are a structured way of collecting information about how people get things done today. Reality maps capture the problems your new product is being designed to solve, and they can be an excellent way to gather qualitative data.

Design maps are created by a design team without the participation of users; their purpose is to allow you and your team to quickly explore the new experiences your product can and should support. In the sections following, we describe how to create and use design maps as part of the *adulthood* phase of an end-to-end persona effort. If you are interested in reality maps and how to use them to gather user data for use during the persona *family planning* and *conception and gestation* phases, see Chapter 10, "Reality and Design Maps," in the original book, *The Persona Lifecycle: Keeping People in Mind Throughout Product Design.*

WHY USE MAPS?

Maps are helpful information-gathering and design tools because they are easy to create, iterate, and read. If they are kept in public spaces, they can become an accessible source of insights into user experiences (either as they exist today or as they are envisioned to become). Unlike prose documents or complex flowcharts, maps make it easy to quickly extract and understand the end-to-end user experience and focus on details of interest.

Design maps are interesting not because they are radical departures from existing methods but because they work well for both creating personas and using them to create new designs. Used with personas, maps can help you understand the experience-related changes (both good and bad) your new product will demand. We love using design maps because:

- *Design maps foster creativity while maintaining focus on user experience.* Design maps focus designers on the holistic experiences that could be built for the personas, rather than on individual tools or features. Design maps allow product designers to create solutions that will work well for users, applying their expertise to the problems they used observation and data collection methods to understand.

- *Design maps are valuable communication and collaboration tools.* Maps depict both the big picture and important details of current user experiences in an accessible format. They allow everyone on a design and development team to understand the user experience as distinct from the system supporting that experience. When you have maps hanging on your walls, it is impossible to lose sight of the big picture of your users' experiences

- *Design maps explore the future.* Because design maps are experiments, you may build more than one to test out different ideas and see which one makes the most sense before you write code or even create paper prototypes.

- *Design maps are the bridge between task analysis and design.* By referring to your personas instead of real users when you start building your design maps, you immediately begin to reap all of the benefits personas offer your team. First, with everyone talking about personas, the team stops focusing on the quirks of individual users and starts thinking about the commonalities among users. Second, when your team shares a vision of the users you are working to help, they can make design decisions based on this vision.

- *Design maps free you from current users' biases.* Design maps allow you to explore innovative processes and methods, and it is important that you be free from current users' habits and biases as you explore the potential for your product. Design maps are a designer's tool, and users should only be involved if they are part of the design team. Design maps should be built using the bird's-eye view of the problem. This view encompasses the problems current users have and the potential of new technologies. Often someone peering into a situation from the outside (you) has the advantage of a fresh perspective and new ideas that users just do not see. The users you work with will have clever ideas that will make even the most seasoned designer say, "Duh, why didn't I think of that?" Don't worry; the personas you have developed will speak for your users. Once you have built a design map (or series of alternative design maps) you can bring users and stakeholders back in to give feedback. It is generally easier for users to give feedback on your design ideas than to ask them to start with a blank slate.

- *Design maps will help you create materials for supporting the development process.* Design maps aren't just an interesting exercise. Once you have created your design maps, you can use them in some very practical ways to support the product development process. In step 3, below, we describe how you can use your design maps to:
  - ○ Create additional scenarios and use cases for exploration and comparison.
  - ○ Conduct walkthroughs of your new design before a line of code is written.
  - ○ Track design changes during the development process.
  - ○ Streamline the communication between the product design and development team and other groups in your organization.

135

Preserve Your Maps

Maps are meant to be big and covered with sticky notes. This makes them inherently difficult to manage as artifacts. Bring tape to your mapping sessions. If you ever try to move a map, or even if you just leave it hanging on a wall, it will shed sticky notes. Take some time at the end of your mapping sessions to reinforce your sticky notes by taping them to the large sheet of paper.

When the map is complete, and it is not changing much any more, consider transferring it into an electronic medium. This can range from taking digital photos of your maps to transcribing all of the sticky notes to create an electronic version. We use Microsoft® Visio® to create electronic versions of our maps and print them on large-format printers. You can also use Adobe® Illustrator® or FreeHand®, or OmniGraffle. As a general rule, pick vector-based software for your electronic mapping.

If your company does not own a large-format printer or plotter and you want to create electronic versions of your maps, you have several options. Print the maps on standard-size paper and tape the pages together to create a large map. It is worth it to see the entire process on the wall. If your company sees enough of these maps, you just may convince someone to invest in a plotter. Alternatively, you can contact your local copy center. Printing on a large-format printer is usually quite expensive, but talk to the manager. Ask if they will give you a better price because your maps will not use as much ink as most large-format, full-color posters and because you will use their services frequently.

The design mapping process

Design maps show the experiences your personas *might* have given various designs for your future product or process. Design maps are experiments in process reengineering. They use a linear format and allow designers to prototype new experiences, from the perspective of the personas. Design maps are built by your team based on their:

- Knowledge of existing processes.
- Understanding of the personas.
- Understanding of the technologies available to incorporate into the product.
- Ability to streamline work processes.

Step 1. Decide which processes you want to map

As you create your design maps, you will focus on capturing the big picture before diving into details. You can try to create design maps for all of the experiences your product will support, but this may prove to be a daunting task. When we create design maps, we create them as follows:

- *Design map for the big picture*—This map shows the entire experience end to end and therefore describes activities in very broad terms. Think of this overview design map as analogous to a map of the United States with a line drawn on it to show the route of a cross-country driving trip. The overview map should give the reader a general sense of direction and the order of progression but should not contain details.
- *Design maps for achieving major milestones*—These maps should fit into the overall map but should explore individual goals and tasks more specifically. In the cross-country trip example, a major-milestone map would be the equivalent of a highway map showing the roads you used to traverse a single state.
- *Design maps for critical details*—These maps should fit into the milestone maps much as the milestones fit into the big picture. These maps explore very specific details of particular tasks, the way an enlargement of a downtown area shows the specific details of the way streets crisscross a city.

The design maps you create should explore the ways your personas achieve the goals you have established for them. Remember that their roles and goals may change in your new designs.

Step 2. Create the maps

Design maps are process flow diagrams created collaboratively using sticky notes. It's really no more complicated than that.

ELEMENTS OF EVERY MAP: TITLES, STEPS, QUESTIONS, COMMENTS, AND DESIGN IDEAS

All maps have five basic building blocks: titles, steps, questions, comments, and design ideas. Titles should identify the type of map (reality or design) and identify the goals or tasks the map depicts. Steps should be arrayed horizontally, with related comments, questions, and design ideas arranged under the steps they reference. You can read across the row of steps to get a sense of the process from end to end (i.e., the steps in a task taken to reach a goal), or you can focus on a subset of the steps and read down the columns to understand related questions and ideas (see Figure 6.7).

Steps (blue sticky notes)

Steps are the "verbs" (or the "backbone") of the process. The facilitator of the mapping exercise places steps horizontally across the map. A good way to elicit steps is to ask, "What do you do next?" Steps are the building blocks of tasks.

Comments (green sticky notes)

Comments are qualifying statements about steps. They are the most flexible elements on a map. Comments can describe behaviors, habits, awareness, or lack of awareness of features or alternative actions or even qualities of objects. If you hear an important piece of information but it is not a step, question, or design idea, record it as a green comment.

For example, in our Megan Delivers the Presentation map (see Figure 6.7), the comment "Megan has already uploaded her slides" is a note about this particular person's actions that could be significant with respect to the rest of the experience. The comment is not a step, but it relates to the step listed above it: "Megan logs into the presentation system." The comment, in this example, serves to remind the facilitator and map readers that, if Megan had not yet uploaded her slides, the process following the green sticky note might look very different.

Questions (yellow sticky notes)

When you first start mapping any process, you will identify many questions—some indicating areas where you need clarification and some that express your mapping participants' issues. In fact, you will probably encounter so many questions that the sheer volume and importance of them will threaten to derail your attempt to map the entire process. Listing the questions on the map allows you to record and move past them quickly so you can capture as much of the process as possible without being derailed. Once you create a map that captures most of an end-to-end process you can loop back and track down answers to the questions you have identified. Questions can either come from the facilitator or the mapping participants. For example, in our Megan Delivers the Presentation map, questions include: "Should we let Megan log on if Ivan hasn't set everything up yet?"

Create a yellow question when:

- You have questions about the process.
- Anyone participating in the mapping session begins to belabor a point.

Design ideas (pink sticky notes)

As you create your map, you will inevitably think of, or be presented with, an assortment of ideas on how to improve the process. Ask anyone who comes up with a design idea to record it on a pink sticky note, place it on the map, and move on.

137

THE "MAPPING TEAM"

Gather the appropriate stakeholders from your team and start creating your design maps. Let the design mapping participants know what you expect of them. The purpose of a design mapping session is to explore and record one end-to-end experience you could create for your personas. For example, Figure 6.8 shows a design map of persona Tanner's registration process on G4K's yet-to-be-built website for kids. The team started the mapping exercise by asking themselves, "Knowing what we do about the way things are done today and the possibilities that are available, how is Tanner going to interact with our new website?"

MAPPING SOMETHING COMPLEX? TRY BRANCHES AND LAYERS

Although we do believe that most experiences can be expressed in a relatively linear fashion, it is also true that many processes branch or depend on very specific interactions among various subprocesses. You can use branching and layering to explore these aspects of your task domain.

Maps tend to look more complex and messier as you add more details to them, as you talk to more people, and as you learn more about existing processes. This makes sense. If there is a good business case for your product, it is probably because someone understood that the current process needed improvement. Your goal should not be to work on the maps until there is nothing left to learn about the process; rather, your goal should be to continue mapping until you believe you have built a solid understanding of the task domain.

Branching

All processes include decision points. Many of these decision points are relatively minor and do not affect the overall process significantly (e.g., Tanner deciding to find a clue for the Skatepunkz game versus the Moneybags game). However, there are some decisions that radically affect the user experience (e.g., whether the child registering is old enough to do so

138

**Design Map:
Tanner signs up on G4kids.com**

Tanner owns the Gigantic game "Skatepunkz"	Tanner sees the G4kids.com address on the Skatepunkz splash screen	Tanner wants to find some of the Skatepunkz secret keys	Tanner goes to the G4kids site to explore	Tanner checks out the 'free Skatepunkz' area of G4kids.com	Tanner thinks the online version of the game is 'pretty lame' since he's so good at the 'real' game	Tanner recognizes the Get A Hint logo from his advanced game play; he clicks on it	Tanner clicks to get the free hint	Tanner...
Tanner's had the game for 3 weeks and he's pretty good			Tanner should be able to use many of the free/G-rated services without permission	G4K tracks Tanner's interests during this session		We probably need some more enticements in case he misses the logos stuff	We need to provide one 'freebie' Skatepunkz hint here	
				If we can track activities in pre-signup sessions, are there any legal/privacy issues?		We can't make this stuff TOO easy to find—the challenge is key		

FIGURE 6.8
A design map exploring how Tanner registers himself on the G4K site. Design maps are created by your team and explore the new experiences you are going to build into your product.

independently or not). When you encounter this type of decision and its consequences, you can:

- Create a new map to express the differences in user experience associated with each choice (or, if there are many, a representative subset of choices). This is a good idea if you think the choice leads to completely divergent experiences.
- Branch your existing map to express the differences in user experience (see Figure 6.9). This is good idea if you think the choice leads to experiences that diverge in the short term and that converge later in the process.

Layering

Branches allow you to depict major decision points and their experiential ramifications for the user. Layers allow you to show disagreement among mapping participants and/or the flow of experiences among various players in the process. In other words, layered maps can:

- Highlight differences in experiences among users with *the same* roles and goals.
- Highlight differences in experiences among users with *different* roles and goals.

Layered maps for users with the same roles and goals. Consider Figure 6.10. In this example, the two layers correspond to two different mapping participants. You might create a map like this if you first map with Herbert and then map with Phyllis, who disagrees with the process Herbert described. Note that the major phases in the process are distinguished. Wherever there are sticky notes for both Herbert and Phyllis, the readers of the map can assume that Herbert and Phyllis disagree on the process. When there are *no* sticky notes in Phyllis's layer, the reader can assume that her description of the process matches Herbert's; for example, Herbert and Phyllis disagree on aspects of Planning the Class and Creating Materials for Students but agree on the process for Creating the Syllabus. If Herbert and Phyllis approached the tasks in the same—or similar—ways, the maps would appear to line up better, with fewer differences between the Herbert process and the Phyllis process. Even at a distance, a layered map makes it easy to see when different users' processes diverge.

139

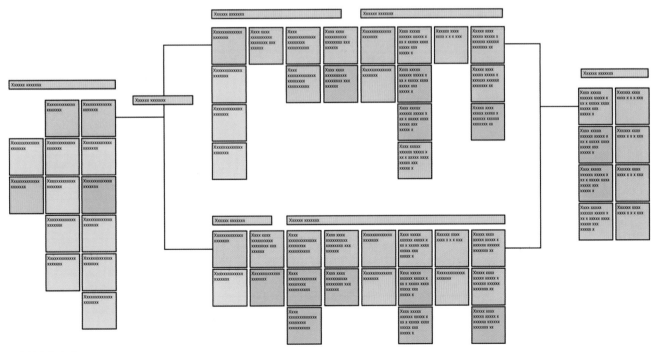

FIGURE 6.9
Map with branches.

Layered maps for users with different roles and goals. Layered maps can also highlight the flow of experience as it moves from one persona to the next. For example, examine Figure 6.11. Unlike Figure 6.10, the layers in this map correspond to users with different roles and goals. This type of layered map can illustrate how responsibilities are handed off among various people. If you create a map like this one, pay special attention to *how* the various people communicate with and depend on one another. These are often experiences that are rich with opportunities for improvement.

MANAGING DESIGN MAPPING SESSIONS

Encourage mapping participants to focus on the *experience*, not on the *tool*. The goal is not to have a map that tells you, "The serial number registration tracking database will feed the score records to the page via ASP," but one that says, "Tanner can see his Skatepunkz high scores on G4kids.com." During design mapping sessions, remind your team to consider the following:

- Do the tasks assigned to personas in the design map correspond to your personas' skills? For example, if Preston the Preschooler is expected to type in a URL address to access the site, he is not being well served by the new design. If Tanner's design map allows him

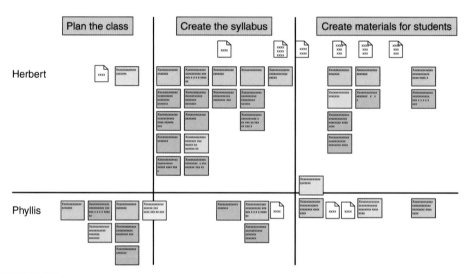

FIGURE 6.10
Layered map showing two alternative approaches to the same basic process.

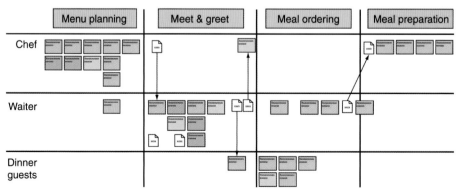

FIGURE 6.11
Layered map showing the experience flow that might occur among a chef, a waiter, and a dinner guest at a restaurant.

Sample Script for the First Design Mapping Session

Welcome, everyone! Thanks for making the time to participate in our design mapping session today. A lot of work has gone into preparing for these sessions. Interviews have been conducted with a number of people who will use our product in different ways. From these interviews, reality maps have been built to describe the way people are doing X today. Personas were also developed to describe the major roles as they are envisioned for people using our new product. We have determined that people have difficulty with X in the products currently available. In the new product, we will work to solve this problem for users. You are all familiar with the reality maps and personas, and we're ready to create a delightful new product for X users everywhere!

For those of you who participated in reality mapping, the process is very similar. We will be creating a giant flowchart, but, instead of charting how users do X now, this time we will record a possibility for how our personas will be able to do X with our new product. We will still use sticky notes with the same color codes: blue for steps, green for comments (anything that tells us more about a step), yellow for questions, and pink for ideas.

We are going to start with a single persona and a single goal and describe what it might feel like to use our software to achieve that goal. Remember, there is not necessarily a right answer. In fact, we may build several design maps that describe different ways a persona can achieve a certain goal. Also, keep in mind that we won't dive into the details during this exercise. This is not the time to decide what color certain buttons should be. Stick to fairly broad brush strokes, and we will settle details in the specifications for each feature that will be informed by this map. As we move to design new experiences, please keep the following questions in mind:

- Are we furthering the goals of the persona with this design?
- Do the tasks the personas perform match their stated skills or skills they are likely to be willing to learn?
- Does the new process we are building provide clear advantages over the old way?

If we can answer "yes" to these questions as we move through the mapping process, we will be on the right track. Okay, let's get started. Let's begin by describing the experience of persona X as he makes coffee for himself and his wife. Are there any assumptions we need to start out with?

to invite his buddies to come play games with him online with just a couple of mouse clicks, you are on the right track.
- Does this new process being constructed in the map offer undeniable advantages to the personas over the old way of doing things?
- Are we assuming things have to be done a certain way just because that is the way they are done now?

As you move through a mapping session, remember to table questions that might sidetrack your work by providing everyone with yellow sticky notes and encouraging participants to write down difficult questions and issues and post them on the map. During your design mapping session, you might hear a comment such as, "Well, if we're assuming Tanner uses the Internet at school all the time, can we assume he's pretty good at navigating websites? If he is, that would make things a lot easier. We would not have to dedicate part of the site to teaching him how to use links." This is a good opportunity to refer to your personas. Do you have information about Tanner's level of Internet experience? How long will it take him to learn the differences between doing things online versus doing things on a PC? Your personas will be able to immediately answer some of these questions. Others will have to go onto to the map to be answered later.

Sometimes you will want to move fairly quickly, placing blue steps across the top of the map and filling in details later. Other times your team might find it more effective to hash out the details under each step before moving to the next one. In either case, you will want to limit mapping sessions to two to three hours each.

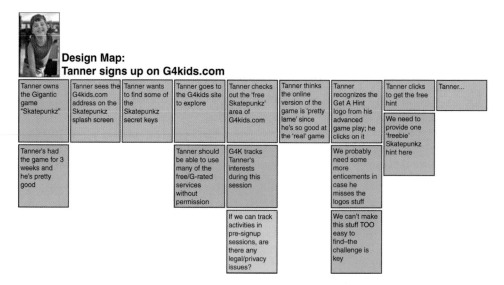

Design Map:
Tanner signs up on G4kids.com

Tanner owns the Gigantic game "Skatepunkz"	Tanner sees the G4kids.com address on the Skatepunkz splash screen	Tanner wants to find some of the Skatepunkz secret keys	Tanner goes to the G4kids site to explore	Tanner checks out the 'free Skatepunkz' area of G4kids.com	Tanner thinks the online version of the game is 'pretty lame' since he's so good at the 'real' game	Tanner recognizes the Get A Hint logo from his advanced game play; he clicks on it	Tanner clicks to get the free hint	Tanner...
Tanner's had the game for 3 weeks and he's pretty good			Tanner should be able to use many of the free/G-rated services without permission	G4K tracks Tanner's interests during this session		We probably need some more enticements in case he misses the logos stuff	We need to provide one 'freebie' Skatepunkz hint here	
				If we can track activities in pre-signup sessions, are there any legal/privacy issues?		We can't make this stuff TOO easy to find—the challenge is key		

FIGURE 6.12
A Design Map exploring how Tanner Registers himself on the G4K site. Design Maps are created by your team and explore the new experiences you are going to build into your product.

After each session, follow up on any questions or issues raised and add answers to the map. It can be useful to convert the sticky-note paper versions of your maps into electronic versions in Visio, OmniGraffle, or a similar tool. This makes it easy for participants to review progress and quickly scan for new material. The electronic versions are useful for printing in various formats and sending to stakeholders for review at a distance. An example of a completed design map is shown in Figure 6.12.

Step 3. Analyze the maps

During analysis you will add labels, compare different user maps, add branches and layers, and evaluate the processes you have captured in the maps. As you analyze your maps, you will also find areas in them that would benefit from further iteration. You will also find aspects of the process that are ripe for improvements.

IDENTIFY AND LABEL INTERESTING ASPECTS OF THE MAP

As you work on your map, you will probably start to discover some important aspects of the process that are not steps, questions, comments, or ideas. As you learn more about the process, you and your team can add symbols to your maps to capture your observations. It's also helpful to keep additional sticky-note colors handy in case you decide to capture some of the following information during a mapping exercise. In my experience, it is helpful to enrich reality maps with symbols (see Figure 6.13) that represent:

- Distinct phases of the process (see Figure 6.14)
- Artifacts or documents that support or are generated by the process
- Problem areas
- Areas that require further exploration
- Places where the process branches or connects to another process you need (or plan to) map

Phase labels

During early mapping sessions, you focus on individual steps. As your map evolves, you may find that your mapping participants have named some of the phases of the process. These phases are collections of individual steps, and the fact that they are seen as cohesive phases

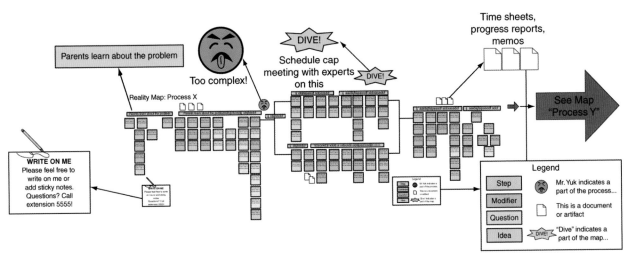

FIGURE 6.13
Additional mapping symbols. Additional symbols can help you highlight requests for contributions, phases in the overall process, problem areas in the process, areas you need to delve for more information, artifacts related to the process, and how the map connects to other maps.

of effort can be important as you develop your designs. For example, you may find that many parents describe some of the phases of implementing online parental controls as:

- Learning about the problem or researching solutions
- Purchasing and installing a solution
- Managing and monitoring access

Record these phases by drawing a line over the series of steps each encompasses and labeling the line (see Figure 6.14).

Artifact indicators

During mapping sessions, your participants may describe various artifacts or documents that support or otherwise relate to their tasks. You can use a document symbol (a rectangle with a "dog ear" on one corner) to indicate the step in the mapped process where an artifact or document is required. In Figure 6.15, you will note that many document icons are sprinkled on the reality map. If you notice that there are quite a few documents required to complete a task that should be relatively automated, you may have found an aspect of the process that is ripe for improvement. If you want to a capture information about artifacts during a mapping session, choose sticky notes in a new color (not blue, green, yellow, or pink) and write the name of each artifact on its own sticky note. You can place these directly on the map near the appropriate step artifacts.

"Mr. Yuk" indicators

Almost every map identifies aspects of a process that could use improvement. A great way to find these areas is to look for stubborn clusters of yellow sticky notes. If you find a series of questions that are clustered and are resistant to being answered, you have probably found a process problem. If you find an aspect of the process that is not in question, but that everyone has ideas about or all mapping participants seem to dislike, you have probably also found a problem area. For internal versions of your map, it is handy to create and use a symbol to highlight that area. In our maps, we use a hand-drawn frowning face that reminds us of the "Mr. Yuk" sticker that used to be applied to indicate the presence of poisons in household cleaners (see Figure 6.16). The Mr. Yuk sticker indicates an area of the map that

FIGURE 6.14
Phase labels.

143

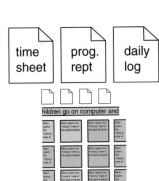

FIGURE 6.15
Artifact indicators.

FIGURE 6.16
Mr. Yuk indicator to highlight complexity.

requires attention during later design mapping sessions. Note, however, that you may want to create versions of your map that contain less incendiary symbols. Subject-matter experts do not always appreciate being told that parts of their processes are yucky. Find a nicer (and more specific) way of indicating a problem in the process on these versions of your maps. If you want to capture Mr. Yuk aspects of a process during a mapping session, assign Mr. Yuk a sticky-note color.

"Deep-dive" indicators

You will identify aspects of the process you are mapping that will need more attention, or a "deep dive." If you find a part of the process you want to take offline or you want to create another mapping session to explore, note this part by placing a deep-dive sticker (see Figure 6.17) on the map. You can use another color of sticky note or create your own symbol. Think of deep-dive stickers as similar to the indicators on street maps that tell the reader to refer to a detailed map in some other area. Like densely crisscrossed downtown streetscapes, some phases of some processes require their own detailed maps. Any time you find yourself creating many "yellow" questions, consider adding a deep-dive indicator to remind yourself to come back and explore that area of the process in depth.

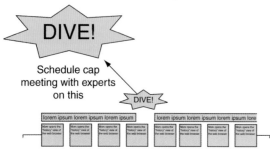

FIGURE 6.17
Deep-dive indicator.

Map connection arrows

You will create different maps for various user roles and goals. It is helpful to indicate how the maps fit together in an end-to-end experience. Use arrows or notes on the maps to show the reader how the maps precede and follow each other to depict the entire experience (see Figure 6.18).

Map legend

Add a legend to your maps so people can read and interpret them without your help. Include short definitions of each symbol and what it stands for on your map (see Figure 6.19). If you create your own mapping symbols, make sure you add them to your legend.

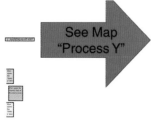

FIGURE 6.18
Map connection arrow.

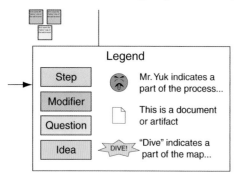

FIGURE 6.19
Map legend.

Step 4. Use design maps to create wireframes

Wireframes tend to evolve naturally from design maps (see Figure 6.20). Once you and your team have agreed on the experience you want to facilitate for your personas, it is relatively easy to use the steps, assumptions, questions, and design ideas in the maps to create wireframes of the product's user interface.

With your team, identify the columns of the design map that go together and should be grouped on a single interface. At this point, the user interface designer or graphic designer should be heavily involved. Consider what information you are collecting from the personas and when you are collecting it so you can plan to display it on the user interface at the right times (e.g., if you have not asked the persona for their name yet, you cannot create a wireframe for a personalized interface).

In Figure 6.21, you can see that the G4K team created very basic wireframes of the G4K.com pages based on the activities they described in the design map "Tanner signs up on G4K.com." As they created the wireframes, they identified a few more questions (note the yellow sticky on one of the early wireframes). As they evolved the wireframes, they continued to reference the original design map to make sure the site design supported the experience design in the design map.

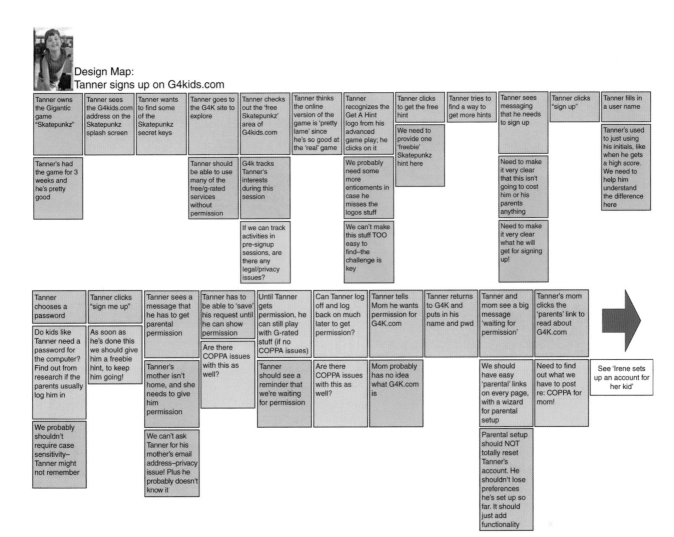

FIGURE 6.20
A completed design map for "Tanner signs up on G4K.com."

145

Step 5. Evaluate and communicate your solutions

Perhaps the most important benefit of design maps (and wireframes) is that they hold and communicate a shared vision of the project for your entire team. Seeing the big picture early on in the project helps motivate everyone toward achieving the common goal of making it real. Design maps enable your entire team to see the product from the personas' points of view, giving the architects of the product the opportunity to understand and empathize with users. A deeper understanding of the planned product and personas early on in the development process can enhance each team member's work on your product—whether they are coding, marketing, managing, testing, funding, or selling it.

USE DESIGN MAPS TO GET DIFFERENT VIEWS OF YOUR PRODUCT IN ACTION

Remember that you can continue to make design maps to explore various solutions your product could support. It is very useful to be able to take these variations to stakeholders for feedback. For example, you could create one design map that shows Tanner getting an account on G4kids.com himself and another showing what the experience would be like if his mother

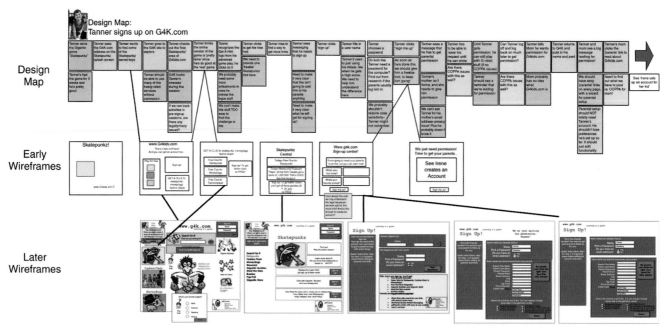

FIGURE 6.21
Wireframes evolve naturally from design maps. You and your mapping team can evaluate which process steps belong together and design the interface flow accordingly.

got the account for him. Comparing these two maps could help development managers understand the resources required to build each option in light of the persona's experience. You may also choose to create a single design map that covers the interactions of all of the personas. This type of map can be very helpful, especially for illuminating communication patterns and getting an overview of "who does what when" across a lengthy process.

HANDY DETAIL

Use Your Maps to Intrigue (and Invite Participation from) Your Coworkers

Maps are intriguing artifacts. They are colorful, and the paper versions that still have sticky notes all over them tend to "flutter" as people walk by. Use these attention-getting aspects of the maps to your advantage. Anyone who stops and reads a portion of the map will begin to understand how real people experience real tasks and have real goals related to your company's product space. Your colleagues may begin to cluster around the maps, and discussions will sprout. People will come into your office to ask you what the heck the big things in the hallway are, and you will be able to tell them that the maps are "windows into the world of our real users." When you post any map, make sure to very visibly note:

- What draft the map is and whether you consider it complete
- The experience it depicts

We have also found it helpful to make new material very visible on the maps. We do this by placing red borders around the notes added from the most recent session (or since the last printing). In this way, interested parties can scan a posted map and quickly see what has been changed or added recently.

Note: Share with Care!

If you choose to share your map, do it carefully. You will have to decide for yourself whether it is appropriate to post your maps in a publicly accessible area and, if so, what mapping symbols should be removed before doing so.

Invite Participation

If you hang your maps in visible places—especially design maps—invite passersby to participate by adding comments, questions, or design ideas (see Figure 6.22). Leave a pile of colored sticky notes and pens for this very purpose. If you are inviting participation on a sticky-note version of the map (in other words, not a digitized version), make sure the sticky notes you leave out are a different color from those already on the map so new comments are not confused with original map elements.

FIGURE 6.22
Invite participation when you hang your maps.

USE DESIGN MAPS TO SUPPORT WALKTHROUGHS AND TO CREATE SCENARIOS AND USE CASES

Design maps (and their associated wireframes) are a perfect document to work from when communicating project plans to stakeholders. Once your design maps are completed, you can use them to perform design walkthroughs of your product with other team members. Have someone read through the map and another person check the prototype or the product to make sure the mapped process is supported by the product's design.

Your design maps will become official historical documents, much like a formal specification document. You can use your maps (and the assumptions they contain about how you think your product should be experienced by the personas) to make sure your product is not swerving in the wrong direction as those inevitable compromises are made during development.

You can use design maps to help communicate and clarify what, exactly, a given feature is and how it works. This is accomplished via *walkthrough scenarios*, which demonstrate the feature in use by the personas in a step-by-step fashion. Design maps show the persona's experience using your yet-to-be-built product from end to end. They are long scenarios, and they are a wonderful source of use cases. After you have decided which design map you are going to follow to build your product, you can pull individual scenarios and use cases out of the maps. Because you have created the maps first, you know that the scenarios you pull out of them fit together seamlessly.

For example, when preparing to write the interface specification for the kids' registration interface for G4kids.com, the product manager can focus in on the "Tanner signs up on G4kids.com" design map. He or she can use subsets of the sticky notes to create an interface document or technical specification document. Using this portion of the design map for reference, the project manager can create a section of the specification document that addresses the technical underpinnings required to support the experiences.

A Picture of a Design Map Could Save You Hours
—Whitney Quesenbery, *Whitney Interactive design* (wqusability.com)

I was asked to review an early version of this chapter and as a result was carrying this chapter around with me for a short period. In a meeting with a new partner, we were struggling to find a way to bring together some very incoherent design ideas from our client. After almost 15 minutes of hand waving, I threw caution to the wind and showed them a complete map as illustrated in this chapter. They immediately got excited—and saw instantly what it would do for us and how it would help us collaborate. It saved me hours.

USE DESIGN MAPS TO EVALUATE DESIGN CHANGES DURING DEVELOPMENT

Even the best and most thorough designs evolve and change during the development process. As your development team begins coding your new product, check in frequently to evaluate what they are building against what you *thought* they were going to build. Use the design maps to test the emerging product. Does the product being built actually support the experience you have designed?

If for some reason the product cannot be created as designed, return to your design maps and evaluate the effect of the changes on your personas' experiences. If you find yourself changing elements of the map to accommodate unexpected design changes, do not despair. It is much better to know sooner than later about these changes and the potential problems they will cause. Reconvene your mapping team—and members of the development staff—to analyze the effects of changes and to tweak the design accordingly. If you cannot solve experience problems with code (perhaps it is too late to fix something you discovered to be broken), you can at the very least create support materials to mitigate the impact on the personas (or, rather, the end users they represent).

USE DESIGN MAPS TO COMMUNICATE WITH OTHER DEPARTMENTS

Teams responsible for product launch and post-launch activities and materials love design maps—especially if they are kept up-to-date and do actually reflect the experiences your product will support. Documentation teams can use design maps as outlines for documentation, testing teams can extract use cases and test cases, marketing teams can build materials that express the value of the new experiences you have created, and so on.

USE PERSONAS TO HELP YOU EXPLORE VISUAL DESIGN SOLUTIONS

How does the visual treatment of your product get specified and created? On some product teams, the developers do it themselves, possibly allowing the development environment to determine the look (e.g., Windows® Forms in Visual Studio® are a set of common control elements used by developers that provide a standard visual style for Windows applications). For others, there are dedicated graphic designers and artists who create a look for the product. In either case, it is useful to have a clear target user to serve as inspiration for the layout, wording, and style choices that need to be specified. Thus, personas can play a role here, too.

Have your team begin its creative process by collaboratively creating style and branding collages on large posterboards, which we call *style* or *mood boards*. Style and mood boards consist of cut-and-paste images that represent your personas. At least one collage is created per persona. As shown in Figure 6.23, style boards can include images of objects and places

FIGURE 6.23
An example of a style-board collage for a teen persona.

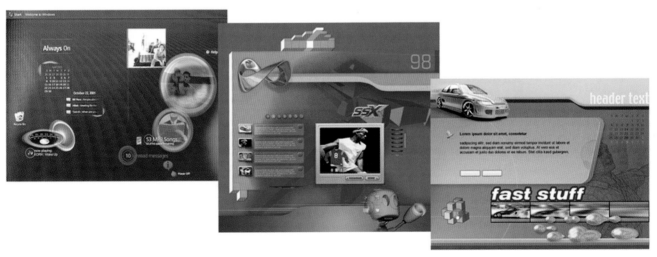

FIGURE 6.24
An example design exploration resulting from the collage shown in Figure 6.23. (Artwork created by Jenny Lam, Greg Melander, Chuck Cummings, and Mark Ligameri.)

(such things as clothing, cars, watches, furniture, home decor, art, and even food products—anything that captures a look or style appropriate for the personas). Your team will then utilize the style boards as the basis for creating exploratory visual treatments across key areas of the product (Figure 6.24).

These design explorations can be evaluated by your product team's stakeholders or by potential users and customers (e.g., in focus group sessions). Doing so will help your team understand what aspects of the visual designs are appealing and how they work together to form a holistic style. For example, what is the preferred color palette? What should the icons and toolbar imagery look like? How do transitions and animations enhance the experience? Based on such in-depth analysis and feedback, your design team can revisit the explorations and combine the visual elements to create a single look and feel for the product.

ADULT PERSONAS AND DEVELOPERS

Before moving on to the next stage in the development process, we want to briefly discuss how you can use personas to facilitate your interaction with the most important members of your team—the developers. Developers (and development managers) are extremely powerful members of your organization. They not only hold many political cards but also make thousands of decisions (of all sizes) throughout the development process that directly affect the user experience of the final product. Thus, it is critical that developers really know the personas and keep them in mind as they make these decisions. In Chapter 5, we recommended that you analyze each of the internal users of persona-related information and their various needs. In this section, we provide a few suggestions to address the issues that might arise as you communicate persona information to developers during *adulthood*.

The first step is to make sure developers buy in to the idea of using personas, and one of the keys to doing this is to make sure they understand that your personas are credible—that they are based on data and that the method has led to good results. Your developers do not have to understand every detail of the data behind the personas (though they will likely ask many questions to ensure that the personas are trustworthy and to be able to recognize the critical differences among them). Developers also do not have to understand all of the ways personas can be used across the organization, but they will need to see a few key uses of personas and hear a few success stories from other companies. Finally, they will want to know exactly what they are supposed to do with the personas—preferably some easy ways to use the personas that will save them time.

Make sure that developers are fully introduced to the personas, and make sure that easy-to-use persona materials are at their fingertips. Give them persona posters to hang in their offices. Your developers have to know the basics of who the personas are and what their goals and needs are with respect to the product being built.

It is important to explain how the personas can affect feature decisions through use of the persona-weighted feature matrix, and it is critical to involve developers in the process. If you have used the matrix in your process, it is helpful to remind your developers that your personas helped the entire team make good decisions on *what* to build and that the data behind the personas is always ready to provide the *why* behind these decisions. Once the *what* and *why* are solid, your developers are free to work their magic on the issues surrounding *how* to build the product.

Remind developers that the personas can help them make some of their decisions. If they are trying to choose between two possible directions their code might take, they can consider the personas. Which code decision is more likely to lead to the easy addition of features the personas would like? Be sure to involve developers in the scenario creation and design mapping process. Make sure your developers have access to these scenarios as they do their work. Furthermore, encourage your developers to create their own walkthrough scenarios as needed to understand the experience they are creating as a result of their work.

If nothing else, personas allow developers to ruminate on such things as, "When Tanner tries to initiate a download from this page, he will." This is a big deal! Even just using the names means that they are using the personas and that they are relating their work decisions to a representation of the user—one that is clear, shared, and based on real data. Your developers will begin to be user centered instead of technology centered. Of course, your developers can use personas more explicitly by employing them in design evaluation, which we cover in the next section.

When there are changes during the course of development (and there will be), the personas can provide the objective voices that should matter most—and this is just as helpful to the development staff as it is to anyone else on the team. They are very helpful as "data-driven justifications" when difficult decisions need to be made. "Tanner needs this feature or he'll never understand how to create an account" is a much more powerful argument than "We're just doing it."

Many of us have been in situations in which suddenly, in the middle of a project, someone decides that there needs to be a new feature added to the product. Perhaps the feature is critical to the success of the product and perhaps it is not, but without good data and personas it is usually a political and opinion-based decision whether to include the new feature. Developers often end up in the middle of these debates by having to explain schedule costs and technical difficulties related to new features. Remind developers that the personas contain a lot of detailed data about the target customers and users of the product, and encourage them to remember the needs of the personas as they participate in debates such as these. Better yet, try to get a persona representative invited to development meetings. New feature X could be a huge sprawling feature, or perhaps it could be a tiny simplified feature. Developers or the persona representative can use the persona descriptions to extrapolate the extent of new feature requirements based on the technical needs.

Finally, if you have trouble getting the development team to use the personas, remember that this is not an end in itself. Your persona effort is about getting everyone to use the personas, but it is also about changing the ways people within your organization communicate and work together. This is a long-term project that will not happen all at once.

STAGE 3. USE PERSONAS TO EVALUATE YOUR SOLUTIONS

As your team settles in on the features and specific solutions it needs to embrace to create a successful product, your personas can help in honing the implementation of these features toward the very best design. In this section, we show you how to use your personas to help with evaluation of your features and solutions through:

- Cognitive walkthroughs and design reviews with personas
- User testing and ongoing user research with persona profiles
- Quality assurance testing and bug bashes

Use personas in design reviews and cognitive walkthroughs

> If you're seeing things through the eyes of a persona, instead of the eyes of a person who's been designing Web sites, it rewires you temporarily.
> —**Christina Wodtke, *Information Architecture: Blueprints for the Web***

Your personas are not done when they have finished helping specify and design the product. They are still raring to go, ready to help you ensure that the product works as it should and is not difficult to use. The personas allow you to get the perspective you need as you review designs and prototypes. Because you will never be a truly objective reviewer of your own product, the personas can help you discover and evaluate problem areas in your design, even before you do usability testing and beta releases with real users. Earlier, we recommended that you conduct competitive analyses using the personas to walk through the user experiences of your competitors' products. You can use the same basic methods now to evaluate the designs you have come up with for your product.

151

There are several formal evaluation methods commonly known to UCD professionals. Two of these are *heuristic evaluation* and *cognitive walkthrough* (Nielsen and Molich, 1990; Wharton et al., 1994; Spencer, 2000). Less formally, these are known as *usability inspections* or *expert reviews* (Nielsen and Mack, 1994). At the core of these techniques is the idea that someone on the development team should step through the product (or portions of the product such as individual features) and reflect on the user experience. Would users know what to do at this point? Would users know that they have made a correct choice?

Design reviews and cognitive walkthroughs are usually done through the eyes of the user, though many times the user is never made explicit or specific. This is where personas can play a part. Personas can serve as the specific user when doing an expert review or cognitive walkthrough. These walkthroughs can be done alone or in group settings. The process for conducting a walkthrough with personas is much like that described earlier in this chapter regarding competitive analysis with personas, except that the focus is your own prototypes or beta product. Rather than recreate that process here, we suggest that you revisit the "Analyze Your Competition Through the Eyes of Your Personas" section and read the example provided below by Joshua Seiden in his "Story from the Field."

Finally, note that it can be helpful to physically act out the actions of the persona with the interface. We referred to this earlier in the chapter regarding scenario-based design. Here, we are recommending it more as an aid in evaluating designs than as an exploratory tool for innovation and insight. This is along the lines of what Salvador and Howells (1998) described as a "focus troupe," in which dramatic vignettes are acted out for evaluation by end users and internal stakeholders.

STORY FROM THE FIELD

Persona-Based Expert Review: A Technique for Usefulness and Usability Evaluation
—**Joshua Seiden, President and Founder,** *Thirtysix Partners*

I've found that personas provide significant benefits during expert review. Personas can function to create a context for the evaluation—the context required to do a meaningful review. Personas also allow reviewers to assess the usefulness of the product, not simply its usability. Persona-based review is a relatively simple technique. You simply perform the evaluation from the personas' perspective and make note of problems as you find them.

Typically, persona-based review can be used in three contexts. It can be used as a rapid evaluation tool. In this case, a persona-based review can take as little as an hour or two. It can be used as a more formal review tool, in which case reviewers may spend a few days researching and modeling and another day or two performing the evaluation. Finally, it may be used as part of a larger design effort to evaluate existing products once a significant research and modeling effort has been undertaken or to evaluate proposed design solutions following that effort.

An Example

I used the method in a recent project—a persona-based expert review to complete a diagnostic review of a website used to make reservations at a popular New York hotel. On this project, my team had no research budget—typical for projects that employ "discount usability" methods. As such, all of our research consisted of a series of e-mail exchanges with project stakeholders. Through our discount research, we generated four personas:

- Our guidebook user, Jurgen, lives in Germany, found our hotel in a guidebook, and accessed the site over a dial-up line. And, though his English is passable, he prefers using the Internet to having an English-language telephone conversation, especially if he can avoid long-distance charges.
- Our package user, John, saw an ad in the local newspaper for a romance package the hotel offers. John lives in New Jersey and likes the idea of bringing his fiancée to the city for a romantic

weekend. He'd like to book a forthcoming weekend and is not particularly date sensitive—any weekend in the next month would work for him—but he is very concerned with the details of the room. Will it really make for the perfect romantic weekend?

- Tim is a Knicks fan who lives in the suburbs and often stays at the hotel after seeing a game across the street at the Garden. He has the most mainstream needs: find a room on a specific night.
- Linda lives in Philadelphia and comes to town occasionally to see long-running museum shows on the weekends. She likes to stay at the hotel because it is close to Penn Station. She's less concerned about specific dates and more concerned with cost savings—but not concerned enough to switch to a different hotel.

We then generated between two and four basic context scenarios for each persona. Context scenarios are abstract, technology-free descriptions of a sequence of events involving the persona. They describe the setting in which the persona interacts with the system, the usage pattern, the major steps the persona takes in order to accomplish the goal, and the end result.

These scenarios were selected to give roughly 100% coverage of the functionality each persona would need. So, for example, each persona had a scenario in which they tried to book a room, but each room-booking scenario was slightly different so as to reflect the unique needs of each persona. Tim's scenario simply involved looking for a room on a specific night for which he had Knicks tickets, whereas John's involved looking for a package, previewing dates and rooms available, and looking at the goody list that came with the package.

With our personas and scenarios in place, the evaluation was a simple matter of stepping through the scenarios from the perspective of each persona and noting problems where we found them. To begin, we made a list of our personas and scenarios. With our four personas, we had about 12 scenarios. We selected the most representative first, but the order was not really important.

We found some problems of usefulness almost immediately; for example, package booking is not available online nor is it possible to modify a reservation online. Instead, users have to cancel existing reservations and create new ones. A handful of other significant features were missing that our personas would need in order to satisfy their goals. So the technique paid off right away, identifying a certain class of problems that many usability inspection methods are incapable of finding.

As we found scenarios the reservation engine supported, however, we were able to use the personas' perspectives to identify problems. For example, none of our personas works in the hospitality industry, yet the website uses industry-specific jargon (such as "run-of-house") to identify available rooms. None of our personas would be likely to understand these terms.

The Benefits

Personas provide two major benefits during expert review. First, the personas function as a context for the evaluation. Personas, by their nature, are a more well-defined construct than "the user." Using personas, reviewers are better able to maintain a fixed and appropriately user-centered frame of reference during the review.

The second benefit comes from using personas during task selection. Task selection is the process of deciding which tasks to review. Because software typically supports many possible tasks, it is usually not practical to try to review every task. So task selection becomes an important part of the review. And, as Molich and Jeffries' (2003) Competitive Usability Evaluations (CUE) studies have demonstrated, task selection has a huge impact on the results of any review. In this method, task selection begins not with what the application allows but with what users consider desirable. These desires are expressed in terms of the personas and scenarios. Task selection thus becomes a matter of identifying the tasks that allow the user to complete the high-level scenarios.

Use personas as a recruiting profile for usability testing and market research

With rigorously defined personas in place, you may be tempted to sit back and enjoy the benefits they provide. Personas do bring a strong source of user centricity to your design and development process, but does this mean you no longer need to include real users in the process? Absolutely not. We strongly believe that user research, usability testing, and market research should continue throughout the development cycle if at all possible. Personas can perhaps ease the burden and cost associated with ongoing user research.

Because personas are meant to serve as your product's target audience, they can and should be used as the recruiting profile for participants in any customer research your team endeavors to complete. Interestingly, doing so not only employs the personas in a specific function but also serves as a communication mechanism that can further your team's understanding of who the personas are (see Chapter 5).

The difficulty in using your personas as a recruiting profile lies in determining the essential qualities of your various personas. Your personas will have many characteristics. Some of these characteristics will be critical to the design and implementation of your product; others will not be as critical.

You will need to develop a set of persona screener questions recruiters can use to find representative participants for your research. To do this, it is helpful to return to your original skeletons of your personas to help determine these essential qualities. Create a draft list of about 10 to 15 characteristics for each persona. Prioritize the list of characteristics, and attempt to remove those that are not truly important to your business or product domain. Be prepared to make compromises in your recruiting requirements, as cost and timeliness are hugely affected by the number of questions asked when screening potential participants. Remember that every question in your screener will eliminate a large population of potential participants. Be willing to make decisions such as, "The 'Tanners' can be either boys or girls as long as they spend 10 hours a week playing some type of electronic game."

It is important to remember that some of your persona details relate directly to data and some are based on assumptions. It is important that you keep close track of which persona attributes are tied to data and which arose from assumptions throughout the development process. This is particularly critical as you apply the persona descriptions as test participant screeners; see "Handy Detail: Ad Hoc Persona Users—Beware Assumption Snowballs!" below.

Now, turn each characteristic into a question that can be easily asked, understood by a potential candidate, and easily answered. Preferably, each question will have a bounded set of potential responses. The following is an example:

- Which of the following activities have you participated in within the past six months?
  a. Surfing the web to compare products and prices
  b. Downloading media (music, photos, video)
  c. Downloading software (games, utilities, and so on)
  d. Posting on an Internet bulletin board or blog
  e. Creating a web page

For each question, determine the criteria that qualify an answer as fitting your persona. In the previous example, a respondent doing three or more activities might indicate a moderately engaged web surfer. (For a further example, see the G4K case study in Appendix C.)

Your goal is to be able to unambiguously tell whether any potential candidate is a good match to one of your personas without taxing the recruiting process with too many questions and options. Amazingly, and even with a very reduced set of recruiting criteria, as you begin to use these participants in focus groups, user tests, field studies, survey panels, and the like, you will readily see their similarity to your personas. We have had team members observe user tests and come away saying such things as, "Wow, that person is such a 'Tanner'!"

As part of the process, it is extremely useful to analyze, categorize, and report your findings by persona. For example, "The 'Tanners' in this study had a difficult time with the registration process, whereas the 'Colbis' breezed right through it." As mentioned earlier, doing so serves to enrich your team's knowledge of your personas and gives them a useful mechanism for understanding and interpreting complex user data.

HANDY DETAIL

Ad Hoc Persona Users—Beware Assumption Snowballs!

Some of you may be using ad hoc personas instead of data-driven personas. Ad hoc personas can help everyone communicate better and make good design decisions, but they should not be treated the same way as data-driven personas. For example, if you recruit usability test participants who closely match your ad hoc-driven personas, you may be artificially biasing your usability results. If it turns out that some of the assumptions built into your personas were wrong, you will have no way of knowing this until you launch your finished product.

Assumption snowballs can still happen even if your personas **are** based on data. Consider Tanner, our tenacious tinkerer. Perhaps one of the developers notices that his own kids, who share some things in common with Tanner, talk of nothing but downloading MP3s. This developer makes the assumption that Tanner must also be obsessed with downloading music, and he begins to talk about Tanner accordingly. After several meetings, everyone begins to think that Tanner downloads a lot of music.

If people start to think that Tanner likes to download music, but they don't seem to be interpreting this extra detail as a reason to rethink all of the product features, you may not have a problem at all. In this case, remember that the purpose of the personas is to build and maintain focus on your users and you still have that.

Once it is time to do usability testing, however, what if this detail finds its way into the participant recruiting documents? You find yourself looking for 9-year-old test participants who download a lot of MP3s, and with some effort you find them. You proceed with your testing and make design changes based on the results. That is fine, right?

Not necessarily. The description of Tanner as a frequent MP3 downloader is flawed, and it could have biased your test results and therefore the design changes you recommended. As it turns out, data show that kids don't tend to get interested in downloading music until they are a little older, and that 9-year-old boys tend to be more interested in games than they are in music. Because you tested a population of kids who download a lot of music, you may have inadvertently made design changes biased toward a very unusual group of users who are a lot less like Tanner than you would have liked them to be.

So, what do you do? You certainly cannot collect data on every aspect of your personas' personalities. However, you and your core team can keep a careful eye on the ways the personas are referenced in product-related documentation. There will inevitably be details that are added to the personas by people not on the core team. It is your job to decide whether these details are likely to veer the product off in the wrong direction. Including the MP3 detail in the usability participant recruiting requirements was a mistake because it was based entirely on assumptions. The resulting design changes would build on this initial mistake, creating a classic assumption snowball that will be difficult to undo.

If you use ad hoc personas, you can avoid assumption snowballs, but you and your core team have to stay on your toes. Every time you decide to use one of the tools in this book, carefully consider which persona attributes are safe to employ. When you create a persona-weighted feature matrix, note where there are debates on the score to give a particular feature for a particular persona, and try to resolve the debate with data if at all possible. When you create a recruiting profile for usability participants, remember that you are narrowing in on a small population of potential users, and stick to generic attributes of your personas (such as age and skill level). Consider creating a value for each of your persona attributes (according to how data driven it is) during the *conception and gestation* phase. When you see an assumption snowball forming, convene your core team and treat the situation as a communication problem. Revisit Chapter 5 for ideas on how to recommunicate the correct persona attributes.

You cannot stop your coworkers from making new assumptions that may or may not be appropriate. What you can do is carefully assess which details of your persona descriptions are data driven enough to drive design decisions.

155

Use personas to focus quality assurance testing and to create test cases

A major part of any development effort revolves around quality assurance (QA). Those on your team responsible for this (generally referred to as "testers" in software development) have a huge job in front of them. They make your product work as designed and intended. To do their job, testers attempt to break the product. They find bugs in the code, clarify the conditions in which those bugs occur, and partner with developers to get the bugs fixed.

Quality assurance teams are often desperate to stay in the loop as product decisions are made, and this isn't always easy to do. Like usability testing, QA is still too often seen as a final, relatively disjointed, step in the development process. Personas and scenarios can communicate critical context, summarize decisions, and clarify product requirements more clearly than most other product development materials. Therefore, they are wonderful resources for the QA team.

We recommend training the entire QA team on the persona process. They will likely see this as an extension of their skills and probably enjoy it as well as obtain information that will help make their test plans more solid. In addition, consider that in the end QA directors have the final power to hold a product up if they consider it unreliable or lacking in performance.

Provide your QA team with the complete set of personas and all supporting data materials. Help them understand that the personas not only represent expected user goals but also contain important information about the context in which the completed product will be used. For example, Tanner's persona profile contains information about the type of computer he uses, the way he accesses the Internet, and so on, and this information is based on real data about the target customer base. Such specificity can help the QA team create product- and market-appropriate test plans.

Use personas and scenarios to inform test cases

The QA team's job is huge because the possible test cases (the scenarios, paths through the product, configurations, and states in which the user could put themselves and cause the code to break) increase exponentially as the size of the code base and the number of product features increase. With many software products, it is virtually impossible to test all possible scenarios and configurations. Personas, like scenario-based design techniques, can help this situation by providing testers with a mechanism for paring test cases down to a reasonable number. The personas serve as criteria by which to judge usage plausibility, likelihood, and frequency of occurrence—and by extension the importance of certain test cases.

The QA test scenarios can be informed or derived from the scenarios used for product design. The scenarios you have already built as part of the planning and design process contain a wealth of information about your expectations for the behavior and affordances of the final product. The QA team can create tests that will help to ensure that the product does perform as expected.

Conduct a persona bug bash

Personas can be utilized to focus less rigorous, but important, "bug bashes." Bug bashes are loosely organized teamwide strolls through the product in search of code bugs, user experience issues, and fit-and-finish problems (typos, visual flaws, redraw issues, slow performance, and so on). They sometimes include non-test-team members (developers, technical writers, program managers, designers, and so on).

To involve the personas, simply divide the bug bash participants into teams, one team per persona. Each team then reviews the persona descriptions and related scenarios and attempts to use the product as if they were the personas reporting bugs as they come across them. After some period of time has elapsed (e.g., four hours on a Friday afternoon), the bugs are counted and evaluated, removing duplicates and nonreproducible issues. The results are then communicated back to the QA team per persona (e.g., "We found 23 'Tanner' bugs and 45 'Colbi' bugs"). Our experience in doing this has been quite positive. The bash participants enjoyed the challenge of trying to use the product as someone else and felt that the quality and types of bugs uncovered were good.

Remember the persona-weighted feature matrix

Finally, note that the persona-weighted feature matrix should be incredibly useful to the QA team. Make sure you schedule time to introduce the team to the matrix, how it was built, and how to interpret its content. Collaborate with the QA team as they decide on and build their test cases. This gives you the opportunity to ensure that the testing focus corresponds to the feature priorities expressed in the matrix.

STAGE 4. USE PERSONAS TO SUPPORT THE RELEASE OF YOUR PRODUCT

Now that your product is getting close to being complete, it is time to turn your attention to details that are not directly related to product development. You have put a great deal of effort into creating and using your personas to design and build your product. Now that the product is almost complete, your personas (and all of the persona-related materials and tools you have created) can be extremely helpful to those responsible for documenting, supporting, and selling your product. In this section, we show you how to you apply your personas toward:

- Documentation, training, and product support materials
- Marketing and sales

Personas can help focus instructional materials, guidebooks, and editorial content

The documentation and product support team is under the gun to produce highly accurate and useful materials that will help real people understand and use the features you are busy building. While the core development team is still writing code, making final decisions, and seeing changes happen, the documentation team is frantic to begin writing so they can meet their deadlines. Everyone on the development team is usually too busy to take much time to give the documentation team the detailed information they need.

Personas and their associated scenarios can help technical writers understand how a product works and who will be using it. Writers can examine the personas and determine which types of editorial, training, and support materials will be most useful to each persona. Scenarios serve as a ready-made list of tasks that must be explained in the support materials that technical writers create. Scenarios will allow writers to understand the "story" of the product and the expected behavior of features and functions long before coding is complete. Alan Cooper and his associates have also noted the role personas can play in the creation of user documentation. Their online article, "Using Personas to Create User Documentation," by Steve Calde, provides several useful tips on applying personas in this way (http://www.cooper.com/journal/2004/12/using_personas_to_create_user.html).

Audience analysis is a well-known concept for the professional writing community (see, for example, Thralls et al., 1988). Clearly, such analysis can be used to guide content selection, organization, and presentation and style. Coney and Steehouder (2000) explored the application of rhetorical theory to persona usage in product and interaction design. They argued that not only readers but also users can actually assume the role of the persona

158

USER PROFILE: BUSINESS BROWSERS

John Fix III

Demographic: Male, 42, married

Occupation: Retail hardware store owner

Personality traits: Friendly, inquisitive, generous

Online habits and behaviors: "I log on every day, numerous times each day for an average of about two hours per day. I have DSL at home, and a T1 connection at work. Work is noisy—it's a busy office—but at home it's quiet, because the PC is in a home office away from the television."

Web history: "I've been using the Web regularly since 1995, but using Internet e-mail since about 1992."

Favorite Web sites: www.theonion.com, ESPN.com, DejaNews.com

Usability pet peeves: Animated ads, pop-ups, code that disables the back button

How do you search? "On a Web site, I usually look for a search option if the item or information I'm looking for isn't immediately visible. I try not to get distracted by other info on the site. I use the back button all the time, usually via the mouse button (I use an MS Intellimouse Explorer)."

What are your typical online goals? "Hmmm, depends on what I'm doing. If it's something work-related, I want to get the info and then get back with my customer or employee. It's made things like finding product information for my hardware store much easier."

FIGURE 6.25
Ilise Benun begins each chapter in *Designing Websites for Every Audience* (2003) with a persona profile.

put forth in an article, website, or software product. In this case, personas can take on a rhetorical role.

As an example, in her book *Designing Websites for Every Audience*, Ilise Benun (2003) used personas in a very direct and explicit fashion to organize the content of the book. Each chapter begins with a unique persona description to set the focus and tone of the subsequent materials (as shown in Figure 6.25).

You can use your personas to create training materials that incorporate the details of their knowledge, goals, and work habits. Imagine bringing your product into a company that has

 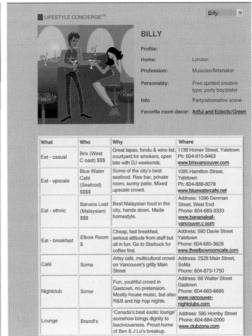

FIGURE 6.26
Opus Hotel concierges (http://www.opushotel.com/services_concierge.html).

been using an older product or process for a long time. Because of your early research to inform your personas, you should know quite a bit about what how they currently get their work done. Your personas and scenarios embody the changes you are expecting in real users' work patterns now that your new product exists.

In addition, you might even consider showing your personas directly to your learners, explaining how they relate to the goals and tasks your product supports. In this way, your personas can literally show your real users what they can accomplish in relation to your product. Although we think that such direct exposure of your personas is not always appropriate or necessary, it is an interesting way to engage your target users.

Using personas in any of the ways described previously requires that your team really understand detailed aspects of how they will use your product, discover its features, and learn its interface and idiosyncrasies. You may need to expand your persona descriptions to include relevant information for your documentation team.

Personas can tailor marketing and sales efforts

Because the marketing and sales teams are not always directly on the development team, they often have to struggle to stay in the loop. During the development process, decisions are made at such a fast pace that no one, even development team members, can keep accurate track of all of them—to say nothing of how each decision will affect the experience of the people who will have to learn about and use the product you are building. During this creative chaos, the marketing team needs to understand enough about what is being built to create materials that will help your company sell the product. These materials should neither radically over- or under-promise features and functionality.

The personas and their associated scenarios can provide the common language between the busy development team and the marketing team. The personas are what these teams can have in common. While developers are busy creating features for the personas, marketing teams are trying to figure out how to sell to them.

In Chapter 11, "Marketing Versus Design Personas," by Robert Barlow-Busch, in our original book *The Persona Lifecycle: Keeping People in Mind Throughout Product Design*, Robert Barlow-Busch provides excellent coverage of using personas for marketing purposes. One specific approach he describes is the "brand ladder." It is a method for explicitly connecting your personas to both your product and your brand.

Like your documentation team, your marketing team may choose to expose the personas as part of a marketing effort. For example, as shown in Figure 6.26, the Opus Hotel website uses user profiles that look very much like personas directly in their user interface (as a part of their website front end). Visitors to the site can select from one of four individual personas ("Billy," "Susan," "Mike," and "Dede") and a couple persona ("Bob and Carol") to serve as their personal concierges (http://www.opushotel.com/services_concierge.html). The inclusion of these profiles helps communicate directly to potential customers who this hotel caters to while positioning itself as the hub for a wide range of activities.

REMEMBER TO DIFFERENTIATE BETWEEN USERS AND CUSTOMERS

Although your personas may represent both your users and your customers, there are situations in which this is not the case. Sometimes the people who will purchase your product are not the same people who will be using it on a daily basis. For example, managers and IT professionals in an organization often make command decisions about what software everyone in the office will use. Although these people are not the intended users of the product, they are critical to the success of the product because they make the purchasing decisions. Likewise, influencers—including market analysts, pundits, and reviewers—can make or break a product before it gets to the purchaser or customer.

Marketing professionals are usually highly sensitized to this distinction and should be able to tell you exactly who your personas represent in this constellation of users, purchasers, and influencers. For small, highly specialized products, the three roles could be occupied by the same person. For large products, the roles almost certainly could *not*. Of course, we believe that personas are a good way of representing users, and they can be a highly effective tool when you explore the differences among the users of your product, purchasers, and influencers. You now have very specific portraits of your users in your personas, and the marketers in your organization should be able to quickly create alternative assumption personas for representing purchasers and influencers.

If you don't distinguish between the users and the potential purchasers of the product, you might run into a problem we think of as the "persona identity crisis." If your organization does buy in to the personas wholeheartedly, make sure they understand that the personas can represent users and purchasers specifically. If the marketing team adopts the personas and builds all of the marketing materials to appeal to the personas, they may actually do the company a disservice—especially if the purchasers of the product are very different people with very different needs. For an excellent discussion of this topic, see Chapter 11, "Marketing Versus Design Personas," by Robert Barlow-Busch, in *The Persona Lifecycle*.

TRANSITIONING INTO LIFETIME ACHIEVEMENT, REUSE, AND RETIREMENT

You have been diligent during your persona campaign, and in return your personas have kept your product team focused and on track throughout the development cycle. As your product goes to market, adulthood for your personas is coming to a close. If your company or product team is like many companies in the industry, you are already beginning to think about the next version of your product. You may be tempted to jump right back into adulthood again, without re-examining your target audience. And why not just do that? You created some great personas and supporting materials, and your team knows these personas and exactly how to use them. Your team probably thought of the personas as helpful and appropriate and are happy to just keep focusing on them. However, before diving into product version 2 and a second persona *adulthood* phase, you will need to ask yourself and your team a few questions. Were all of this time, money, and energy worth it? Was your end product good? Was your decision making better, faster? It is time to validate your efforts.

Perhaps more important, you will need to think again about why your team would build another version of your product. Does the current version satisfy your users? Has the market changed, or your competition? Will your target audience change? In relation to that change, will your personas retire from use? Can you reuse some of their content? These questions and many others are explored in Chapter 7.

SUMMARY

An overriding message of this chapter is that *adulthood* is key. If you have not come to this conclusion yet, you will once you attempt your first persona effort. Personas cannot just be "thrown over the wall" once *family planning, conception and gestation*, and *birth and maturation* are done. You will have to keep track of them like you would any employee. You will need to make sure they know what to do and ensure that they are actually doing it. Identifying and providing specific uses for your personas go a long way toward making that happen. Hundreds of decisions are being made every day by your product team as they plan, build, and promote your product. They can make those decisions with your target customers in mind or without them. Much of the time, such decisions are made via implicit assumptions, known only to the single decision maker. Personas can help your product team be user centered. They can take part in those decisions to make the implicit become explicit. They can help move an entire team in a user-focused direction.

How personas are used depends greatly on where you are in the development cycle, as well as on who is using them. Early on, executives are interested in the bigger picture, the product vision, as well as competitive marketplace, product marketing, messaging, and positioning. They are also interested in cost of development and time to market. Program managers and product planners are interested in defining functionality (i.e., features and user interfaces). Usability specialists are interested in scenarios and tasks, participant recruitment, interaction issues, and products that are useful, usable, fun, and good sellers. Interaction designers are interested in user interfaces, format behaviors, inflection, and style. Once things get moving, developers (programmers) are interested in architecture, implementation, and work resourcing. A little later, QA testers are interested in bugs, crashes, test scripts, and edge cases. Technical writers (user assistance/education) are interested in the documentation development process, documenting the application, and being in the loop with program managers, designers, and developers. And, finally, once the product is nearing release, the marketing, sales, and support folks are eager to work their magic to make the product a business success.

You can use some or all of the tools presented in this chapter to ensure that your personas provide the right information to the right people at the right time—so that ultimately you end up building the right product!

Each tool provides a different utility and helps different team members at the appropriate time in the development cycle. Again, the most important thing to remember here is that you are not done once your personas have been created. The real effort and payoff occur throughout the development cycle.

We believe there are many more persona tools out there waiting to be created or already in use. It is important to understand what your team needs and how knowledge about target users can be a part of that. Be creative and flexible in employing your personas. Your team will likely find that personas are not only useful and informative but also fun and inspiring.

CHAPTER 7

Persona lifetime achievement, reuse, and retirement

WHAT ARE LIFETIME ACHIEVEMENT, REUSE, AND RETIREMENT FOR PERSONAS?

The complete persona lifecycle positions your persona team as the "first-in/last-out" members of the product development team. You will be first in as you collect and express data about target user populations to your executive team to support their strategic work. You will be last out as you help manage the transition from the end of one project to the beginning of the next. In this sense, this last phase of the persona lifecycle is both critical and too often ignored.

For a variety of reasons, persona efforts tend to peter out rather than end in a managed, measured, and organized manner. Consultants are usually not paid to stick around long enough to manage the personas at the end of a project, and in-house teams are usually more concerned with ramping up for the next project than they are with tidying up loose ends from the previous one. Being first-in/last-out on projects means that you will probably end up with responsibilities that straddle two projects. You will be completing your work on project A even after you have begun your work on project B. That is no simple task. It is certainly easier to simply move on to project B; however, we argue that an organized approach to measuring and managing the end of a project can yield significant benefits.

The final persona lifecycle phase is about measurement, regaining control of the persona effort as a whole, and preparing for the future. As the leader of your persona core team, you have two primary tasks at the end of your persona effort:

- Measure the lifetime achievement of your personas (their value), including the return on investment (ROI) of the persona effort.
- Manage the organization's transition to a new project with regard to user-centered design (UCD) and target audiences, which will involve reusing, retiring, or in some way reincarnating your personas.

In this chapter, we cover both of these topics in depth.

STEP 1. MEASURE THE RETURN ON INVESTMENT OF YOUR PERSONA EFFORT

One of the most common questions we are asked about personas is if they actually work. And, if they do, how can you tell if they were worth the effort? Answering these questions is difficult. What counts as proof of the method is different for different people, products, and companies. There is no single case study or research study that proves their effectiveness rigorously; however, as you have seen, examples of their effectiveness and value are scattered about the industry. This is why this section includes so many stories from the field describing success stories from persona practitioners.

Measure the ROI of the persona effort

The work you do during this phase to prove the ROI of the persona effort, both quantitatively and qualitatively, will empower you as you continue to introduce user-centered methods into your organization. Now is your chance to help your organization understand why it was so critically important to understand users and their goals before diving into product design or redesign (and thus why your work as a user-experience professional is valuable). In the most recent edition of *Cost-Justifying Usability* (Bias and Mayhew, Eds., 2005), contributors Wilson and Rosenbaum refer to three distinct measures of ROI:

- *External ROI*—Measurable ways UCD work helped make the company money
- *Internal ROI*—Measurable process improvements and savings in the organization
- *Social ROI*—Perception that the UCD team and their methods were helpful during product development, whether or not this helpfulness is measurable

We think this is a helpful way of thinking about the ROI of personas, because we believe personas can help you create a product that is likely to:

- Be more successful and require fewer support costs (bottom-line improvements)
- Help you streamline your design and development efforts (process improvements)
- Improve the way your company communicates about and focuses on your users

You will see that these three topics are major themes in this chapter.

The work you did during the family planning phase will help you measure ROI

Earlier, we recommended that, during the *family planning* phase of the persona lifecycle (see Chapter 3), you do some "organizational introspection" to understand current product- and process-related problems you might be able to solve with your persona effort. In addition to identifying ways in which your products could be more user centered, we suggested that you ask the following questions:

- How user focused is your company?
- How does your organization think and communicate about users?

Questions you asked during *family planning*	Questions you will ask during *lifetime achievement*
What resources do we have for personas and other UCD activities?	How much did the persona effort actually cost?
What product problems do we want to solve with personas?	Has the product improved? How much, and in what ways?
What process problems do we want to solve with personas?	Has the process improved? In what ways?
How can we ensure that the personas will be accepted and used by our colleagues?	Were personas perceived as helpful? Has the company's focus on users improved? In what ways?

FIGURE 7.1

The work you did during the family planning phase is highly related to what you will do to assess the lifetime achievement of your personas.

- How is user information incorporated into the product design and development process?

As shown in Figure 7.1, the work you did during the family planning phase is highly related to what you will do to assess the lifetime achievement of your personas. If you can apply quantitative values to the answers, you can illustrate the ROI of your personas.

It is time to decide whether or not you satisfied the goals you established in your action plan. You will need to go a bit deeper than just stating whether or not you met your goals. If you did satisfy some (or, even better, all!) of the goals in your action plan, you can work to express the benefits of achieving these goals in quantitative and qualitative terms. We believe you can express the full range of persona-related ROI by answering the following questions:

- How much did your persona effort cost?
- In what measurable ways did the personas improve your product? (related to Bias and Mayhew's external ROI)
- In what measurable ways did the personas improve your design and development processes? (related to Bias and Mayhew's internal ROI)
- Is your company more user centered with personas than it was before? (related to Bias and Mayhew's social ROI)

Consider these four questions while looking back at the resources and goals your team identified for your persona effort during *family planning*.

STEP 2. DECIDE HOW TO MANAGE THE TRANSITION TO THE NEXT PROJECT

During the final phase of the persona lifecycle, you will not only measure the value of your personas but also decide what to do with them as you move on to your next project. So far, most of the content of this book has been about how to create personas and keep them alive. Now it is time to reconsider the personas you have created as you transition to a new project, which could mean helping your colleagues to *forget* the personas. Persona are easy to remember and easy to empathize with, which makes them great when you need them and tough to send packing when the time comes to move on to a new project.

In most cases, you will decide to use some combination of direct *reuse* (using them again without alteration), *reincarnation* (using them again without alteration), and *retirement* (discarding or completely replacing some of the personas). If your persona effort has been a success, retirement and reincarnation can be a bit tricky. To make room for the next set of personas, you will need to help your organization let go of the personas they have come to know so well.

Reclaim ownership and control of your personas

During the *adulthood* phase, you relinquished control of your personas to a certain extent. You sent them out into your organization to do the work they were born to do. People have been using (or not using) them, and your ownership of the personas has probably become a bit hazy. It is a good thing to allow and encourage others to feel ownership of the personas during *adulthood*, but it is time for you to step in again as your product is completed and you begin the transition to the next project.

Evaluate your data. Are the data still valid for the next project?

Before you decide what to do with your personas, you need to revisit the data sources you used to create them. If you are about to start work on the next version of the product you have just released, it is likely that many (but probably not all) of your data sources are still relevant and you can reuse entire personas or some of the information in the personas. If you are moving on to create a completely different product or if there have been major shifts in strategy, perhaps only a few of the data sources (e.g., those that relate to your company or to the general product space in which you work) may still be relevant. Review your original data sources to determine:

- Are the data still up-to-date? As a rule of thumb, if the research you conducted to inform your personas is more than a few years old, you should consider collecting new data.
- Has your product or customer domain changed so much that the data are no longer relevant?
- What *portions* of the existing data are still relevant?

As you review your data sources, also keep an eye out for factoids you did not use originally but which may be relevant in your next project. In addition, take the time to see what new information is available since you created the personas, and work with your team to integrate the new data into the existing personas.

Decide to reuse, reincarnate, or retire your personas

Once you have decided how much of your old data is appropriate for your new project, you are ready to decide how to retire or reuse your personas. In our experience, there are three possibilities:

- Reuse existing personas intact and promote or demote them (from primary to secondary, and *vice versa*) as appropriate for your next project.
- Reincarnate your personas by reusing some or all of the data, incorporating new data, and creating new or significantly updated personas.
- Retire your personas and start over.

REUSING YOUR PERSONAS

If you are building a new version of your product, or a new product for the same audience, you might find that many of your personas can be reused. Your personas could be reused by the same team that used them originally, by a new design and development team, or perhaps by a team in some other part of your company, such as marketing, sales, or product support.

When you created your personas, you assimilated your data, created persona skeletons, prioritized the skeletons, and built some or all of the skeletons into full personas. When you move on to the next version of your product, you can reevaluate the primary versus secondary classification for each of your original personas. You might decide to demote one of your primary personas and promote one of your secondary personas. This promotion/demotion is especially useful if you are building a new version of the same project but your company has decided to focus on a slightly different user base. In addition, you can revisit some of the persona skeletons you created but never developed for the first project. It is possible that one of these would be just right for the new project. If so, you have a tremendous head start and can simply build up the skeleton into a full persona.

REINCARNATING YOUR PERSONAS (REUSING SOME OR ALL OF YOUR DATA)

Even if your original set of personas is no longer relevant as you move onto your next project, some of the original data are often reusable. We like to think of this data reuse as either *reincarnating* or *evolving* your personas. Reincarnation describes the reuse of key data in a new persona. Evolution describes significant changes to existing personas, usually in logical, meaningful ways.

REINCARNATING PERSONAS

If some of the data in your personas are still relevant, but the personas you originally created are not, you can create reincarnated personas by reusing some of the data in new personas. If the products you develop serve users in a specific market segment or industry, you will find many data sources that stay relevant no matter what project you are working on. If the data sources are still relevant but the particular personas you have created are not, it is important to do some research and find some additional data sources.

Once you have collected the appropriate set of data (which will include sources you have already used), you can revisit the processes described in Chapter 4 and reassimilate data points according to the issues you are finding related to your new project.

As you create your reincarnated set of personas, be aware that many of the people who used the original set of personas probably did not have a thorough knowledge of all details in the foundation documents. Some of your colleagues may only know the persona names and a few basic details about each.

If the new personas you create out of data you are reusing are different only in very particular details, it might be difficult for your colleagues to understand why you are using new personas at all. On the other hand, if your colleagues did not know the first set of personas very well, they may not be aware that many of the details in the two persona sets are similar. As you introduce your new set of personas, try to find ways of making them more engaging and of clearly communicating the details critical to the product design. In addition, make sure that the important differences between the reincarnated personas and the original personas are clearly communicated, and not just in the long foundation documents. Even summaries of personas built from reincarnated data sources usually benefit from statements such as, "Unlike 'Mary' [the original persona], 'Ginny' never telecommutes. Her boss simply won't let her."

RETIRING YOUR PERSONAS

You might decide that you do not want to reuse or reincarnate your personas or their underlying data at all. There are many reasons to *retire* personas before moving on to the next project:

- The current project is significantly different from the last project.
- The users' goals have changed.
- Your company adopted a new strategy or is targeting a different user base.

- There are significant changes to the environment in which your product will be used, such as new technologies or new competitive products that have changed the landscape (e.g., the advent of streaming media and broadband in the home, or Bluetooth® technology for computing).

When you determine that a persona or set of personas is no longer relevant, it is a good idea to officially retire the personas before moving on. Why officially? Why not just take down the posters and start working on a new set of personas? Because if you have done your job well, you have made the personas incredibly memorable and all your work has paid off. People in your organization have absorbed various amounts of information about the primary personas and are accustomed to thinking about them. If you try to introduce a new set of personas on top of an old set you run the risk of confusing your team, which will destroy the clarity personas are supposed to provide.

You cannot reach into your colleagues' heads and erase everything they know about the personas you have been using, but you have to find a way of helping them move past the old personas and let go of the (no longer relevant) information they contain. This can be as simple as an e-mail announcement that the old set of personas is retiring (including why). If you are moving on to a totally different product or a new strategy, most of your colleagues would know about the switch, and the retirement announcement will make sense to them. Use this as an opportunity to invite feedback from the team on the ways personas helped or did not help them do their jobs. You can use this feedback to tweak your customized persona lifecycle the next time around.

Alternatively, you could plan for a richer persona retirement experience. Consider persona *retirement* an opportunity and excuse to celebrate the end of the project with your team. Create new posters that describe the ways the personas are using the newly completed product. You might even want to bring your persona models so you can take pictures of them using the product or even invite them in person to a retirement celebration. Plan to follow up over the following months with short updates from the old personas, describing their use of the product and perhaps even the problems they are having with it (which you can easily gather from your product support team). If there are other celebratory activities at the end of the project (such as a team dinner or some other activity), you can include some fun persona-related activities, including:

- Give prizes to colleagues who gave up pet features for the sake of personas.
- Reward developers who have said things such as, "I did it for 'Helen'!" or, "Bob would never use that."
- Recognize the people who suggested or implemented a successful new feature based on a persona's needs.
- Describe product successes based on personas. ("We have had over 100 e-mails from 'Lauras' who love these new features.")
- Invite your team to self-congratulate for using personas (self-congratulation is very motivating!) and end the project and persona effort with a flourish. Help your colleagues remember the persona-related work as fun and something to look forward to in the next project. Personas are supposed to be engaging, helpful, and perhaps even stress relieving, so it is a good idea to associate personas with fun.

SUMMARY

User-centered designers will face the task of proving their own worth for the foreseeable future, and part of this challenge is to quantify the value of the work we do. User-centered designers have to start thinking about new projects long before anyone else does, and they have to spend some time proving the ROI of UCD methods—especially if the methods are time consuming or expensive. As a rule, the earlier you think about measuring and expressing ROI the better. There are ways to begin measuring ROI during every phase of the persona lifecycle, and we encourage you to use some of the ideas we have included in earlier chapters to develop your own measures.

Well-crafted and appropriately applied personas can yield product and process improvements we can identify and measure to help quantify the value of the persona effort and, more generally, of the UCD process. As you evaluate the ROI of your own efforts, take the opportunity to publicize your successes and analyze reasons for problems or process failures.

The activities we recommend at the end of one project also function to prepare you for the next project. Regaining control over the personas and evaluating the success of the effort will help you be even more successful in your next effort. The lifetime achievement, reuse, and retirement phase provides an excellent opportunity to touch base with your core team members and with other stakeholders to talk about how things went. As you dive back into *family planning* you will want to predict the new issues you will encounter. This final lifecycle phase is a great time to have a postmortem to talk about what improved, stayed the same, or worsened during or due to your persona effort.

Whatever you do during this life phase, make an event of it. Take the opportunity to celebrate accomplishments as you prepare the team for the next project and the next set of personas.

The lifetime achievement, reuse, and retirement phase is the least understood of all of the persona life stages, in part because the persona method is fairly young. People are still just trying to figure out how to get started. We look forward to hearing from more practitioners on how you measure ROI, what becomes of your personas at the end of a project, and how you transition between one project and another as the persona cycle of life begins again.

Ad hoc persona example

COMPANY: ACME PROFESSIONAL ASSOCIATION FOR CPAs

GARY GETTING STARTED
Quote

Yeah, I could build a career being a CPA, but is it the right thing for me? It's been a lot of work to get where I am and maybe it's crazy to change plans now, but I'm already so burned out!

Recommended priority: primary

Gary is exactly who we want to help. If we help him now, he will be loyal to us for the rest of his career. Also, he is radically underserved by other organizations.

MEET GARY

Gary is 25 years old and has been working for a CPA firm for 3 years. He just earned his CPA certification last year, but he's burned out from working too many hours in recent months and is questioning whether he's made the right career choice. When it's not tax season, Gary goes out a couple of nights a week with other young people he works with, but he's met few other people since he moved after college. Even though he theoretically has "flex time," Gary blames his lack of outside involvement on his crazy work hours. Gary is also questioning whether he should be doing something more meaningful with his life, whether within or outside of his career.

Gary's employer chooses the continuing education courses he gets to attend and pays for his professional association memberships. His employer is also encouraging Gary to get involved on boards or in leadership positions outside of the organization to advance his career.

Gary's goals
- I want to figure out what I really want to do with my life.
- If I decide to change careers, I want to figure out what my options are!
- Whatever I end up doing, I want to build it into a career.

- I want my work life to be less overwhelming.
- I want to meet more people … both professionally and socially.
- I want to find some activities to participate in that benefit society at-large and that I can accommodate to my schedule.
- I want discounts on purchases that benefit me personally, rather than professionally.

Gary's questions in his own terms

- Where can I find and interact with people like me?
- Where can I find career and personal development resources?
- Are there value-adds to membership that will benefit me personally?

How we want to answer Gary's questions

- The Acme Society of CPAs is the best place to connect with people like you.
- We have a number of sponsored programs that are fun and will fulfill your community service and personal development goals.
- We have many volunteer opportunities that are flexible enough to work within your time constraints that will support your career development goals.
- We are the best portal to connect you with other discount opportunities to benefit you personally.

What we think Gary should know

(Oh, by the way, did you know we also do *x* and *y* and can be helpful in *a* and *b* ways …?)

- *Even if you decide to change careers*, we're here to help. There are lots of ways the hard work you've done so far can benefit you in other careers.
- The CPA designation positions you well for many career options.
- There are fulfilling careers available for CPAs both in traditional and nontraditional roles.
- We have numerous educational opportunities that will also assist you in fulfilling your goals, available in various formats, including online. You have the opportunity to "try before you buy" by taking an online class without paying (you don't pay until you take the test for credit).

Data-driven persona example

Tanner is an intense 9-year-old boy who loves computers, games, and gadgets of all types. He's an entertainment enthusiast and active gamer. Generally speaking, he just loves to play. Tanner is familiar with G4K game titles and is a likely frequent visitor to the G4K site to seek out new ways to entertain himself. Tanner has significant influence over his parents' spending on family fun. Note from the authors: Tanner was created several years ago, when many of these data sources were relevant. We do not recommend using 'old' data sources when creating new personas.

DESCRIPTION

Tanner, a 9-year-old boy, is a fourth-grade student at Montgomery Elementary School, a public school. He lives with his mother and father (Laura and Shane Thompson) in a suburb of Chicago, Illinois. Tanner has been using computers[1] at school since kindergarten[2] and has had a family computer[3] at home for 2 years. He has been using the Internet[4] in the computer lab at his school[5] for some time but only recently got Internet access[6] at his house (6 months ago through his family's AOL account[7]). Even though Tanner loves to be physically active (riding his skateboard and bike, playing in the yard and nearby creek, participating in organized sports, etc.), Tanner thinks computers are really, really fun and prefers the PC[8] to television.[9] He uses the PC mostly to play games[10] and surf the Web for stuff, but he occasionally does research[11] for school projects. His favorite computer game of the moment is The Sims™ 2,[12] which his uncle gave him for his birthday (his mother and father usually just buy him educational games). He also really likes Moneybags,[13] which he just got for his birthday, and RollerCoaster® Tycoon 3.[14] Since his dad[15] likes computer sports[16] games[17] such as NBA Live 2005,[18] Tanner sometimes play those with him, but[19] it

[1] Computer use begins at an early age. About three-quarters of 5-year-olds use computers, and over 90% of teens (ages 13–17) do so. About 25% of 5-year-olds use the Internet, and this number rises to over 50% by age 9 and to at least 75% by ages 15 to 17 [28].

[2] The youngest students were more likely than older students to report that they used computers at school. In 1996, 72% of fourth graders reported using a computer at school at least once a week, compared to 47% of eighth graders and 50% of 11th graders. However, eighth and eleventh graders were more likely than fourth graders to report using computers every day [12].

[3] One strong incentive for parents to have Internet access is for their children. The vast majority of parents believe that their children need to know about computers and the Internet in order to succeed [20].

[4] Forty-five percent of America's children—or more than 30 million of those under the age of 18—have Internet access. Fully 73% of those between the ages of 12 and 17 have Internet access, and 29% of those under 12 have been online. Eighty-two percent of those living in households with more than $75,000 in income now have Internet access, compared to 38% of those in households earning less than $30,000 [27].

[5] Ninety-five percent of all U.S. public schools had computers with Internet access in 1999. Within those schools, 63% of instructional rooms had computers with Internet access [39].

[6] Parents are more likely to have broadband and wireless Internet access and are more willing to embrace these access capabilities in the future, thereby creating a lucrative market for online service providers [26].

[7] AOL captures about 42% of access market; other ISPs have 37%. Not included in the "other" category are MSN®, EarthLink®, CompuServe®, AT&T™, and Prodigy [41].

[8] Given a choice of six media, one-third of children ages 8 to 17 said that the Web would be the medium they would want to have if they couldn't have any others. Television was picked by 26% of kids, telephone by 21%, and radio by 15% [16].

[9] When they are first beginning to use media, boys and girls spend the same amount of time watching TV, reading, listening to music, and using computers. They develop the same basic media-use skills and do so at roughly the same age. By the time they are in the 4- to 6-year-old range, however, there is a difference between boys and girls when it comes to video games, with boys being more likely to play and to play for longer periods of time [25].

[10] Fifty-two percent of boys ages 9 to 17 play games [11]. Other research has claimed that 90% of U.S. households with children rent or own video or computer games and that U.S. children spend an average of 20 minutes a day playing video games [33].

[11] All of the kids in the G4K home site visits used the Internet for school project research [29]. Also, 29% of 9- to 17-year-olds used the Internet to do their homework [11], and 8.3% of first- to eighth-grade kids used a home computer for school assignments [39].

[12] The Sims 2 was fifth on *Game Developer Magazine*'s list of the top 20 PC first-person action game titles for the week of 2/11/05 [43].

[13] According to internal G4K research, focus groups and sales data show that boys 9 to 11 years old chose to play Moneybags over other G4K titles [18].

[14] RollerCoaster Tycoon 3 was number two on Game Daily Kids' list of the top 20 children's entertainment software titles for the week of 1/05/05 [42].

[15] Of all adults with access to a computer at home, men continued to exhibit marginally higher rates of use than women (72% versus 70%). Considering computer use at any location, there is no longer a gender gap [10].

[16] Three out of four Internet users have sought information about a hobby or interest online. The number of hobby seekers increased by 40% between March 2000 and January 2002—from 65 million to 91 million [21].

[17] Those who have played games online increased by 45%—from 29 million in March 2000 to 42 million in June/July 2002 [21].

[18] NBA Live 2005 was number one on *Game Developer Magazine*'s list of the top 20 PC sports game software titles for the week of 4/12/05 [43].

[19] Mothers differ from other groups in the way they use the Internet; they praise the medium because it allows them to do research or write e-mail in 5- to 10-minute chunks of time [6]. Time savings is one prominent reason behind increased use of the Internet by parents, especially for shopping. Further, 59% of mothers regularly multitask to save time versus only 43% of men. Still, mothers are more likely than fathers to say they "surf for the fun of it" [7].

is really his mother[20] who spends the most time online with him. Tanner has a GameBoy Color™[21] and saves up his allowance to buy new games for it, but his parents say he can only play GameBoy for half an hour each day (they tell him "it will rot his brain").

Tanner is fairly involved with his school soccer team; he plays forward, not because he's fast but because he never runs out of energy (he simply has a lot of energy to expend, all of the time). In addition to soccer and other organized school activities, he likes to build things with LEGO® bricks (he wants to collect all the Star Wars® LEGO sets), play board games, ride his skateboard with friends, and just run around the neighborhood. He watches Dragon Ball Z® episodes as much as he can, and avidly follows the Chicago Fire[22] (big pro soccer team) with his dad. Although his parents limit his TV time, they make a point to watch *Malcolm in the Middle*[23] together every week.

TANNER'S GOALS AND DESIRES[24]

- Be accepted and sought out as a friend by neighborhood kids and schoolmates.
  - Impress his friends with knowledge and skills[25] related to the video and PC games they play (e.g., find out new hints for Dragon Ball Z[26] before his friends do).
- Stay entertained (i.e., not bored).
  - Please his parents and teachers but get schoolwork[27] done fast so he can play.
  - Watch his favorite movies and TV shows, extending his interest in these things online (searching for info, chatting with others).
  - Find really fun but free online games[28] so he can have fresh experiences without having to ask for money[29] to buy stuff.
- Have cool stuff[30] and do cool[31] things.
  - Find out the best prices[32] on Nintendo 64s to show to his mom (so maybe she'll get him one for his next birthday[33]).

175

[20] With 46% of them buying online, mothers are becoming an increasingly important segment of online purchasers to target. This is in comparison to 41% of all online women purchasers. Online mothers are also very loyal consumers; once they find a brand that they like, 70% find it difficult to change [26].

[21] Thirty-seven percent of Americans who own consoles or computers reported that they also play games on mobile devices such as handheld systems, PDAs, and cell phones [44].

[22] Boys are more likely than girls to go online to play games (52% versus 43%) and to get sports information or scores (40% versus 15%) [11].

[23] Ten of 15 households mentioned watching regularly scheduled television shows together. Among those mentioned were *Malcolm in the Middle*, *Seventh Heaven*, *The OC*, and *America's Funniest Home Videos* [29].

[24] All goals were derived as underlying themes from the G4K site visits [29].

[25] At age 9 or 10, children begin to think in abstract terms and become more focused on interactions with others. By 5 to 6 years of age, children have already formed their identities, can play cooperatively, and have developed fine motor skills. By age 9, a child's world has expanded beyond the immediate surroundings [3].

[26] Overall, boys are more interested in technology, seeking out game-playing resources, building Web pages, downloading software, and even downloading music files. Teen boys largely use the Internet for game playing and game-playing advice [18].

[27] The number of children age 12 and under going online for entertainment and games more than tripled between 1998 and 1999, reaching 9.2 million and surpassing homework as the most popular activity in this age bracket. Growth has been exceptionally fast among boys age 12 and under [1].

[28] The popularity of online games has risen since 1999 when only 18% participated. A 2003 poll revealed that more than one-third of frequent game players go online to play—up from 31% in 2002 [9].

[29] Thirty-one percent of parents would allow their children to purchase online if they could control the amount spent, although only 11% of parents were aware of services that allow parents to allocate money for kids to spend online [2].

[30] Kids seem to be highly aware of the age appropriateness of the products and media content around them. Boys in particular were very vocal about not wanting to do something or use something that was clearly intended for a younger audience [29].

[31] More than half (54%) of teens said that the Internet helped them find out what's cool in fashion and music that they like. Younger girls, 12- to 14-years-old, were the most likely (64%) to say that the Internet helped them to find fashion and music; 59% of frequent users (those who go online every day) were also more likely to have used the Internet to find out what's cool [17].

[32] More than 8 out of 10 Internet users have researched a product or service online [21].

[33] Eight percent of online parents whose children go online indicated that they had made purchases as a direct result of information retrieved by their kids [7]; 15% of children have retrieved information online leading to a purchase by the parent [2].

- ○ Make his parents get broadband (their dial-up connection is "sooooo slooooow").
- ○ His dream is to convince his parents to go to Disney World® and Universal Studios during spring vacation.[34]

WHAT DOES TANNER WANT FROM G4KIDS.COM?

- Tanner knows all about G4K because he already loves our games. He loved the G4K *Peter Plane* and *Hallie Helicopter* interactive books series when he was a kid, and now G4K Moneybags and G4K Skatepunkz are two of his favorite games. He expects G4Kids.com to be very cool!
- He will likely seek out our site for game hints, new product information, and especially direct entertainment.
- Tanner has a short attention span and little patience. He will leave the site if we do not quickly engage him and provide enduring fun experiences.

TANNER'S COMPUTER AND INTERNET USAGE
School Use

Before Tanner had a computer at home,[35] he would sign up for free time on the computer in his classroom[36] as often as he could.[37] The kids in his class get 10-minute turns, and they have to use one of the teacher's choices of educational games,[38] which seem quite limited to him[39] (the computer is a Power Mac® G4, and the teacher[40] keeps Kid Pix™, HyperStudio®, and a bunch of JumpStart™ and Blaster® math and reading stuff on it). Now that he has a computer at home, he has better games there and so doesn't fight for the classroom computer as much.

On Thursdays at school he spends an hour in the school computer lab.[41] He always has to start out practicing his typing (they use Read, Write & Type™[42]) and then most of the rest

176

---

[34] Thirty-four percent of online parents said their use of the Internet improves the way they plan weekend outings and family trips; 27% said it improves the way they shop for birthday and holiday gifts; 26% said it improves the way they spend time with their children; and 19% said it improves the way they care for their children's health [20].

[35] More school-age children use computers at school than have access to them at home [8]. Sixty-six percent of teenagers who are online have access from home, while 60% have access from school, 30% have access from both home and school, and only 11% have access from some other location [2].

[36] Much like a school-issued textbook or a traditional library, students think of the Internet as the place to find primary and secondary source material for their reports, presentations, and projects. This is perhaps the most commonly used metaphor of the Internet for school—held by both students and many of their teachers alike [24].

[37] Students think of the Internet as one way to receive instruction about material that interests them or about which they are confused. Others view the Internet as a way to complete their schoolwork as quickly and painlessly as possible, with minimal effort and minimal engagement. For some, this includes viewing the Internet as a mechanism to plagiarize material or otherwise cheat [24].

[38] Sixty-six percent of public school teachers reported using computers or the Internet for instruction during class time [19].

[39] Two-thirds of teachers agree that the Internet is not well integrated into their classrooms, and only 26% of them feel pressure to use it in learning activities. Forty-four percent of teachers cited lack of knowledge about how to use the Internet as the reason for not logging on, and 78% of teachers cited lack of time as the number one reason for not logging on to the Internet [14].

[40] More than 8 out of 10 teachers (84%) believed that computers and access to the Internet improve the quality of education [14].

[41] In 1996, 79% of fourth graders, 91% of eighth graders, and 96% of 11th graders reported using a computer at home or at school to write stories or papers, a substantial increase from 1984. The percentage of students who used a computer to learn things also increased between 1984 and 1996 for all three grades [12].

[42] Elementary school teachers were more likely than secondary school teachers to assign students practice drills using computers (39% versus 12%) and to have their students use computers or the Internet to solve problems (31% versus 20%). Secondary school teachers, however, were more likely to assign research using the Internet (41% versus 25%) [19].

of the time is taken up with a class assignment using the Internet, HyperStudio, Word, or Excel®.[43] Tanner really likes it[44] when his teacher gives an Internet assignment[45] and he can go online to find out something. Even though the teacher says the Internet is an unlimited resource,[46] they're only allowed to go to certain sites, such as PBS® or Encyclopaedia Britannica®, and sometimes he can't even get to those because the filter the school uses screws up.

Tanner and his friends don't[47] use instant messaging[48] as much as some of the girls[49] in his class do. He doesn't e-mail[50] very often either, but mostly because he doesn't have his own e-mail account[51] (the whole family shares one e-mail address), but occasionally (at his mother's urging) he'll reply to notes from family[52] members.

Tanner at Play

Tanner likes using the computer at his home, because he gets to play around[53] and do what he wants.[54] He uses the computer at home to go online about three times a week,[55] mostly on Saturdays or Sundays and occasionally on a weekday when he doesn't have soccer practice. His mom says he has to do his homework first,[56] before he gets on the computer for fun on a weekday, but if he has to do some research for a report[57] or look up words he might use Encarta™ or go online with his parents' AOL account to search the Web.

[43] Forty-one percent of teachers reported assigning students work that involved computer applications such as word processing and spreadsheets to a moderate or large extent, 31% of teachers reported assigning practice drills, and 30% reported assigning research using the Internet to a moderate or large extent [19].

[44] Young people believe that online use benefits them in a number of ways. Forty-four percent said it had increased their interest in current events, while 36% thought it had improved their writing or language skills. Altogether, 33% thought that it had improved their performance as a student overall. Online use benefits kids' relationships as well, with 39% saying it has improved the quality of their friendships. Virtually no online young people said that online use negatively impacted these areas of their lives [11].

[45] Online- or PC-based homework or school assignments are more common as the age of the child increases. Browsing or informal learning activities are now performed by over 5 million children age 12 and under, three times as many as were doing this in 1998. Growth has been somewhat faster among boys and children age 9 to 12 [1].

[46] Seventy-five percent of teachers said the Internet is an important tool for finding new resources to meet new standards [14].

[47] Just over 3 million children age 12 and under go online for e-mail or chat. E-mail and online chats are the second most popular activities among online teenagers, surpassing entertainment and games. However, very few children age 8 and under go online for communications purposes, and this number hasn't grown appreciably in the past year. This activity segment has an even split between boys and girls, with growth being faster among teenage girls over the past year [1].

[48] Communication tops the list of favorite online activities. Three out of the five activities most engaged in by young people involve communicating with friends and family—writing letters or notes to friends (59%), using instant messages (52%), and writing letters or notes to relatives (36%). Other popular activities include playing games (48%) and getting information about rock stars or music groups (35%) [11].

[49] Girls are more likely to go online to socialize than boys (68% versus 50% among 9- to 17-year-olds) [11].

[50] Only 32% of 9- to 11-year-olds e-mail friends [11].

[51] Almost half of all online parents share access with a spouse or partner [7].

[52] Of 9- to 17-year-olds, 36% say they go online to write letters or notes to relatives "very often" or "pretty often" [11].

[53] Young people display a strong interest in a range of new online activities, including sending and receiving pictures from family and friends online (78%), downloading music or songs online (76%), having a live video conference with a friend online (70%), and watching short cartoons or video clips online (63%) [11].

[54] Younger children are more likely than older children to go online to play games (58% of 9- to 11-year-olds versus 40% of 15- to 17-year-olds) and to get information about TV shows (23% versus 13%) [11].

[55] Online use grows as young people get older. The amount of time per week young people report spending online increases as they mature: 2.8 days per week for 9- to 11-year-olds to 4.5 days per week for 15- to 17-year-olds. Eight out of ten young Internet users (79%) say they go online, on average, at least an hour daily [11].

[56] Half or more of online young people said that their parents have rules about going online only after homework is completed [67%], limiting the amount of time spent online [51%], or checking with an adult before going online [50%]. Younger children were most likely to say their parents set rules (76% of 9- to 11-year-olds), although half (52%) of online teens between the ages of 15 and 17 also said their parents set rules for them about going online [11].

[57] Fifty-five percent of 9- to 17-year-olds said they prefer to use the Internet as a resource for homework [11].

Not surprisingly, most of Tanner's time on the computer is spent playing PC games,[58] both online[59] and off. Once he gets into a Half-Life™ game he can stay involved with it for hours. His mom will usually have to say, "That's enough," and make him go outside. Several times a week, he goes online to play instead of starting a more traditional PC game.

When Tanner goes online for fun[60] he likes to surf around for just about anything that comes to mind,[61] and he'll stay online for at least an hour[62] or so. Because of the ISP they use, he usually starts at AOL Kids and uses familiar links[63] there, or he sometimes goes to Yahooligans™ and uses their categories to get back to favorite sites. He sometimes checks out the scores[64] and stats for the Chicago Fire and the Cubs, and he goes to links for DragonBall Z® stuff, GameBoy® games, and Half-Life 2 (to look up cheat codes that his friends have told him about). He often tries out new games[65] on Yahooligans, Nick, Disney, or LEGO and has downloaded music.[66] Generally, his online[67] activity is more like a flowing stream of consciousness[68] rather than a planned event; if something catches his attention, he's off to it until something else does. His bedroom reflects this[69] disposition, as the walls littered with posters, printouts, and other artifacts representing his varied interests.

Tanner and the Family Computer

The family's 56k modem is sometimes too slow and makes surfing frustrating. not to mention that sometimes he gets disconnected from AOL[70] (often in the middle of a game or something cool). Slow connections and getting kicked off really make him mad. He doesn't

[58] Boys and girls use computers almost equally but for different activities. While 42% of girls used the household computer for word processing, only 36% of boys did. In addition, 79% of girls played games on the home computer compared with 87% of boys [10].

[59] Younger children are most likely to go online to play games (58% of 9- to 11-year-olds versus 40% of 15- to 17-year-olds) and to get information about TV shows (23% vs. 13%) [11].

[60] Young people prefer online to television and telephone. The centrality of Internet use can be seen in the degree to which it has supplanted other favorite activities. Sixty-three percent of those surveyed preferred going online to watching television, and 55% chose going online over talking on the telephone [11].

[61] The number of online Americans who said that they sometimes go online for no particular reason, just to browse for fun or to pass the time, increased by 444% from 2000 to 2002. These recreational users of the Web grew from 54 million in 2000 to 78 million in January 2002 [21].

[62] Sixty-nine percent of online youth-access websites are related to favorite hobbies. This compares to the 78% of adults who search for hobby information. Boys are more likely to go to hobby websites than girls, with 76% of boys having ever done this, compared to 62% of girls [17].

[63] Nine to 11-year-olds spend an average of 1.15 hours online per session [11].

[64] Kids in our site visit study around this age were less likely to add sites to favorites; they tended to just recreate the actions that got them to a specific page in the first place. For example, if they found what they wanted from their home page, they'd simply try to remember the path and repeat it the next time [29].

[65] Forty percent of 9- to 17-year-old boys said they go online "pretty often" to get sports information or scores [11].

[66] The popularity of online games has risen since 1999, when only 18% participated. A 2003 poll revealed that more than one-third (37%) of frequent game players went online to play, up from 31% in 2002 [9].

[67] More than half of the children (53%) in that age bracket (ages 12 to 17) have downloaded music. It was particularly popular with online boys, some 60% of whom said they downloaded music compared to 47% of girls. Some 73% of older boys (ages 15 to 17) had downloaded music. There was some evidence that the prevalence of downloading increased with age; for example, 44% of kids between the ages of 12 and 14 had downloaded music, and fully 61% of those 15 and 17 years of age had done so [23].

[68] Forty-one percent of tweens said that they do other things while surfing the Internet. Some split their attention between surfing and talking on the phone, eating, or listening to music. Still others said they watch TV while working at their computer [4].

[69] Both boys and girls spent significant effort making their bedroom (and sometimes playroom) personal and unique. There was clearly a need to identify themselves and make a statement [29].

[70] Most of the families in our site visits reported being very frustrated because they were often disconnected or dropped in the middle of a session [29].

have much patience[71] for slow sites, so if a Web page is loading slowly he often clicks the "back" button or opens another browser window and finds a different link to follow.[72] In addition to broadband, Tanner really wants his parents to get a new PC for the house (so he can get the old one for his room[73]). His parents are considering it, mostly because they are tired of Tanner messing things up.[74]

Tanner knows his mom is worried[75] about what he might see on the Internet.[76] That is one reason[77] why their PC is placed in the family room.[78] He hasn't really been interested in going into chat rooms, but his mom said she wouldn't let him anyway, and he has to ask one of his parents before he can go online. He's a little worried that his parents might turn on the parental controls[79] or get some other filtering software like "the dumb one at school," but they haven't gotten around to doing it yet. He knows he's not supposed to look at anything "gross" and his mom checks in periodically[80] when he's online to make sure he's not into anything bad. His mom likes to sit with him[81] when he goes online for school stuff[82]—she gives him ideas[83] on where to look for certain things[84] and helps him type in search questions. Sometimes she even plays games[85] and online activities with him.[86] He helps his

[71] We witnessed lots of kids being impatient with slow-loading pages, and many times they assumed that the page was down or broken if nothing happened quickly [29].

[72] Across our site visits, kids of all ages just don't show a lot of patience—or at least they are highly excitable and easily distracted. Regarding Internet behavior specifically, they won't wait for pages to load. Instead, they either click on a different link, type a new URL, or open a completely new browser and get distracted with something else [29].

[73] Only 25 of the 103 (24%) computers in the sample were located in a private space—a parent's or child's bedroom. This placement is surprising, in part, because so many of the families in the sample got their computers for their children. Families were more likely to place the computer in public spaces, such as the dining room, kitchen, family room, spare room, or basement (50% of computers) or in a semiprivate space, such as a study; these computers had adult owners but could be used by all household members (26%). This made it difficult to use the computer for tasks such as e-mail, finances, or word processing that require a degree of peace and quietness [15].

[74] Parents often complained that their kids "messed up" the computer regularly, by freely tinkering with settings, downloading unknown items, and installing all kinds of applications [29].

[75] Eighty percent of parents surveyed thought that Internet filtering was a good idea. Parents worried about their kids seeing pornography (81%) or violence (74%) on the Internet [26].

[76] Online teens, as a group, are generally much less concerned than parents about online content and do not feel as strongly that they need to be protected [17].

[77] Many parents selected a public place precisely because it denied privacy to their children as they used the Internet. By placing the computer in a public place, parents could casually inspect what their children were doing online. As they walked past, they could see what was on screen, for example, and ask questions about their children's behavior [15].

[78] While 75% of tweens (7- to 14-years-old) had a computer at home, one-fifth of the older ones (13 and 14) had a PC in their own bedroom [4].

[79] Another tool that parents use to control what their children see and do online is to actually sit down and surf alongside their children. Close to 7 out of 10 parents (68%) reported sitting down at the computer with their children. More mothers than fathers reported sitting down at their computers with their children. Interestingly, 34% of parents who said that they "do not go online" said that they do sit down and go online with their children [17].

[80] Some parents used the public location of the computer as a deterrent, believing that their children would be less likely to visit sexually explicit websites or converse with strangers in chat rooms if their behavior was subject to parental oversight. Conversely, children lobbied to have the computer placed in their rooms because of the privacy it afforded them [15].

[81] A majority of young people (56%) said they go online sitting together with their parents. The younger the children, the more likely they are to say they go online together with their parents—two-thirds (67%) of 9- to 11-year-olds said so, compared to half of 15- to 17-year-olds (49%) [11]. Nine out of 10 parents "always or sometimes" surfed the Internet with their kids [4].

[82] Across studies, it has been found that younger children prefer and spend more time playing education games than do older children [13].

[83] Seventy-four percent of 9- to 11-year-olds said that their parents give them new online ideas [11].

[84] More than 8 out 10 Internet users have searched the Internet to answer specific questions [21].

[85] A range of age groups are getting in on the gaming action, and the activity is becoming quite popular with women [9].

[86] Parents' use of online content is closely linked to things their kids want to do online. This is especially true for children under 12 who go online [7].

mom out sometimes,[87] too; for example, he showed her[88] the Ask Jeeves® site that they use at school. She really liked it.[89]

Tanner wishes he could play games[90] more often than he actually gets to; however, his mom limits his time playing PC or online games[91] as well as with the GameBoy, particularly if it is something that she thinks is not very educational or social. He has a few friends who have a Nintendo® game console that they play with together,[92] and he wants one *really badly*.[93] He talks about it all the time and points out prices and cool games[94] (even educational ones) to his parents.[95]

RESEARCH REPORT REFERENCES

1. Cyber Dialogue, *The Internet Consumer: Online Children*, December 1999 (http://www.cyberdialogue.com/).
2. Cyber Dialogue, *Cyberfacts: Teenagers on the Internet*; summary datasheet in PDF format, based on data from the American Internet User Survey (http://www.cyberdialogue.com/; http://mslibrary/research/mktresearch/findsvp/pages/AIUS.htm).
3. Dina Demner, *Children on the Internet*, April 2001 (http://www.otal.umd.edu/UUPractice/children/).
4. Media Awareness Network, *Children's Internet Use (Canada)*, October 2000 (http://www.media-awareness.ca/english/resources/research_documents/statistics/internet/childrens_internet_use.cfm).
5. Robert Brooks and Lynne S. Dumas, *Curiosity: Five to Eleven*, Sesame Street Workshop, 2007 (http://www.sesameworkshop.org/parents/advice/article.php?contentId=75002).
6. Rachel Konrad, *Why Net Marketers Love Mom*, May 2002 (http://news.cnet.com/2100-1017-900615.html).
7. Internet Consumer Industry Brief, *Families Online*, February 1999 (http://www.cyberdialogue.com/).
8. U.S. Census Bureau, *Home Computers and Internet Use in the United States*, August 2000 (http://www.census.gov/population/www/socdemo/computer.html).
9. Robyn Greenspan, Gamers growing up: the big picture demographics, *CyberAtlas*, August 29, 2003 (http://cyberatlas.internet.com/big_picture/demographics/article/0,,5901_3070391,00.html; http://cyberatlas.internet.com/).
10. U.S. Census Bureau, *Computer Use in the United States*, October 1997 (http://www.census.gov/population/www/socdemo/computer.html).
11. Roper Starch Worldwide, Inc., *America Online/Roper Starch Youth Cyberstudy 1999*, November (http://corp.aol.com/press/roper.html).
12. National Center for Educational Statistics, *Student Computer Use: Indicator of the Month*, ED433008, August 1999, Education Resources Information Center (http://nces.ed.gov/pubsearch/pubsinfo.asp?pubid=1999011).
13. Ellen Wartell, June H. Lee, and Allison G. Caplovitz, *Children and Interactive Media: An Updated Research Compendium*, 2002 (http://www.digital-kids.net/modules/downloads/file_archive/final_compendium_ac.pdf).

[87] Ninety-one percent of those parents say they supervise their kids' online sessions some of the time and 62% all of the time [7].

[88] Young boys in this study promoted themselves as the household "computer guru." A quote from one 11-year-old participant: "I sometimes have to hang out while my parents try to use the computer—just in case they get confused or something." However, observation of actual skill and knowledge indicated that parents and children are actually not that different in this regard [29].

[89] Among adult users of home computers, 70% used them for word processing, the most common use. Other common uses included games (54%), e-mail and communications (44%), bookkeeping/finances/taxes/household records (44%), and working at home (34%) [10].

[90] Use of home computers for playing games and for work on school assignments is common. A majority (59%) of 5- to 17-year-olds use home computers to play games; 46% use computers to connect to the Internet and 44% to complete school assignments. Middle-school-age and high-school-age youths (ages 11–17) use home computers to complete school assignments (57–64%), to connect to the Internet (54–63%), and to play games (60–63%) [28].

[91] Claiming computer time was a heated issue in many of the families we visited. Families did not sit down calmly at the beginning of the week to schedule time slots together. According to our informants, they watched where the computer sits, trying to figure out each other's plans and fighting for a seat [15].

[92] PC gaming and general PC usage, as opposed to gaming consoles, were treated as individual activities. Game playing with dedicate consoles was more social in nature [29].

[93] Boys in our study tended not to care about brands. They knew specific products (and either loved or hated them), but they didn't particularly know or care who made them. As an example, in one family, even though they had one specific gaming console that they seemed to enjoy, the two boys in the family repeatedly discussed wanting specific games made only for other platforms. Girls, on the other hand, tended to appreciate not just specific products but the companies that made them. They expressed interest in having other products by the same specific company or brand [29].

[94] A majority of parents (77%) thought teens, who represent a very lucrative market, should be allowed to shop online [26].

[95] Nearly two-thirds (63%) of parents planned to purchase at least one computer video game in 2003, as did 56% of all Americans under age 45 [9].

14. Michael Pastore, Teachers say Internet improves quality of education, *ClickZ*, April 5, 2001 (http://www.clickz .com/734761).

15. David Frohlich and Robert Kraut, *The Social Context of Home Computing*, 2003, (www.hpl.hp.com/ techreports/2003/HPL-2003-70.pdf).

16. Dick Halpern, *More Kids Say Internet Is the Medium They Can't Live Without*, April 5, 2002 (http://www .sriresearch.com/press/pr040402.htm).

17. Pew Internet & American Life Project, *Teenage Life Online: The Rise of the Instant-Message Generation and the Internet's Impact on Friendships and Family Relationships*, June 20, 2001 (http://www.pewinternet.org/Press-Releases/2001/The-Rise-of-the-InstantMessage-Generation.aspx).

18. Jupiter Communications, *Targeting Teens Is a Gender Game*, August 2000 (http://us.mediametrix.com/data/ teensconcept.pdf).

19. Cassandra Rowand, Teacher use of computers and the Internet in public schools, *Education Statistics Quarterly*, April 2000 (http://nces.ed.gov/pubsearch/pubsinfo.asp?pubid=2000090).

20. Pew Internet & American Life Project, *Parents Online*, November 17, 2002 (http://www.pewinternet.org/reports/ toc.asp?Report=75).

21. Pew Internet & American Life Project, *America's Online Pursuits: The Changing Picture of Who's Online and What They Do*, December 22, 2003 (http://www.pewinternet.org/reports/toc.asp?Report=106).

22. Pew Internet & American Life Project, *The Ever-Shifting Internet Population: A New Look at Internet Access and the Digital Divide*, April 16, 2003 (http://www.pewinternet.org/reports/toc.asp?Report=88).

23. Pew Internet & American Life Project, *The Music Downloading Deluge: 37 Million American Adults and Youths Have Retrieved Music Files on the Internet*, April 24, 2001 (http://www.pewinternet.org/reports/toc.asp?Report=33).

24. Pew Internet & American Life Project, *The Digital Disconnect: The Widening Gap Between Internet-Savvy Students and Their Schools*, August 14, 2002 (http://www.pewinternet.org/reports/toc.asp?Report=67).

25. Victoria J. Rideout, Elizabeth A. Vandewater, and Ellen A. Wartella, *Zero to Six: Electronic Media in the Lives of Infants, Toddlers and Preschoolers*, Kaiser Family Foundation Report, Fall 2003 (http://www.kff.org/ entmedia/3378.cfm).

26. Cyber Dialogue, Online parents: gateway to a new generation, *The Internet Consumer*, 7, 2000 (http://www .cyberdialogue.com/index.html; http://mslibrary/research/mktresearch/FindSVP/indbriefs/ic-ib-2000-07.pdf).

27. Pew Internet & American Life Project, *More Online, Doing More: 16 Million Newcomers Gain Internet Access in the Last Half of 2000 As Women, Minorities, and Families with Modest Incomes Continue To Surge Online*, February 18, 2001 (http://www.pewinternet.org/reports/toc.asp?Report=30).

28. Matthew DeBell and Chris Chapman, *Computer and Internet Use by Children and Adolescents in 2001*, National Center for Education Statistics, October 2003. (http://nces.ed.gov/pubSearch/pubsinfo.asp?pubid=2004014).

29. *G4K Home Site Visits (Summer 2004): Visit Notes for 15 Homes with 1 or More Children Between the Ages 5 and 12* (\\g4k\user_research\site_visits\summer_2004).

30. Anne Kleiner and Laurie Lewis, *Internet Access in U.S. Public Schools and Classrooms: 1994–2002*, National Center for Education Statistics, October 2003 (http://nces.ed.gov/pubsearch/pubsinfo.asp?pubid=2004011).

31. Pew Internet & American Life Project, *The Internet and Education: Findings of the Pew Internet & American Life Project*, September 1, 2001 (http://www.pewinternet.org/reports/toc.asp?Report=39).

32. Pew Internet & American Life Project, *Consumption of Information Goods and Services in the United States: There Is a Trendsetting Technology Elite in the U.S. Who Chart the Course for the Use of Information, Goods, and Services*, November 23, 2003 (http://www.pewinternet.org/reports/toc.asp?Report=103).

33. Pew Internet & American Life Project, *Let the Games Begin: Gaming Technology and Entertainment Among College Students*, July 6, 2003 (http://www.pewinternet.org/reports/toc.asp?Report=93).

34. Pew Internet & American Life Project, *Cities Online: Urban Development and the Internet*, November 20, 2001 (http://www.pewinternet.org/reports/toc.asp?Report=50).

35. Pew Internet & American Life Project. *Spam: How It Is Hurting Email and Degrading Life on the Internet*, October 22, 2003 (http://www.pewinternet.org/reports/toc.asp?Report=102).

36. Pew Internet & American Life Project, *Tracking Online Life: How Women Use the Internet To Cultivate Relationships with Family and Friends*, May 10, 2000 (http://www.pewinternet.org/reports/toc.asp?Report=11).

37. Pew Internet & American Life Project, *Broadband Adoption at Home: A Pew Internet Project Data Memo*, May 18, 2003 (http://www.pewinternet.org/reports/toc.asp?Report=90).

38. MSN Kidz Usability Test, IDIS #7285. \\minerva\usabilit\reports\7285\MSNKidsReview.doc

39. Thomas Snyder and Charlene Hoffman, *Digest of Education Statistics, 2000*, National Center for Education Statistics, 2001 (http://nces.ed.gov/pubsearch/pubsinfo.asp?pubid=2001034).

40. Susan Solomon, Content for kids, *ClickZ*, July 9, 2002 (http://www.clickz.com/experts/design/cont_dev/article .php/1381161).

41. *Internet Service Provider Review*, G4K Marketing Group, 2005.

42. GameDaily (http://www.gamedaily.com).

43. *Game Developer Magazine* (http://www.gdmag.com/).

44. Robyn Greenspan, Games people play, *ClickZ*, May 31, 2002 (http://www.clickz.com/stats/sectors/software/ article.php/1152221).

45. *Get-in-the-Game News* (http://www.gignews.com/).

46. E3 Expo online news (http://www.e3expo.com/).

47. *Firing Squad: Home of the Hardcore Gamer* (http://www.firingsquad.com/).

48. *G4K Holiday Usage Focus Groups*, December 2004 \\G4Kmarketresearch\reports\12-18-2004.doc.

Case study: G4K (games 4 kids) kids' web portal

INTRODUCTION

This case study provides detailed examples connecting all of the lifecycle phases and demonstrating more holistically how personas can be used in building a product from end to end. A fictional company—Gigantic for Kids, Inc.—has been generated to serve as the basis for this case study. This G4K case study will illustrate some of our main points.

Who is G4K?

G4K currently specializes in children's software, across the areas of entertainment (games) and education. The company's products are distributed through traditional "brick and mortar" retail outlets as well as third-party Web retailers.

What is G4K trying to achieve?

Gigantic has been exploring the viability of the Internet, both to market and distribute its traditional shrink-wrap software products as well as to extend its product offerings and business/revenue model. As part of this new strategy, its corporate website, www.G4kids.com, is soon to become a "destination" site for kids, providing children-oriented entertainment, news, and merchandise primarily related to G4K's existing software offerings. While this is not a major departure from its normal business (seen simply as an opportunity to build stronger customer loyalty and deeper branding), the company is also flirting with the possibility of partnering with other children-focused merchants, potentially offering joint promotions, advertising, and sponsorship (e.g., sponsoring children's events or promoting other noncompeting brands or goods such as clothing, skateboarding equipment, soft-drink companies, and retailers). While the company does understand its market related to shrink-wrapped software products, which tend to be focused very tightly to specific age groups, they have never dealt with something that potentially spans all of the company's customers at once. The task is daunting.

What does this case study provide?

This case study tells the story of Gigantic's effort to redefine its existing corporate website into a children's destination site. It follows Gigantic's modest user experience team, which consists of two people (an interaction designer and a graphic designer who have recently been moved off of a game development team in the company) as they attempt to create and use personas for the first time. The case study provides stories and situated examples that illustrate major points introduced throughout this book.

G4K PERSONA FAMILY PLANNING

As the G4K portal project got under way, several people across the company (people who had been working directly on one or more G4K games) were asked to participate in the design and development of their Web portal. Ingrid, an interaction designer and the company's only person responsible for usability testing, was one of these folks. She had heard about personas at a professional conference and recently saw an article on the Internet highlighting a persona success story. She thought the technique would be useful to try here. Ingrid ran the idea past her close colleague, Graham (a graphic designer), and together they agreed to do it.

The persona technique was brand new to G4K. Not many people at the company had ever heard of it. What's more, while user testing and a few other UCD techniques were sometimes incorporated in the development of G4K products, the notion of doing any kind of user profile was simply nonexistent. They knew they had their work cut out for them.

Putting together the core team

The first step was to discuss the technique with the project lead, Paula. She thought the idea was a bit overboard (not really needed), but it might be useful for some aspects of their work. So, Paula said she would help out a bit with it. Ingrid and Graham knew how busy Paula was going to be, so they decided to use her time sparingly. Paula would be both a part-time contributor to the effort and a stakeholder (a key recipient of the end product of the personas).

Ingrid and Graham also approached Michael, the company's only market research professional. Michael had key knowledge of both market trends and customer segments that would be crucial for appropriately defining and prioritizing the personas. He also understood the business better than most people at the company. Michael was not directly assigned to the portal project but would be a key part-time participant in the effort.

Finally, Ingrid and Graham approached Theo, one of the company's technical writers. Theo had written a range of content for G4K, from user guides to marketing copy and website text to storyline content directly in their game products. Theo was no stranger to thinking about target audiences and was intrigued by the notion of personas. The portal project was one of many things on Theo's work list, so his involvement here, like several of the others, was going to be somewhat limited.

Paula, Michael, and Theo would all be active participants in the persona efforts; however, due to their time limitations and focus, they would need to do this on an "on-call" basis. For this reason, Ingrid and Graham would be the ones truly responsible for getting everything done and would likely handle any of the grunt work that needs to happen.

THE PERSONA CORE TEAM

- *Ingrid*, an interaction design/usability person from the games group
- *Graham*, a graphic designer

THE PERSONA ON-CALL TEAM

- *Paula*, the project lead for the new website
- *Michael*, a market researcher
- *Theo*, a technical writer

Creating the Action Plan

The G4K core team created the following high-level schedule by working backward from the launch date and other significant project milestones. The entire development cycle is extremely aggressive for this team—6 months from start to finish.

RESOURCES FOR OUR PERSONA EFFORT

- First 2 weeks—Half-time effort for core team members
- Remaining weeks—2 hours per week for core team members
- Use of printing facilities in design department (e.g., color printer)
- Permission to expense $200 for persona-related costs

PRODUCT PROBLEMS WE WANT TO SOLVE WITH PERSONAS

- Other companies have Internet portals for kids. We're behind. How can we create a product that's world class and worthy of the G4K brand in such a short time?
- How can we recreate some of the key experiences built into our G4K games into an Internet experience? The technologies are very different.

PROCESS PROBLEMS WE WANT TO SOLVE WITH PERSONAS

- We need to deal with the incredibly fast turnaround required for online portal development (unlike game development schedules).
- We've never done Internet delivery of a product. Personas are necessary to help us understand our existing users in a completely new domain.

- We need to communicate different needs to development staff unfamiliar with Internet-related issues.
- We need to leverage the efforts of our very small team.
- We need to leverage the efforts of people not directly on our team but whose help and expertise are needed.

THE G4K PERSONA TEAM FIND SOME MUCH NEEDED DATA FREE WEB-BASED DATA SOURCES

When the G4K team set out to find data relevant to the development of their project domain, they didn't know quite where to start. They had all sorts of information about kids, parents, and shrink-wrapped games but nothing except assumptions when it came to kids and the

Phase	Activity	When Completed	Related Project Milesones
Family planning	Organizational introspection Data collection	2 weeks from now	Vision complete (business plan, corporate strategy)
Conception and gestation	Data organized, persona creation complete, evaluation and prioritization by stakeholders complete, validation complete Begins evangelizing persona effort around organization	1 month from now	Requirements complete (system architecture, functional requirements)
Birth and maturation	Persona effort introduced to team Initial posters and communication artifacts delivered to team Personas used in storyboards, scenarios, design walkthroughs, etc.	2 months from now	Feature specification complete (design complete) GOAL: Use personas in feature prioritization decisions
Adulthood	User testing with personas as recruiting profile Personas used in Q/A test case selection Persona knowledge enrichment artifacts delivered	3 months from now	Beta 1 complete (core features intact, but not polished)
Adulthood	Iterative user testing and Q/A testing continues User assistance team begins writing documentation based on persona profiles	4 months from now	Beta 2 complete (core features polished; secondary features intact)
Adulthood	Personas introduced to support team Marketing begins to explore messaging and advertisement channels considering personas	5 months from now	Release to operations (design complete, no further changes allowed unless they are show-stopper bugs)
Adulthood	Support team uses personas to categorize customer issues/complaints/requests	6 months from now	Live to web (site launch)
Lifetime achievement	Persona core team measures ROI of persona effort	6 to 7 months from now	Site maintenance; planning for next release

FIGURE C.1
G4K's persona action plan.

Internet. So, they opened a Web browser and searched on terms such as "Internet behavior," "PCs & kids," "statistics software usage," etc., because G4k was primarily interested in children's Internet behaviors. They discovered that an ocean of data awaited them. Here are a few of the key resources they found that helped them identify specific studies and larger collections of data:

- U.S. Census Bureau, *Computer Use and Ownership* (http://www.census.gov/population/www/socdemo/computer.html)
- Pew Internet & American Life Project (http://www.pewInternet.org/)
- Cyberatlas, The World's Leading Resource for Internet Trends & Internet Statistics (http://cyberatlas.Internet.com; http://www.nua.com/surveys/)
- Complete Guide to Internet Statistics and Research (http://Internet-statistics-guide.netfirms.com/)
- Consumer Internet Barometer™ (http://www.consumerInternetbarometer.us/index.htm)
- Demographics and census data (http://www.usg.edu/galileo/Internet/census/demograp.html)
- InfoQuest! Internet Surveys and Statistics (http://www.tbchad.com/stats1.html)
- Websense Internet Use Statistics (http://www.websense.com/management/stats.cfm)

From these sources and others, the G4K core team found 30 relevant research studies. Many of these were available on the Internet for free. Some had to be purchased from a research

187

G4K Kids Portal project: Data resources

1. The Internet Consumer: Online Children. (December 1999). Inte
2. Cyberfacts: Teenagers on the Internet (summary data sheet in pd http://www.cyberdialogue.com/, (internal MS - http://mslibrary/rese
3. Children on the internet, http://www.otal.umd.edu/UUPractice/chil
4. Children's Internet Use (Canada). Media Awareness Network. ht
5. Curiosity: Five to Eleven (R. Brooks & L Dumas). Sesame Street http://www.sesameworkshop.org/parents/advice/article.php?conte
6. Why Net Marketers love mom. http://news.com.com/
7. The Internet Consumer Industry Brief: Families Online (February
8. Home Computers and Internet User in the United States (August 2000). US Census Bureau. http://www.census.gov/, http://www.census.gov/population/www/socdemo/computer.html
9. Gamers Growing Up. The Big Picture Demographics. http://cyberatlas.internet.com/
10. Computer use in the United States (October 1997). US Census Bureau. http://www.census.gov/, http://www.census.gov/population/www/socdemo/computer.html
11. The America Online/Roper Starch Youth Cyberstudy 1999 (Nov. 1999). http://www.corp.aol.com/press/roper.html, http://www.corp.aol.com/press/study/youthstudy.pdf
12. Student Computer Use – Indicator of the Month, National Center for Educational Statistics (August, 1999). http://nces.ed.gov/pubsearch/pubsinfo.asp?pubid=1999011
13. Children and Interactive Media. Wartell, Lee, and Caplovitz (Nov 2002). Markle Foundation.
14. Teachers say internet improves quality of education. Cyberatlas. http://cyberatlas.internet.com/
15. The social context of home computing. Frohlich and Kraut (April 2002).
16. More Kids say internet is the medium they can't live without. http://www.sriresearch.com/press/pr040402.htm
17. Teenage Life Online: The rise of the instant-message generation and the Internet's impact on friendships and family relationships. (June 20, 2001). Pew Internet & American Life Project. http://www.pewinternet.org/reports/toc.asp?Report=36
18. Targeting Teens is a gender game (August 2000). Jupiter Communications.
19. Teacher Use of Computers and the Internet in Public Schools, Education Statistics Quarterly – National Center for Education Statistics. http://nces.ed.gov/pubsearch/pubsinfo.asp?pubid=2000090
20. Parents Online. (November 17, 2002). Pew Internet & American Life Project. http://www.pewinternet.org/reports/toc.asp?Report=75
21. America's Online Pursuits: The changing picture of who's online and what they do. (December 22, 2003). Pew Internet & American Life Project. http://www.pewinternet.org/reports/toc.asp?Report=106
22. The Ever-Shifting Internet Population: A new look at Internet access and the digital divide (April 16, 2003). Pew Internet & American Life Project. http://www.pewinternet.org/reports/toc.asp?Report=88
23. The Music Downloading Deluge: 37 million American adults and youths have retrieved music files on the Internet (April 24, 2001). Pew Internet & American Life Project. http://www.pewinternet.org/reports/toc.asp?Report=33
24. The Digital Disconnect: The widening gap between Internet-savvy students and their schools (August 14, 2002). Pew Internet & American Life Project. http://www.pewinternet.org/reports/toc.asp?Report=67
25. Zero to Six: Electronic Media in the Lives of Infants, Toddlers and Preschoolers (Fall 2003). Kaiser Family Foundation. http://www.kff.org/entmedia/3378.cfm
26. Online Parents: Gateway to a New Generation, Cyber Dialogue, The Internet Consumer, Year 2000, Vol.7. http://www.cyberdialogue.com/index.html. (internal MS - http://mslibrary/research/mktresearch/FindSVP/indbriefs/ic-ib-2000-07.pdf)

1. The Internet Consumer: Online Children. (December 1999). Interactive Consumers. Cyber Dialogue. http://www.cyberdialogue.com/
2. Cyberfacts: Teenagers on the Internet (summary data sheet in pdf format; based on data from the American Internet User Survey). http://www.cyberdialogue.com/
3. Children on the internet, http://www.otal.umd.edu/UUPractice/children/

FIGURE C.2
A list of some of the data sources G4K found.

	G4K Market segmentation	Internal Market Research	Sources purchased from agency	Sources found via web searches	More data needed
Kids online					
How many kids are online?	√				
What are the demographics of kids online?				√ Search terms: "Kids online" and "schools online"	
How do kids get online? Do they have their own accounts?				√	Need more
What do kids like to do online?		√	√	√	
Kids and entertainment					
What do kids do for fun?				√	Need more
How much time do kids have for fun (vs. school?)			√	√	
The family and the computer					
Where is the computer in the house?			√	√	
How many computers are in the house?			We should buy this!	√	
How many are using the computer?				√	
Parents and their concerns					
What are parents concerns re: the Internet and their kids?					Can't find enough recent stuff!
How do parents control access to the Internet?			√	√	
What benefits do parents perceive re: the Internet for their kids?				√	Need more

FIGURE C.3

G4K's "Data Collection by Topic" spreadsheet. The G4K team used this spreadsheet to keep track of whether they had data to answer persona-related questions; green cells indicate that a type of data was found in a particular set of sources

Personas Data Source Index

Category	Description	Date	Author	Source #	Incorp. into Personas?
Kids Online	G4K Market Segmentation	oct 2003	Market Research	01	
	Wired elementary schools in the Boston area	aug 2003	Persona team	02	
	Agency Report: Kids online 2002	jan 2002	Agency	03	
	"Kids Count" http://www.aecf.org/kidscount/	2003	Annie E. Casey Foundation	04	
	CLIKS online data http://www.aecf.org/cgi-bin/cliks.cgi	jun 2003	Persona team	05	
	Analysphere kids online: privacy and content regulation http://www.analysphere.com/23Apr01/kidz.htm	apr 2001	Analysphere	06	
Kids and entertainment	kids entertainment.com	2003	Kid's Entertainment Industry	07	

FIGURE C.4

Create a data source index. Note that this example includes the category for the data, a link to the primary source, the date of creation and author, source number, and a final column for whether and when the source was used in the creation of the personas. You will use the final column during the *conception and gestation* phase to keep track of which data sources have been mined for their persona-related information.

firm. They made printed copies of each report, distributed them among their core team members, and created a numbered list so each study could easily be referred to as they used these resources in the *conception and gestation* phase.

G4K PERSONA CONCEPTION AND GESTATION

During the *family planning* phase, the G4K persona core team was able to get a good sense of how personas could be used to enhance the portal project team's specific design and development process. They are now eager to create personas.

They collected a lot of existing data (much of which was free) and uncovered many assumptions about users from the project team and execs. They executed some very enlightening field research and now have a slew of interesting flow charts, graphs, photos, quotes, and observation notes. They feel like they've explored as much as they can about the ways their future customers will potentially use their product; however, they also feel a bit overwhelmed at the prospect of combing through all of the data sources they've amassed. They know they must plow ahead to begin the work of conception and gestation in the persona lifecycle: evaluating and organizing data, creating and prioritizing persona skeletons, and enriching those terse abstractions to create complete persona foundation documents.

The team discusses user categories

Let's take a look at how G4K thinks about user categories and their relation to roles, user goals, and user segments. Historically, G4K has focused on four categories of users—children in four different age/grade groups—and they also make a big distinction between boys and girls (thus doubling the number of distinct user categories to eight). Thus, they have the following eight categories of users:

- Preschool and kindergarteners (girls, boys)
- First and second graders (girls, boys)

189

- Third through fifth graders (girls, boys)
- Sixth through ninth graders (girls, boys)

Obviously, they consider children as their users; in other words, children are the people who directly use their software products. But children don't have the direct power to purchase G4K products. Thus, G4K also considers five types of customers in their business model:

- Parents
- Educators (teachers, specialists, and educational administrators)
- Librarians (or library administrators)
- Retailers and partners (typically business managers or product specialists at toy store outlets)
- Industry analysts, investors, and other influencers (individuals, investment capitalists, agencies, and institutions that G4K needs to stay on top of)

As mentioned previously, their current website (www.G4kids.com) was created to communicate the corporate image and vision, promote the mass sale of products, and more generally serve the needs of their customers. It was not thought of as a destination site for their users.

In the meeting to discuss categories of users for the creation of their destination site (www .G4kids.com), the stakeholders agreed that users would be the primary focus (all eight categories), along with parents and teachers. The other three types of customers would still be served, but only through the existing corporate website.

This was an important and freeing decision for the persona core team; however, this wasn't good enough. The persona core team needed to push back a little bit on the stakeholders. They didn't think they could easily distinguish and target all ten categories at once (eight classes of children, parents, and teachers). So, they asked the stakeholders to brainstorm a bit regarding other ways of conceptualizing segments, roles, and goals. They explored a few interesting dimensions of their users along the way. The following groups were discussed in detail.

Possible categories of G4K users by role
- The child as a game player
- The child as a learner/student
- The parent as guardian/monitor/investigator
- The parent as purchaser/enabler
- The teacher as direct educator/assistant/learning partner
- The teacher/administrator as curriculum advisor/determiner

Possible subcategories of G4K users by goal
Kids
- Have fun/be entertained
- Feel independent
- Get better at a game than another kid
- Excel at school (please my parents and teacher)
- Make and maintain friends

Parents
- Make good choices for my kids
- Not have to worry about my kid on the Internet
- Make sure my kids don't screw up my computer
- Be sure my kids are being productive with their time
- Build my kids' self-esteem

Educators
- Get a lot without huge time investment
- Be on the cutting edge, but not fall behind
- Get new ideas and find content that is relevant and interesting
- Please the parents by what I provide to the kids
- Stay within budget
- Look and be professional

Possible subcategories of G4K users by segment
Kids
- Age—Young children/kids versus school-age children versus teens
- Users versus nonusers of our existing software products/games
- Homes with computer/Internet access versus access only at school or the library
- Girls versus boys
- Sitters (play indoors—TV, PC, gaming) versus physically active kids (sports-minded, like being outdoors)

Parents
- Computer savvy/not
- Highly involved/not so involved
- Age/generation (X-Gen parents, baby boomers)
- Moms versus dads versus grandparents versus guardians
- Educational background

Educators
- Years of experience
- Access to technology
- Fear or embracement of technology/computers
- Education level
- Grade/subject taught

In the end, the stakeholders felt that a good starting point for personas would be a simplified combination of user roles and segments. Everything they discussed felt important to them, but the only categories they knew they wanted to capture from the start were children, parents, and educators. So, they decided to keep it simple and let the data confirm the categories and determine whether additional subcategories would be needed.

IDENTIFYING FACTOIDS AND TRANSFERRING THEM TO STICKY NOTES

As discussed earlier, the G4K persona core team amassed over 25 relevant research studies and had conducted a series of observational site visits with families who use their products and the Internet. Because they had so many data documents, the team decided to do the data filtering process prior to their assimilation meeting. To ease the load, they distributed the documents across the five core team members (roughly five or six documents per person). They then agreed on a general rule that no document would get more than about 30 minutes of a person's time. So, in total, the data filtering took roughly 3 hours of each team member's time. During the process, each person independently scanned through his or her assigned reports and marked findings that seemed critical to their audience and overall project. Figure C.5 shows the resulting highlighting in one such document—one of the market research reports relevant to their domain which they found for free on the Internet.

As a second step, they met as a group for an hour to transfer the resulting highlighted information onto sticky notes. They did this together in case there were questions about the

192

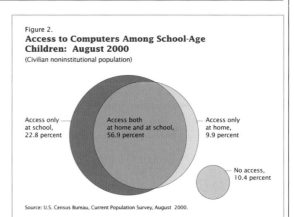

While 38 percent of White non-Hispanic children and 35 percent of Asian and Pacific Islander children used the Internet at home, just 15 percent of Black children and 13 percent of Hispanic children did.[5]

More school-age children use computers at school than have access to them at home.

School is a major influence on children's access to computers. Among children of school age (6 to 17 years), 2 in 3 had access to a computer at home in 2000. However, 4 in 5 actually used a computer at school.

More than half of school-age children had access to computers both in school and at home (57 percent). However, many children had access in only one location or the other. Of them, far more had access in school than had access at home. Twenty-three percent of school-age children had access to a computer only at school, compared with just 10 percent who had access only at home. Adding all three groups together, 9 in 10 school-age children had access to a computer somewhere, leaving just 10 percent of children who had no access to a computer in any locale (Figure 2).

Schools level the playing field by giving computer access to children who have none at home.

For children 6 to 17 years old, computer use at school was more nearly equal across different income, race, or ethnic groups than computer access at home (Figure 3).

School-age children in family households with incomes of $75,000 or more had the highest rates of home

[5]The proportions of home Internet users among Asian and Pacific Islander and White non-Hispanic children were not significantly different. The proportions of home Internet users among Black and Hispanic children were also not significantly different.

computer access, at 94 percent, compared with those with incomes below $25,000, at 35 percent (a difference of about 60 percentage points). But at school, while 87 percent of those with the highest incomes used a computer, 72 percent of those with the lowest incomes did so, a difference of only 15 percentage points.

Figure 3 illustrates a similar equalizing effect observed among children of different racial or ethnic groups. At home, access varied from high to low by 41 percentage points. However, at school the range was much smaller, just 14 percentage points.

The net result of the effect schools have in giving computer access across income, racial, and ethnic groups is a leveling of the computer access that children of different groups have compared to what they would have had if home were the only place available for them to use computers. The absolute percentage-point gap in total computer access between children from family households with the highest and lowest incomes was only about one-third as large as the gap in

home access between these two groups. Similarly, the overall computer access gap between White non-Hispanic school-age children and Black or Hispanic school-age children was just over one-third the size of the gap between these groups in home computer access.[6]

ADULT ACCESS TO COMPUTERS AND THE INTERNET

More adults have computers and use the Internet at home than ever before.

More than half of all adults 18 years old and over, 55 percent, lived in a household with at least one computer in 2000, compared with only 46 percent in 1998. Thirty-seven percent of all adults used the Internet at home, compared with just 23 percent in 1998 (Table C).

The oldest adults had the lowest rates of home Internet use. Only 13 percent of those 65 years old or over used the Internet at home.

[6]The proportions of overall computer access among Black and Hispanic school-age children were not significantly different.

U.S. Census Bureau   5

FIGURE C.5
Data highlighting in a quantitative market research report. (Adapted from U.S. Census Bureau, 2001.)

inclusion of specific facts and what surrounding details might need to be captured. Figure C.6 shows an example of some of the facts that were pulled from one of the field study reports (qualitative findings).

Across the many research documents, they amassed over 500 sticky notes containing important findings, or "factoids" (about 15 or so factoids per research article). They were now ready to do the assimilation exercise.

ASSIMILIATING FACTOIDS

Earlier, the G4K team decided that a simple set of categories (children, parents, and educators) was an appropriate starting point for the assimilation exercise. These three category labels were placed in large print on the meeting room walls. They each gathered

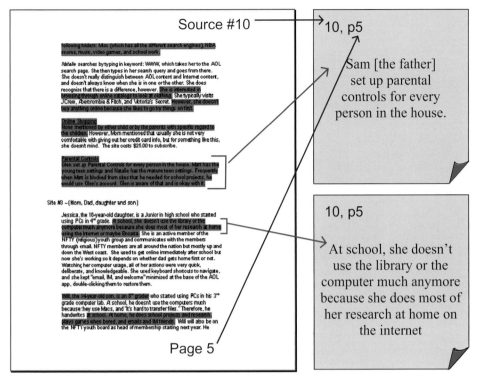

FIGURE C.6
An example of two factoids identified in a qualitative research document (field study report) and transferred to sticky notes.

their sticky-note factoids and started the process. Working simultaneously, they began posting sticky notes on the wall under one of the three major category labels. For each sticky note, the team member would look at the posted sticky notes and decide if the note was related or unrelated to those notes. If related, they posted their sticky notes in or near the other notes. If unrelated, they posted their notes separately to possibly form the beginning of a new group of notes.

During the assimilation exercise, they began noticing that many factoids were very specific about behaviors and interests related to specific ages, which was not a surprise for them. So, they put up some additional labels to mark the age groups that were emerging. "Tweens" was one of these emerging groups (ages 9 to 12); they found the word "tween" occurring over and over again in factoids related to this age range. They also began putting labels on the smaller clusters of notes that were forming, as shown in Figure C.7.

As the majority of the factoids got placed, the team found many meaningful clusters and subclusters; there was a big division around gender for the older children (those from 9 to 12 years old) as well as for parents (moms versus dads), but not for younger children. As they expected, their original main categories of users remained stable throughout the exercise, but some of the groupings of factoids got moved around, relabeled, or even distributed as the group gathered insights through the process.

Whenever a cluster got too large (that is, it contained more than ten sticky notes) someone on the team would attempt to split it up into subclusters. For example, initially a large cluster of factoids about the general activities of teens had formed, but then the team found many ways to divide these into meaningful clusters. "Teen activities" became "teens and school," "teens and social activities," "teens and the Internet," "teens and gaming," etc.

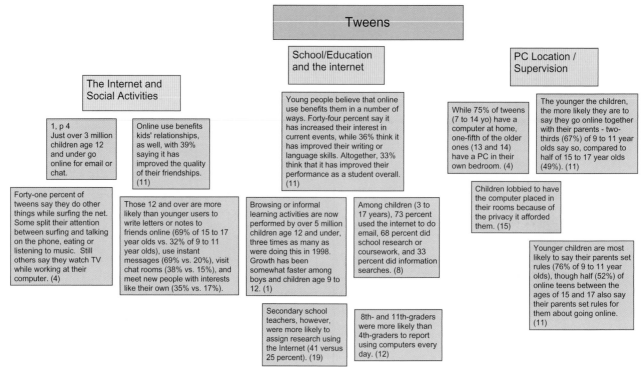

Tweens

School/Education and the internet

The Internet and Social Activities

PC Location / Supervision

1, p 4
Just over 3 million children age 12 and under go online for email or chat.

Online use benefits kids' relationships, as well, with 39% saying it has improved the quality of their friendships. (11)

Young people believe that online use benefits them in a number of ways. Forty-four percent say it has increased their interest in current events, while 36% think it has improved their writing or language skills. Altogether, 33% think that it has improved their performance as a student overall. (11)

While 75% of tweens (7 to 14 yo) have a computer at home, one-fifth of the older ones (13 and 14) have a PC in their own bedroom. (4)

The younger the children, the more likely they are to say they go online together with their parents - two-thirds (67%) of 9 to 11 year olds say so, compared to half of 15 to 17 year olds (49%). (11)

Forty-one percent of tweens say they do other things while surfing the net. Some split their attention between surfing and talking on the phone, eating or listening to music. Still others say they watch TV while working at their computer. (4)

Those 12 and over are more likely than younger users to write letters or notes to friends online (69% of 15 to 17 year olds vs. 32% of 9 to 11 year olds), use instant messages (69% vs. 20%), visit chat rooms (38% vs. 15%), and meet new people with interests like their own (35% vs. 17%).

Browsing or informal learning activities are now performed by over 5 million children age 12 and under, three times as many as were doing this in 1998. Growth has been somewhat faster among boys and children age 9 to 12. (1)

Among children (3 to 17 years), 73 percent used the internet to do email, 68 percent did school research or coursework, and 33 percent did information searches. (8)

Children lobbied to have the computer placed in their rooms because of the privacy it afforded them. (15)

Younger children are most likely to say their parents set rules (76% of 9 to 11 year olds), though half (52%) of online teens between the ages of 15 and 17 also say their parents set rules for them about going online. (11)

Secondary school teachers, however, were more likely to assign research using the Internet (41 versus 25 percent). (19)

8th- and 11th-graders were more likely than 4th-graders to report using computers every day. (12)

FIGURE C.7
Some example clusters of factoids for the tweens group (ages 9 to 12).

194

Finding unexpected clusters

The core team found several clusters that didn't specifically relate to any of their preconceived notions of users and their characteristics. For example, they found an interesting cluster of factoids that included information on the placement of the family computer in the home and the behavior of various family members to the computer. They even found some clusters consisting of government policies and laws, including laws related to targeting minors and collecting any kind of information from them via the Internet.

IDENTIFYING SUBCATEGORIES OF USERS AND CREATING SKELETONS

During the assimilation exercise, the G4K core team discovered many of clusters of factoids related to each of the initial three main categories. Before they began the assimilation exercise, the G4K team knew that kids tend to behave very differently depending on their ages (after all, G4K is a game software company, with lots of experience with kids). Their assimilated data corroborated this basic notion. What they didn't know upfront was how kids behave *online* and which age groups were the best targets for the Internet portal project. They also didn't know that tweens would factor so much in the data; G4K had never used the term *tween*, and this was a new concept for the organization.

The team also discovered clusters of information about gender differences in kids of different ages. Generally, they found that boys and girls differ in terms of activities and interests; for example, girls are more active in social activities but don't differ in the overall amount of PC or Internet use. Interestingly, differences in gender were much stronger as kids got older.

The G4K team expected to find differences between kids at school and kids at home or in their leisure time. While they did find factoids on these topics, the factoids didn't cluster in a way that suggested that kids have different goals or roles at school and home when it comes to online activities.

Subcategories that were most meaningful and unique

KIDS

The G4K team created a list of the meaningful subcategories they found in the assimilated data for kids, with loads of interesting clusters of findings for each one. The resulting groups were not surprising to the team. After evaluating these possible groups and the data in the clusters (particularly related to gender differences), they decided that six subcategories would be enough to represent the general category:

- 3- to 5-year-old boys and girls combined (not meaningful enough gender differences)
- 6- to 8-year-old boys and girls combined (not meaningful enough gender differences)
- 9- to 12-year-old boys (tweens)
- 9- to 12-year-old girls (tweens)
- 13- to 15-year-old boys (young teens)
- 13- to 15-year-old girls (young teens)

PARENTS

In the clusters of data describing parents, the G4K team was quite surprised to find that there were several distinct clusters of data related specifically to mothers (in addition to the clusters related to parents), data that were specifically about mothers and their attitudes regarding kids and online activities. In fact, much of the data indicated that female adults (moms) were a stronger target for considering G4K design issues than adult males (dads). Other factors, such as the number of children in the household, seemed to play only a small role in determining activities, interests, and other factors related to the G4K domain; however, single- versus multiple-adult households did show some interesting differences. Ultimately, the G4K team decided on one subcategory of parents that was important and unique:

- Parents (usually moms) who take a very active role in their children's use of computers and the Internet

EDUCATORS

Regarding the domain of teachers, they found that computer access was a fairly common thing in most schools, but newly hired (recently trained) teachers showed a greater affinity toward the use of technology in the classroom. They were more comfortable with computers and thought that providing children with related experiences was important. The team found that some teachers avoid technology in the classroom (for a variety of reasons), and, while almost all schools have PC and Internet access, not all of them have such capabilities directly in the classroom. Thus, there were several possible subcategories of teachers:

- Newly hired teachers with in-classroom PC/Internet facilities and an interest in promoting and exploring new technologies for education
- Established teachers who had a desire to control or expand their curriculum but were less versed in technology
- School librarians or educational specialists that run a centralized computer facility for the entire school

From these ten subcategories of users, the persona team assembled ten skeletons, defining their core attributes using the associated clusters of factoids, respectively.

DISCUSSING PRIORITIES

Now that the G4K core team had ten skeletons resulting from the assimilation exercise (six kids, one parent, and three educators), they needed to get input from their stakeholders. The core team arranged a 1-hour meeting with the stakeholders.

During the meeting, they first reviewed the initial subcategories and resulting skeletons for each major category separately. For kids, the stakeholders were not quite convinced that gender could be collapsed for the younger age groups. So, the core team provided the clustered factoids and some of the original data reports to help the stakeholders understand their reasoning.

With regard to parents, the stakeholders were surprised that only one group emerged but understood that it would not be useful to target parents who were not likely to visit the site. The core team suggested that one parent target could be used to explore multiple reasons for visiting the site (e.g., surfing together with a child, buying a present for a child, snooping around using the browser history to view sites that a child had visited recently). The stakeholders agreed this would be adequate.

The stakeholders also agreed that the educator skeletons were all good targets, but the core team pressed them to identify which of the three educator categories would be most fruitful to focus on. After some deliberation, the stakeholders came to believe that only focusing on one would cover the needs of the others. They felt that the first segment (newly hired teachers with an affinity for technology) would be the most appropriate.

Once they moved past these initial issues, the core team asked the stakeholders to prioritize the skeletons by discussing aspects of frequency of use, size of market, potential revenue, and strategic importance. Considering these factors, they devised a loose prioritization scheme by collectively assigning percentages to subcategories such that they equaled 100%. The results were as follows.

Kids (75% focus total)
- 5%—3 to 5 years of age, boys and girls combined (key targets for G4K's early educational products but not able to use the Internet alone)
- 25%—6 to 8 years of age, girls as a growth market (an important strategic target interested in creativity and education but somewhat less influential than older users; G4K has game products that are popular with younger girls but no offerings that are strong in this category)
- 30%—9 to 12 years of age, tween boys (current users of G4K shrink-wrap games and the Internet who are focused on entertainment; the most frequent visitors and likely to influence purchase decisions of parents)
- 15%—13 to 15 years of age, early-teen boys (more hard-core gamers; tough audience to please but important for branding and market influence)

Parents (15% focus total)
- 15%—Parents (usually moms) who take a very active role in their children's use of computers and the Internet (involved parents, especially moms, are more likely to be aware of the G4K brand and tend to participate in online activities with their kids)

Teachers (10% focus total)
- 10%—Newly hired teachers with in-classroom PC/Internet facilities and an interest in promoting and exploring new technologies for education (interested and capable of exploring online content and activities but perhaps not aware of the G4K brand)

The most surprising result of this prioritization exercise for the persona core team was that the stakeholders reduced the skeleton count by two, realizing that two of the skeletons were not critical for initial success. That is, for this first version of the portal site, it made the most sense to focus on audiences already familiar with the G4K brand and those with a propensity for gaming. Thus, two of the six kid skeletons were put on the sideline and would only be considered at a later date.

COMPLETING THE PERSONAS

G4K's persona core team created six personas to help with the development of their children's portal site.

Tanner Thompson (the tenacious tinkerer)—An intense 9-year-old boy who loves computers, games, and gadgets of all types. He's an entertainment enthusiast and active gamer. Generally speaking, he just loves to play. Tanner is familiar with G4K game titles and is a likely frequent visitor to the G4K site to seek out new ways to entertain himself. Tanner has significant influence over his parents' spending toward family fun.

Colbi Chandler (the creative child)—A charming 7-year-old elementary school girl who loves to do anything imaginative, crafty, or fun. She enjoys reading and writing and has always loved school. Colbi will be an occasional visitor to the G4K site, lured there because of the creative content and because her friends go there. Colbi is the little sister of Austin.

Austin Chandler (the active competitor)—An athletic 13-year-old boy who is interested in anything competitive or challenging. Austin loves to play sports of all kinds and is a disciplined achiever. Austin plays video and PC games for the sense of competition and the thrill of victory. Austin will likely come to the G4K site to seek out new games, hints, and tips as well as worthy opponents.

Preston Pasquez (the precocious preschooler)—A bright-eyed and inquisitive 3-year-old boy who is intrigued by anything new. He loves his parents' PC, but his mother, Irene, won't allow Preston to play on the PC by himself, especially when it is connected to the Internet. Irene will always be present to help Preston visit the G4K site.

Irene Pasquez (the involved parent)—Mother of Preston and, in one word, engaged. Irene is vigilant and involved with Preston to the highest degree. She loves to spend time directly interacting with and fully focused on Preston. She believes that the PC is a vital tool to help educate her children and stimulate mental development. Irene actively seeks out good experiences on the PC for Preston. She will visit the G4K site on occasion but as an ever-present partner with Preston. She is not currently aware of the GK4 brand or specific products.

Elaine Evans (the enlightened elementary school teacher)—A young and relatively new elementary school teacher who loves what she does and takes it very seriously. Elaine has interest and direct training in promoting technology as an educational tool for children. She sees the PC as a vital tool for today's youth and tomorrow's leaders. Elaine is vaguely aware of the G4K brand but doesn't have any direct experience with G4K products.

From the priorities assigned by the stakeholders, you can see that Tanner and Colbi are the primary personas for this G4K development effort. Irene and Austin are secondary targets. Elaine, the enlightened educator, and Preston, the 3-year-old, are tertiary targets.

A complete example foundation document for Tanner is provided in Appendix B.

G4K PERSONA BIRTH AND MATURATION

During *conception and gestation*, the G4K persona core team analyzed their data, created several skeletons, and enriched the ones selected by their stakeholders into full personas. They are eager to show off the fruits of their labor to the rest of the team. Since the team is fairly small and the development cycle is short, their efforts here will be minimal. Even so, they want to make sure that their personas—*Tanner* (the tenacious tweener), *Colbi* (the conscientious student), *Austin* (the active investigator), *Paige* (the precocious preschooler), *Yvonne* (the involved parent), and *Elaine* (the enlightened teacher)—don't get ignored once development ensues.

The core team is also nervous about introducing the persona method into their larger organization. During the *conception and gestation* phase, they had several debates about the value of the personas and how the personas should fit into the development process. The core team knows they are going to get some push-back from their colleagues on using this new technique; everyone is under pressure due to the fast release schedule and the discomfort of working in a relatively unfamiliar domain. The design process hasn't waited for the personas to be finished, and the core team feels a bit like they're trying to jump onto a moving train.

Creating a Communication Strategy

During the *family planning* phase, the G4K core team created an action plan. Now that they are ready to introduce the personas to the rest of the portal team, they know they need a more specific communication strategy. While the core team has been working on the personas, others on the portal team have been working hard to identify requirements. The G4K team knows they can't ask the rest of the product team to redo any of the work that's been done without the aid of personas; instead, they have decided to create a strategy to make the most of the personas for the rest of the product development process (see Figure B.8). To them, this means embarking on a communication campaign to very quickly express the value of the personas in time for the persona names to be included in the final versions of requirements and specification documents. The core team also hopes the personas will help once development gets under way; they know that there will have to be some serious feature triage if the portal is to be launched in time.

GOALS FOR THE G4K COMMUNICATION CAMPAIGN

- Support the action plan we created during *family planning*.
- Bring the personas to life in the minds of all colleagues who influence the design and development of the G4K kids' website as fast as possible—no one is going to stop what they're doing for this.
- Progressively disclose the right information to the right people at the right time to ensure that the user data embedded in the personas are understood and absorbed. We have limited resources, so we need to try to be efficient in introducing the personas to the various teams we hope will use them.
- Make sure everyone who is introduced to the personas knows how we hope they will use the personas in their everyday jobs. This means we have to be very specific about the changes to our usual design and development processes and documents.

199

FIGURE C.8
A section of the G4K core team's communication strategy.

Who	What	When	How
Stakeholders who have advised us on our persona effort to date	Evangelism about the persona method and our personas	Tomorrow or as soon as we can get on their calendars. Before we begin presenting to the other audiences listed in this document	Meeting to describe our work to date—Create slides on user-centered design, personas in general, and how and why we created our personas. Any more than this won't work. Prepare our proposed schedule for rollout of persona information and how we hope it will be used (perhaps a version of this strategy document?).
All	Introduce the persona method and put it in context for this project	As soon as possible	Pizza-party kickoff meeting—Use the five intro slides from stakeholder meeting if they worked well. Buzz generators—Create intro posters. Get someone to post intro posters all over halls while we do kickoff meeting.
Product managers	Information about each persona's roles and goals	As soon as possible	Ask product managers and other product designers what info they need to feel comfortable including persona names and roles in all requirements and specification documents.
Developers	Basics about this set of personas (introduce them to the people)	After requirements docs are complete and have been presented to development staff	Create comparison facilitators and enrichers; focus on the aspects of the personas that are clearly tied to data about large groups of people (characteristics of Abby as "a mom," elements of Tanner that are familiar from our shrink-wrapped products). Provide clear information about how these personas will have different expectations for the portal than they do for shrink-wrapped games. Explain the persona method, including some specific examples of how we'll use the personas (persona-weighted feature matrix, replacement of "actor" and "user" in scenarios for the Web site)
User testers, QA team, user support team	Core team assumes that these audiences can use same info as developers for the time being. Later, they might need additional information.		

THE G4K PERSONA EFFORT ELEVATOR PITCH

The G4K team created an 'elevator pitch' to quickly explain the persona effort to their collegues:

> G4K creates great games because we know what kids and their parents want from games. The G4K portal can only be great if we know what kids and their parents want from the Internet. We're creating specific descriptions of kids and parents—via personas—to capture everything we know and need to learn to create the G4K kids' portal. Our personas are going to allow all of our data, in the shape of real kids and real parents, to sit in on every meeting, in every office, and influence every decision we make about the portal.

G4K PERSONA ARTIFACTS

See Chapter 5 for examples of the artifacts used by the G4K team during *birth* and *maturation*.

G4K PERSONA ADULTHOOD

During *birth*, the G4K persona core team introduced the persona method and the G4K personas to the portal team and executive staff. There are some new persona posters on the walls, and people around the company are beginning to talk about target users. The persona core team is eager to see the personas being used toward the development of G4K's new website. They have several specific uses in mind already and have begun to contact team members who will be involved in those activities.

The development cycle will be short (in fact, some of the coding has already begun!), so the use of personas will have to be tactical and carefully targeted. Still, the core team knew from previous development efforts that a real focus on users has been difficult to achieve; if the personas help even just a little bit, the effort will be worthwhile.

USING PERSONAS FOR COMPETITIVE ANALYSIS

The G4K team needed to get very smart very fast about the kinds of things that appeal to kids—and their parents—on the Internet. They decided to do some research about other sites that were already trying to do something similar to what they wanted to achieve with their kids' site. They looked for websites that seemed:

- Designed to appeal to kids Tanner's age and their parents
- Focused on children's games or on "edutational" content

They found many websites and decided to look at a few of them through the eyes of Tanner Thompson, the tenacious tinkerer, and Irene Pasquez, the involved parent. Two of the sites they chose to review were www.scholastic.com and www.strangematter.com. They convened the persona core and on-call teams in a conference room with a projector.

The G4K core team is comprised of:

- *Ingrid*, an interaction design/usability person from the games group
- *Graham*, a graphic designer

The persona on-call team is comprised of:

- *Paula*, the project lead for the new website
- *Michael*, a market researcher
- *Theo*, a technical writer

First, they made sure that everyone was still familiar with the important details of Tanner. Then Theo, the technical writer, was assigned to be Tanner during the review. Ingrid started by projecting the Scholastic home page (see Figure C.9) and asking Tanner/Theo what he thought and what he'd do.

Here's a segment of the dialog during the walkthrough at G4K:

Tanner/Theo. Well, this is kinda boring. What am I supposed to do here? Get ready for an A+ test session?! What test? I hate tests. I'm outta here. But if I have to stay … let's see what else there is. Harry Potter, that's kinda cool. But I already have all those books. There's shopping stuff over here but who has money? Besides, who the heck would spend it here anyway? Maybe my mom, I guess. There's a Kids button over there with some dorky kids on it. I guess I could click that. What are the other ones? Families, Teachers, Administrators, Librarians … whatEVER. But, hmmm, wonder if there is any cool secret teacher and administrator stuff behind those. Nah. I guess I'll try the Kids button.

Ingrid. What would you expect to see if you click that button?

Tanner/Theo. I don't know. I guess something for kids.

FIGURE C.9
The www.scholastic.com home page (March 20, 2004).

FIGURE C.10
The www.scholastic.com/kids page (March 20, 2004).

FIGURE C.11
The www.strangematterexhibit.com home page (March 20, 2004).

Ingrid then clicked the "kids" button, which projected the page www.scholastic.com/kids on the wall (see Figure C.10).

Tanner/Theo. Oh, this is better. Looks like it's got some cool stuff on it. I like the looks of that Deltora dinosaur thing. And there's a Harry Potter poster! I don't have one of those! There's definitely stuff I can do here.

etc. …

203

Key Findings

After the Scholastic walkthrough, the G4K team talked about what they found. They agreed that the Scholastic site was really built more for Irene than for Tanner and that Tanner might even leave the site before he ever found the Kids section because he wasn't immediately engaged by the home page. They decided this decision on Scholastic's part probably was totally in line with their own business objectives. For the G4K site, the team decided that their home page would have to be designed to engage Tanner immediately. Irene, they decided, would be willing to look a little bit harder for the area of the site dedicated to her, but if Tanner didn't like it right away their own site wouldn't succeed.

After they finished walking through the Scholastic site, they moved on to look at the Strange Matter site (http://www.strangematterexhibit.com/) (Figure C.11).

Ingrid. So, Tanner, tell me about this page. What do you think? What are you going to do here?

Tanner/Theo. Those buttons in the middle are cool—I like that one that says CRUSH STUFF! I want to click that one right now!

Ingrid. What would you expect to happen if you clicked that?

Tanner/Theo. I'd want to be able to crush stuff! Duh. (At this point, Theo the technical writer was really getting into being Tanner!)

Ingrid clicked the "Crush Stuff!" button and the results projected on the wall (Figure C.12).

Tanner/Theo. Cool. Okay, I'll pick the "Chipper vs. Bauxer" one, though I really don't know what that is. I do know that I better get to see something being crushed soon.

Ingrid clicked the "Match 3" area and the results were projected on the wall (Figure C.13).

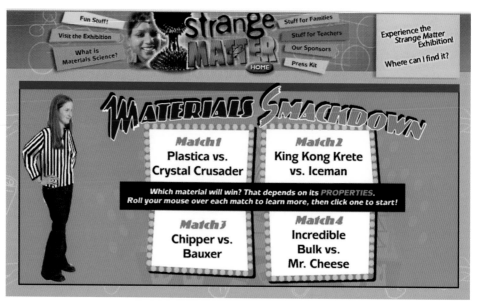

FIGURE C.12
The result of hitting the "Crush Stuff" button at www.strangematterexhibit.com/properties.html (March 26, 2005) was loading a page called "Materials Smackdown." Each of the four "Match" areas showed a set of two materials to be matched against each other in a crushing machine.

FIGURE C.13
Wood versus aluminum being crushed at www.strangematterexhibit.com/properties.html (March 26, 2005).

Tanner saw Figure C.13 and excitedly pulled the lever to start the crushing match.

Tanner/Theo. CRUSH IT!!! CRUSH IT!!! This is *cool.* I want one of those crushing things for my room.

After the match, Tanner sees an information bubble pop up on the screen (Figure C.14).

Tanner: Oh here's the boring teaching part. Wait a sec. There's something about airplanes.

etc. …

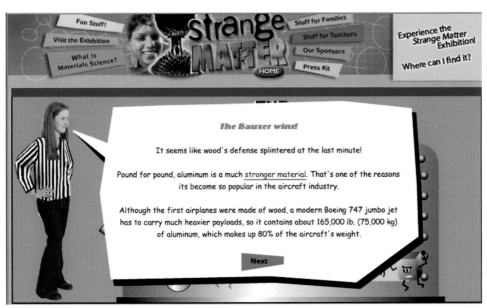

FIGURE C.14
After the match, the site displays an explanation of the different properties of the materials that were crushed (www.strangematterexhibit.com/properties.html; March 26, 2005).

Key Findings

The G4K team got a lot of ideas for Tanner from the Strange Matter website. They realized that Tanner probably wouldn't do a lot of reading but would be interested in some text if the key words were right; he would read if he had a good reason to do so. The team liked the way the Strange Matter site used carefully crafted, minimal text at just the right times to capture Tanner's attention and keep him moving through the site. They were surprised to find that Tanner was totally okay with just a few options—they had assumed that sites for kids had to be like many of their G4K games—full of lots of options and buttons on every screen. The team also liked the way the Strange Matter home page put everything in Tanner's terms and expected Irene to work around these terms; for example, Irene would have to realize that the "Stuff for Families" button was the best path to get the information that she'd be interested in.

USING PERSONAS FOR FEATURE BRAINSTORMS

Ingrid and the G4K persona team called together several key stakeholders from the kids' portal development team to hold a feature brainstorming session (about eight people in all). This included the company's VP, who had been the initiator and champion on the portal project. Ingrid reserved a meeting room for 2 hours and planned to hit each of the primary personas as well as the secondary personas during this session, spending no more than 20 minutes per persona.

As the session started, she reminded everyone of the brainstorming ground rules (most notably, that all ideas are good—the more, the better) and then reintroduced the personas. Recall that Tanner Thompson is the "tenacious tinkerer." He loves to play but he has a short attention span. He is reasonably skilled with using computers and definitely can tinker around with something until it works (or breaks). He is an active user of G4K products and has several favorite titles and characters from the G4K series.

The 20 minutes allotted for Tanner slipped into 30 minutes, and the ideas were still flowing. Ingrid had to force the group to move on to the next persona. They generated about 30 feature, service, and experience ideas for Tanner. Below are a few of the interesting ones:

- Braniac Bonuses (G4K.com tokens)
- BuddyMail or "Gigantic Buddies" (a protected messaging service for registered users)
- Daily game hint
- E-mail reminders/notifications for kids' events
- Kids' event promotions and ticket purchasing
- G4K stories (embellishments of well-known G4K characters)
- G4K flash games (simple online versions of the G4K shrink-wrap games)
- Game feedback (ratings by users)
- Personal game score history
- Long-term teams for repeated online game play
- Meet the Idols/Stars (column)
- Pop Polls (pop-up animated surveys on popular topics)
- Registration for kids
- Search companion (animated search helper for kids)
- Site customization (per-user content, style, layout selection)
- Toy and gizmo reviews with "fun" ratings
- Trial versions of G4K games for download
- *Wowzers!* e-zine (online magazine for kids)

CREATING A PERSONA-WEIGHTED FEATURE MATRIX

The G4K portal team created a persona-weighted feature matrix to help them prioritize their feature set and make a few much-needed cuts. Figure C.14 shows their first run-through with scoring the features in the matrix. There are clearly some "winning" features and some that will have to be deprioritized. For example, it seems the team would be crazy not to do simple flash versions of the current G4K titles and also have trial versions of their games available on the site. BuddyMail and Creation Corner scored highly as well. At the other end of the scale, adding "send to" link capability to their site's pages seems like a bad idea now. Interestingly, the registration feature scored somewhere in the middle. It is not a hot feature, though, because of Children's Online Privacy Protection Act (COPPA) regulations (see http://www.ftc.gov/ogc/coppa1.htm); this is one feature they'll have to think about very carefully.

The G4K team then did a technical feasibility analysis. BuddyMail, which scored high, will require a lot of work to do properly. That feature is probably one they will put on the back burner for now. The search companion also required some technical feats that the team was not prepared to meet. Because it didn't score as well in terms of user value, they will also put it on the version *x* list.

USING A SCENARIO COLLECTION SPREADSHEET

At G4K, the product development team was now moving fast. The core team felt like there was good buy-in for the persona effort, but everyone was now heads-down and working on their own projects and it was difficult to tell how people were using the personas (and if they were using the personas correctly!). One day, Ingrid (the G4K information architect) looked through a spec for one of the product features and found several scenarios written about Tanner, the tenacious tinkerer; a few about Irene, the involved parent; and one about someone named "Jimmy." There was no persona named Jimmy! She began to worry that something was going wrong.

Ingrid called the project manager for the new website. They decided to create a scenario collection spreadsheet. Together, they gathered all of the walk-through scenarios from every existing feature specification document for the G4k portal into a single spreadsheet. This

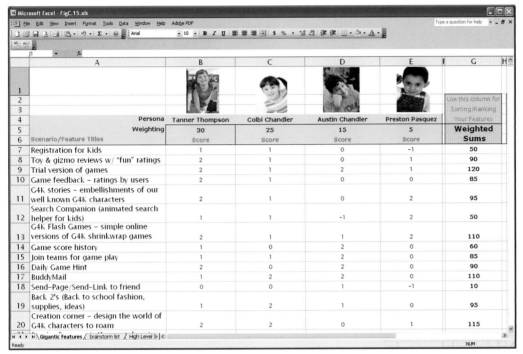

FIGURE C.15

The G4K persona-weighted matrix. (Note that for simplicity of presentation, we included only the kid personas in this example.)

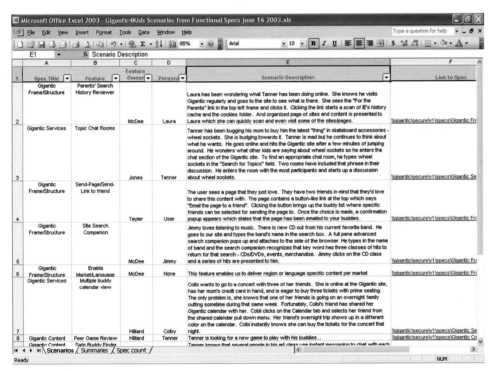

FIGURE C.16

G4K's scenario collection spreadsheet.

required a lot of manual copying and pasting from document to document, but it turned out to be worth the effort. They noticed (see Figure C.16) that one of the development managers seems to have made up his very own set of personas! They set up meetings to go over all the wayward scenarios and make sure that they fit the primary personas for the project.

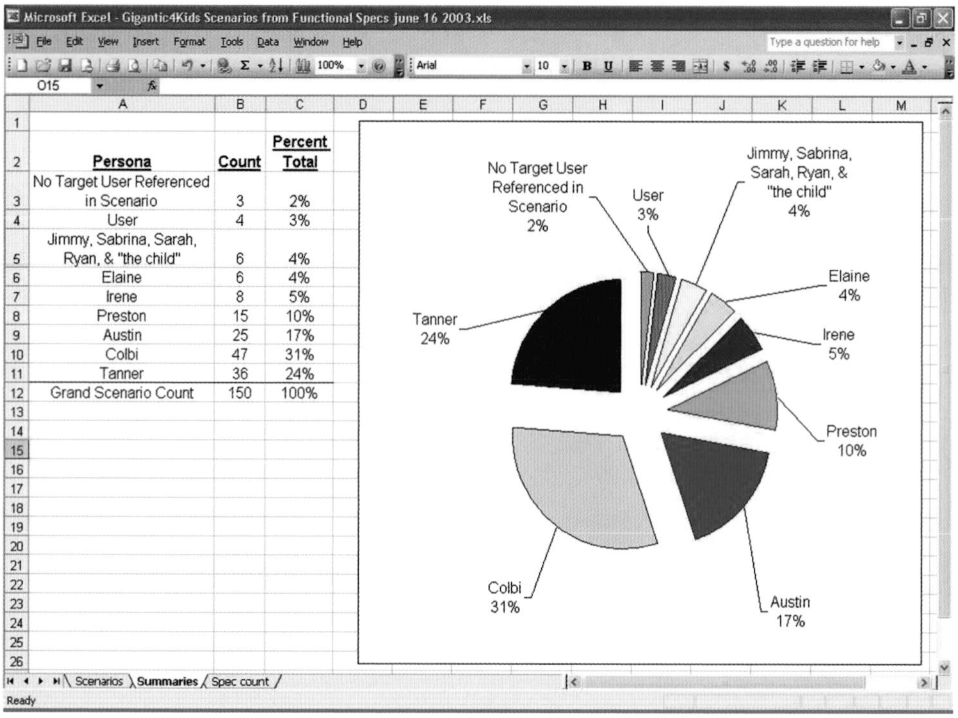

Persona	Count	Percent Total
No Target User Referenced in Scenario	3	2%
User	4	3%
Jimmy, Sabrina, Sarah, Ryan, & "the child"	6	4%
Elaine	6	4%
Irene	8	5%
Preston	15	10%
Austin	25	17%
Colbi	47	31%
Tanner	36	24%
Grand Scenario Count	150	100%

FIGURE C.17

The G4K scenario collection spreadsheet "scenario count per persona" view.

Ingrid decided to sort the spreadsheet by persona. She looked at all the scenarios for Tanner, then all the scenarios for Irene, and so on. She found that some of the Irene scenarios had taken too much liberty with Irene's ability and interest in troubleshooting. Ingrid knew she needed to review those scenarios with the feature owners.

Using scenario counts as a rough guide

Ingrid could now do a simple scenario count per persona and create a pie chart to illustrate the results (shown in Figure C.17). It is *not* clear in the chart that Tanner, the tenacious tinkerer, is the most important persona. With only 36 scenarios written with Tanner as the actor/agent, Colbi, the creative child, overshadowed him with 47 scenarios (roughly 31% of the total scenarios).

Ingrid understood why this has happened—Colbi was a very cute, endearing persona! Most of the project team had a soft spot for Colbi. However, Ingrid knew that Tanner was actually more important to the product than Colbi, so she followed up with the various development teams to make sure they weren't spending time on fun features for Colbi at the expense of features for Tanner.

Structuring user research based on personas

The team at G4K had some prototypes they wanted to test, and it was time to bring in some usability test participants. They decided they wanted to bring in real Tanners, Colbis, and Irenes to see how they liked the prototypes. The core team got together and tried to identify five key characteristics of each of these personas so they could create screening documents that they could send to a test participant recruiter. It was a tough meeting; everyone knew Tanner, Colbi, and Irene pretty well at this point and it was hard to imagine broadening the description of any one of them ("how can Tanner *possibly* be a girl? He's just such a *boy*!").

G4K.com Persona Screeners

G4K

Tanner Thompson
Colbi Chandler
Austin Chandler
Preston Pasquez
Irene Pasquez
Elaine Evans

Tanner Thompson (questions answered by parent about child)

- **Child is Elementary school-aged**
  Question: How old is your child?
  Required Answer: Must be between 8-10 years of age.

- **Household has a computer at home w/Internet connection used by children**
  Question: Do you have a PC with a connection to the Internet in your home that your children use?
  Required Answer: Yes. Reject if answer is "yes, but I don't let the kids use it."

- **PC used by child regularly**
  Question: How often do your children use the PC? (daily, several times a week, several times a month, rarely)
  Required Answer: Several times a week or daily.

- **Child loves PC (rate the following statements as true or false)**
  Question: Which of the following statements describe your child related to the PC:
  Statement 1: My child fights/begs for PC time (T or F)
  Statement 2: My child prefers the PC over Television (T or F)
  Statement 3: My child amazes me with their knowledge of the PC/Software (T or F)
  Statement 4: My child is continually dragging me to the PC to show me something they did or found (T or F)
  Statement 5: I have to encourage my child to do other activities than using the PC (T or F)
  Required Answer: Must answer "True" to at least two of the statements above.

- **Uses PC to play games & surf web**
  Question: Your child uses the PC to do the following things:
  Activity 1: Play PC games (yes or no)

FIGURE C.18
The G4K usability test participant screening document for Tanners.

It seemed important for the Tanners to be current owners of at least one G4K game title, but they also knew that recruiting participants based on such a criterion would be very difficult.

There was a lot of debate, but finally everyone agreed on a set of questions they could use to screen for potential Tanner participants (see Figure C.18). The team knew they could always add screener questions or revise them at a later date if they weren't producing adequate participants for their usability sessions. They also knew that other questions could be asked during a usability session to get further clarity on participants, even if they didn't screen on those responses.

As the G4K marketing team prepared the portal launch effort, they used this same set of screener questions to focus market research toward the personas. Ultimately, they focused their advertising efforts on the media outlets they knew Tanner already accessed: *SportKid* magazine, cereal boxes, and perhaps even Saturday morning television programming. They could also harvest lists of registered owners of G4K shrink-wrapped games.

Phase	Activity	When Completed	Related Project Milesones
Family planning	Organizational introspection Data collection	2 weeks from start of persona effort	Vision complete (business plan, corporate strategy)
Conception and gestation	Data organized, persona creation complete, evaluation and prioritization by stakeholders complete, validation complete Begin evangelizing persona effort around organization	1 month from start of persona effort	Requirements complete (system architecture, functional requirements)
Birth and maturation	Persona effort introduced to team Initial posters and communication artifacts delivered to team Personas used in storyboards, scenarios, design walkthroughs, etc.	2 months from start of persona effort	Feature specification complete (design complete) *GOAL*: Use personas in feature prioritization decisions
Adulthood	User testing with personas as recruiting profile Personas used in Q/A test case selection Persona knowledge enrichment artifacts delivered	3 months from start of persona effort	Beta 1 complete (core features intact, but not polished)

FIGURE C.19

The G4K persona effort action plan. During family planning, the G4K team created this action plan, which includes elements that they can use to measure the ROI of their effort at the end of the project.

G4K MEASURES THE ROI OF THE PERSONA EFFORT

The G4K portal team was excited to have launched their new site. They are roughly on time and on budget, but they had to cut a few features and live with a few known bugs to make it happen. They were confident that those things would be worked out in subsequent updates, and plans were already under way for more significant enhancements to the site, so the persona core team would have to work fast to evaluate the appropriateness and accuracy of their current personas toward any new development.

Even though the traffic to the site was minimal initially, the executive staff believed that the effort was successful—simply because the site existed. The persona core team knew that they could lend a hand in assessing how successful the effort and site really are. Along with this, they planned to look at how useful the persona method was in this development effort.

Returning to the action plan to measure success

During family planning, the G4K core team created an action plan, which included the resources and amount of time they estimated for the persona effort and the process and product issues they hoped the personas would address (see Figure C.19). To measure the return on investment (ROI) of the G4K persona effort, the G4K core team can return to each of these estimates and plans to evaluate the success of their personas.

The G4K team can compare the time estimates they included in the action plan (see Figure B.19) to the actual time it took to create and support the personas:

- Were their estimates regarding core team members' required time commitments accurate?
- Were their estimates of the calendar time required for each life phase accurate? They could add another column to this table to show the actual time it took to complete each task.
- If they missed their planned dates, what were the costs of missing the deadlines they originally set?
- Were some of the related project milestones completed before the personas were available to influence the decisions they contained?

These measures are important. If the persona effort was perceived as being unsuccessful, and you had hoped to use personas in another project, evaluate whether the problems were related to timing problems rather than weaknesses of the persona approach as a whole.

MEASURING PRODUCT IMPROVEMENTS

The G4K persona team worked on the first version of the G4K kids' Internet portal; the improvements they hoped for were stated as problems they predicted and wanted to avoid through their use of personas. These problems were reflected in several aspects of their action plan, including the 'elevator pitch' and the 'product problems we want to solve with personas':

- Elevator pitch: G4K creates great games because we know what kids and their parents want from games. The G4K portal can only be great if we know what kids and their parents want from the Internet. We're creating specific descriptions of kids and parents— in personas—to capture everything we know and need to learn to create the G4K kids' portal. Our personas are going to allow all of our data, in the shape of real kids and real parents, to sit in on every meeting, in every office, and influence every decision we make about the portal.
- Product problems we want to solve with personas:
  - Other companies have Internet portals for kids. We're behind. How can we create a product that's world class and worthy of the G4K brand in such a short time?
  - How can we recreate some of the key experiences built into our G4K games into an Internet experience? The technologies are very different.

These elements of the action plan reflected key concerns of the G4K team at the beginning of the project. The G4K team was afraid that their unfamiliarity with the Internet would result in a product design that was difficult to build and unappealing to their intended audience. They had a small team, a short deadline, and a development staff that felt as if they already knew everything they needed to know about the intended users of the new product (e.g., the kids who play G4K games). The persona core team knew that if they relied on existing assumptions about users and traditional development processes, the new G4K Internet portal might fail. They hoped personas would allow the team to focus on the information that was appropriate to the portal project, whether that information was leveraged from existing knowledge or was new and domain specific.

The G4K team decided to look for ways to assess the impact of the personas on the product by restating the problems they wanted to solve such that the answers were in some way measurable.

Problem expressed in the elevator pitch: The G4K portal can only be great if we know what kids and their parents want from the Internet.

To construct an answer:

- How much new information did we find out about what kids and their parents want from the Internet (vs. from shrink-wrapped games)?

211

- Can we trace how much of this information affected the design of the portal and in what ways?
- Which are the most popular ("great") and least popular elements of the portal? Are the popular elements the ones for which design decisions are traceable to the data we collected?

From the statement of product problems to solve with personas

Problems expressed in the product problems to solve with personas: Other companies have Internet portals for kids. We're behind. How can we create a product that's world class and worthy of the G4K brand in such a short time?

To construct an answer:

- Can we get measures of what parents and kids think of the G4K portal versus the other portals that were already out there?
- How, specifically, does our portal take advantage of lessons we learned from analyzing the competitors' portals from the point of view of our personas?
- In what ways is our portal different from our competitors' portals? Can we trace the decisions to create these differences back to the data reflected in our personas?
- Do industry influencers and/or internal stakeholders think that our new portal is inferior, as good as, or superior to our competitors' sites?
- Did we meet our schedule for building and deploying our portal? Were there decisions we made as we triaged the development work that we can trace to the use of personas?
- Is the portal satisfying the business objectives that fueled the project and were reflected in the personas?

How can we recreate some of the key experiences built into our G4K games into an Internet experience? The technologies are very different.

To construct an answer:

- What are the key experiences built into our games that we wanted to reflect in the portal?
- Did the personas help us create Internet versions of these key experiences (that are still familiar even though they are implemented differently)?

MEASURING PROCESS IMPROVEMENTS

The G4K team was highly invested in making the new Internet portal a success, but they were worried about the intense schedule and lack of resources. The persona core team knew that intense schedules were likely to cause flare-ups and turf wars in the team, because everyone would be trying to work quickly under a great deal of pressure. The G4K core team hoped the personas would allow the team to be both focused and highly collaborative.

In their action plan, the G4K team listed several process-related challenges that they hoped to mitigate with the personas:

- We need to deal with the incredibly fast turnaround required for online portal development (unlike game development schedules).
- We need to leverage the efforts of our very small team.
- We need to leverage the efforts of people not directly on our team but whose help and expertise are needed.

The G4K core team decided to measure the impact of the personas on the design and development process by surveying the portal team to ask them such questions as:

- What, if anything, helped us meet (or caused us to miss) important milestones in the project schedule?
- How did you make decisions when there wasn't time to meet with the entire team?

- Were there more or fewer last-minute changes than in other projects you've worked on? What were they?
- What are you most proud of in our finished portal?
- What do you wish we could change?
- What would you do differently if we were creating another version of the portal?

They also surveyed the borrowed resources from other teams; they asked these people to describe the target users of the Internet portal. Through these surveys, the G4K team knew they would collect information that they could use to assess whether the personas:

- Helped the team meet the tight deadline and in what ways
- Helped coordinate the efforts of the main team and of the borrowed resources (without having them get in each other's way)
- Communicated and maintained focus on the goals and needs of the targeted users of the portal (and the ways they were different from users of other G4K products)

PREPARING PERSONAS FOR THE NEXT PROJECT

As mentioned earlier, the G4K portal team launched their portal, but not without some compromises. Generally, the project was considered a big success by the broader company and key stakeholders. After evaluating some aspects of ROI and gathering feedback on the method from colleagues, the G4K persona core team deemed that the persona effort was also a success. Now some of the other groups in the company are starting to ask "How did you do that?" and "Can we use your personas for our next game?"

Because of this, the core team has already been looking at ways to reincarnate their kid personas and create a couple more that are appropriate for other projects that are not specifically about Internet delivery of content. Further, they plan to reuse and extend the parent and teacher personas for the next version of the site, because they feel smarter about the domain now. They know they didn't do much for educators in their current release, so they hope to strengthen this aspect of their site without decrementing the focus on kids.

In the meantime, they are using the existing personas to get new team members up to speed, as the new portal is successful enough to inspire their executive team to assign more people to the Web portal team.

213

Benun, I. (2003). *Designing websites for every audience.* How Design Books.

Beyer, H., & Holtzblatt, K. (1998). *Contextual design: A customer-centered approach to systems designs.* San Francisco, CA: Morgan Kaufmann.

Carliner, S. (September/October 1998). Future travels of the InfoWrangler. *Intercomm, 45*(8), 20–24.

Carroll, J. (Ed.). (1995). *Scenario-based design: Envisioning work and technology in system development.* New York, NY: John Wiley & Sons.

Carroll, J. (2000). Five reasons for scenario-based design. *Interacting with computers, 13*(1), 43–60.

Coney, M., & Steehouder, M. (2000). Role playing on the Web: Guidelines for designing and evaluating personas online. Technical Communication, Third Quarter.

Cooper, A. (1995). *About face 1.0.* Foster City, CA: IDG Books Worldwide.

Cooper, A., & Reimann, R. (2003). *About face 2.0: The essentials of interaction design.* Indianapolis: Wiley Publishing, Inc.

Cooper, A. (1999). *The inmates are running the asylum: Why high-tech products drive us crazy and how to restore the sanity.* New York, NY: Macmillan.

Donahue, G. M. (January/February, 2001). Usability and the Bottom Line. *IEEE Software*, 31–37.

Garrett, J. J. (2002). *The elements of user experience: User-centered design for the web.* Berkeley, CA: New Riders.

Hackos, J., & Redish, J. (1998). *User and task analysis for interface design.* New York: John Wiley and Sons.

Kuniavsky, M. (2003). *Observing the user experience: A practitioner's guide to user research.* San Francisco, CA: Morgan Kaufmann.

Mayhew, D. (1999). *The usability engineering lifecycle: A practitioner's handbook for user interface design.* San Diego, CA: Morgan Kaufmann Publishers.

McQuaid, H., Goel, A., & McManus, M. (2003). When you can't talk to customers: Using storyboards and narratives to elicit empathy for users. *Proceedings of the 2003 international conference on Designing pleasurable products and interfaces.* New York: ACM Press.

Mikkelson, N., & Lee, W. O. (2000). *Incorporating user archetypes into scenario-based design.* Proc. UPA 2000.

Molich, R., & Jeffries (2003). Comparative Expert Reviews, CHI 2003 Proceedings.

Moore, G. A. (1991). *Crossing the Chasm: Marketing and selling high-tech products to mainstream customers.* Berkeley, CA: New York: HarperCollins Publishers (Revised in 2002).

Nielsen, J., & Mack, R. (Eds.). (1994). *Usability inspection methods.* New York: John Wiley & Sons.

Nielsen, J., & Molich, R. (1990). Heuristic evaluation of user interfaces. *Proceeding ACM CHI '90 Conference* (Seattle, WA, 1–5 April), 249–256.

Preece, J., Rogers, H., & Sharp, H. (2002). *Interaction design: Beyond human-computer interaction.* New York, NY: John Wiley & Sons.

Salvador, T., & Howells, K. (1998). Focus troupe: Using drama to create common context for new product concept end-user evaluations. *Proceedings of CHI 98.*

Spencer, R. (2000). The streamlined cognitive walkthrough method. *ACM-CHI 2000 Proceedings*, April 1–6, 353–361.

Thralls, C., Blyler, N., & Ewald, H. (1988). Real readers, implied readers, and professional writers: Suggested research. *Journal of Business Communication, 25,* 47–65.

Upshaw, L. (1995). *Building brand identity: A strategy for success in a hostile marketplace.* New York: John Wiley & Sons.

Vredenburg, K., Isensee, S., & Righi, C. (2001). *User-Centered design: An integrated approach.* Upper Saddle River, NJ: Prentice Hall.

Walden, D. (1993). Kano's methods for understanding customer-defined quality: Introduction to Kano's methods Fall. *Center for Quality Management Journal, 2*(4).

Wharton, C., Rieman, J., Lewis, C., & Polson, P. (1994). The cognitive walkthrough method: A practitioner's guide. In *Usability Inspection Methods*, Nielsen, J., & Mack, R. L. (Eds.), New York: John Wiley & Sons, 105–141.

Wilson, C. E., & Rosenbaum, S. (2005). Categories of ROI and their practical implications. In R. G. Bias & D. J. Mayhew (Eds.), *Cost-justifying usability.* San Francisco: Morgan Kaufmann Publishers.

215

217

223